MINDING
the LIGHT

"I found this book a breathtaking reading experience, a series of shocks of recognition, as I discovered in it the unacknowledged and most essential foundations for all of my own most cherished pedagogical practices."

—Sheridan Blau, Director, South Coast Writing Project
and Literature Institute for Teachers, University of California, Santa Barbara;
Author of The Literature Workshop: Teaching Texts and Their Readers

"Minding the Light represents the kind of thoughtful reflection about teaching that refreshes our commitment to classroom life and that helps us see with new eyes why our work there matters. The book's intellectual generosity and easy grace make it an important contribution to our ongoing conversations about teachers and their craft."

—James Marshall, Associate Dean, Teacher Education and Student Services, University of Iowa

"In higher education, the pressures to be expert and always in the know are great, yet the need to remain intellectually open and to cultivate such openness in students is paramount. These educators take up the challenge of making more space for the process of learning, and use Quaker values and insights to pursue the humility and honesty it seems to require. Their 'attitudes' of equality and community and the methods they give rise to seem to push out the walls of academic classrooms and disciplines to create places that serve the larger self and the larger good. From here, we might see more students able to realize their potentialities and the tracked and tiered system of both secondary and higher education fall away."

—Diana Oxley, Assistant Professor, Research Associate,
Center for Educational Policy Research, University of Oregon

"Minding the Light: Essays in Friendly Pedagogy is a clear-minded contribution to the conversation about ethical, authentic teaching. These authors speak from a place of deep integrity to the hearts of other educators, offering wisdom and insight about teaching from the best in ourselves to the best in our students."

—Ann Faulkner, Co-director, Center for Formation in the Community College

"Quakers believe that everyone has access to the 'inner light.' It is a belief I treasure in part because it is pivotal to authentic education. This superb collection of essays focuses that light on a variety of critical issues in teaching and learning, dispelling a lot of darkness in the process. *Minding the Light* illumines pedagogy in ways that will deepen the practice of anyone who claims the vocation of teacher."

—Parker J. Palmer, Author of The Courage to Teach *and* Let your Life Speak

MINDING
the LIGHT

STUDIES IN

EDUCATION & SPIRITUALITY

Peter Laurence and Victor Kazanjian
General Editors

Vol. 6

PETER LANG
New York • Washington, D.C./Baltimore • Bern
Frankfurt am Main • Berlin • Brussels • Vienna • Oxford

MINDING
the LIGHT

Essays in Friendly Pedagogy

Anne Dalke • Barbara Dixson
EDITORS

PETER LANG
New York • Washington, D.C./Baltimore • Bern
Frankfurt am Main • Berlin • Brussels • Vienna • Oxford

Library of Congress Cataloging-in-Publication Data

Minding the light: essays in friendly pedagogy /
edited by Anne Dalke, Barbara Dixson.
p. cm. — (Studies in education and spirituality; v. 6)
Includes bibliographical references and index.
1. Society of Friends—Education. 2. Quakers—Education.
3. Teaching—Religious aspects—Society of Friends. 4. Teaching—Religious
aspects—Quakers. I. Dalke, Anne French. II. Dixson, Barbara. III. Series.
LC571.M56   371.071'96—dc21   2002156043
ISBN 0-8204-6357-4
ISSN 1527-8247

Bibliographic information published by **Die Deutsche Bibliothek**.
Die Deutsche Bibliothek lists this publication in the "Deutsche
Nationalbibliografie"; detailed bibliographic data is available
on the Internet at http://dnb.ddb.de/.

Cover art by Sharon Burgmayer
Cover design by Dutton & Sherman Design

The paper in this book meets the guidelines for permanence and durability
of the Committee on Production Guidelines for Book Longevity
of the Council of Library Resources.

© 2004 Peter Lang Publishing, Inc., New York
275 Seventh Avenue, 28th Floor, New York, NY 10001
www.peterlangusa.com

Printed in the United States of America

ೞ

To our friends in the Friends Association for Higher Education,
in whose good company this book arose,
and from whom it goes out.

C8 Table of Contents

CB Acknowledgments

We are grateful to Sharon Burgmayer for "Diffraction," the painting on our cover; to Alexa Antanavage, for her capable and efficient work in preparing this book for publication; and to Bryn Mawr College for the grant in spring 2003 which paid our preparation costs.

Excerpts from *The Journal of George Fox,* by George Fox are reprinted with permission of Cambridge University Press.

Excerpts from *Servant Leadership: A Journey into the Nature of Legitimate Power and Greatness,* by Robert Greenleaf, © 1977 are reprinted with permission of Paulist Press.

Excerpts from "Warrior with Words: Towards a Post-Columbine Writing Curriculum," by G. Lynn Nelson, © 2000, by the National Council of Teachers, are reprinted with permission.

Excerpts from *The Thought of the Heart and Soul of the World* by James Hillman, © 1992, are reprinted with permission of Melanie Jackson Agency, L.L.C.

Excerpts from *Their Eyes Were Watching God,* by Zora Neale Hurston, © 1937 by Harper & Row, Publishers, Inc., are reprinted with permission.

Excerpts from *The Journal and Major Essays of John Woolman,* by John Woolman, © 1971, are reprinted with permission of Oxford University Press.

Excerpts from *The Courage to Teach: Exploring the Inner Landscape of a Teacher's Life,* by Parker Palmer, © 1998, are reprinted with permission of John Wiley & Sons, Inc.

Excerpts from *Christian Faith and Practice in the Experience of the Society of Friends,* published by London Yearly Meeting, © 1960, are reprinted with permission of the Yearly Meeting of the Religious Society of Friends (Quakers) in Britain.

೦೩ Part One
Original Seeking: Invitations into the Conversation

☙ Introduction
"Minding the Light":
A Range of Quaker Pedagogies

Anne Dalke and Susan McNaught

If there is, or can be, a spiritual unity in the aims of Friends education at every level, it would seem to manifest itself less in a single comprehensive educational philosophy than in the creation of a particular kind of atmosphere or climate from which all aspects of school life…take their form and meaning.

Paul Lacey, *Growing into Goodness: Essays on Quaker Education* (1998)

The essays in this collection center around the question, "What is Quaker pedagogy?" They grew out of conversations at the 2000 conference of the Friends Association for Higher Education at Earlham College, where we repeatedly asked one another, "What is Quaker education?"—and where there was much talk about Quaker pedagogy, about Quaker ethos, about what we mean by "that which is distinctly Quaker." There are some important distinctives that frame this faith and its various expressions, including our approaches to education. And yet, although simplicity is a core value of the Society of Friends, definitions are not usually simple things. Because the Society of Friends is noncredal, there is no easy list of beliefs. Although Quakers have long been known for their strong support of education, we do not have a set of elaborate educational principles. "Quaker pedagogy" may even be an oxymoron.

Yet as we described, reflected on and reexamined our practices of Quaker education, first at the conference, then in preparing the essays for this volume, we also came to discern our shared underlying beliefs. We began with practice, and worked back to understanding (though for some of us, the process worked in the other direction: We began in belief or in doubt, out of which grew our practice). Steven Garber says that all ideas have "legs," that there is always a connection between worldviews and ways of life. What we believe about the world and why we believe it frame how we move and function in it, how we live our lives. Quaker educational practices express our Quaker philosophy of life, and the label is finally less important than the work we are all trying to do.

Quaker pedagogy is less a visible, outward result than a fundamental attitude. Each of us seeks to honor that which is of God in each other. This involves a centering of spirit, an approach to students and colleagues, a certainty that the teacher is an instrument. As many of these essays testify, this kind of work is possible for those who do not teach in Quaker institutions and may be even more crucial there because they lack a structure of support.

How, then, do Quaker distinctives work in multiple settings? All of the teachers who speak in this volume are aware that good teaching and good learning cannot be reduced to technique, that the process grows from the identity and integrity of the learners and their teachers. Our students learn only when they risk opening themselves. They are more likely to be willing to risk when we provide a safe place for them to do that. As teachers, we must risk, too, demonstrating what Parker Palmer calls the "courage to teach": the courage to keep our hearts open in those very moments when our hearts are asked to hold more than they are able, so that teachers, students, and subjects can be woven into the fabric of community that learning and living require. We risk in order to discover connections.

The task of Friends' worship, as all these teacher-authors understand it, is to "mind the Light." We all focus, in worship, on what we call the "inward teacher," the intuitive wisdom available to us all. This is a joyous undertaking, but not an easy one, and Friends enter worship with a sense both of humility and expectation of one another's gifts. This, too, is the way that we approach the process of learning and teaching, with a mind for the Light and with a sense of the expansiveness of the task. We invite you to join us in the search.

CR Chapter One
The Spiritual Roots of Quaker Pedagogy[1]

Steve Smith

Nowhere in the contemporary world is the influence of the Religious Society of Friends more publicly evident than in the field of education. Numbering worldwide fewer than 300,000 members, Quakerism[2] has nevertheless been the source and inspiration for a remarkable number of fine educational institutions at all grade levels, from preschools through K12 to college and universities.[3] Though the greatest number are located in the United States, Friends' schools are found not only in England but also in Australia, Bolivia, Costa Rica, Japan, Kenya, and Palestine. Despite retaining a distinctively Quaker flavor, most of these schools cater to a clientele that is largely non-Quaker; at many Friends' schools, only a small minority of students, faculty, and administrators are themselves Friends. When several distinguished Quaker-related schools and colleges are ranked among the very best in the world, and when a President of the United States and First Lady choose while in office to send their daughter to a select Quaker school,[4] to say nothing of the many less well-known but nevertheless fine schools at all levels that carry on the tradition of Quaker education, one may well ask what accounts for this remarkable record of success. Why has the Religious Society of Friends proved so fecund in fostering educational institutions of high quality and remarkable inclusiveness?

Afire with spiritual awakening, consumed with burning concerns for social and economic justice, the earliest Friends in seventeenth-century England initially took only small steps toward a uniquely Quaker approach to education.[5]

Yet over time, their growing interest in the creation of educational institutions rooted in the spiritual life of Friends flowered into the rich offerings that are available today. Not coincidentally, Friends were pioneers in coeducational and racially integrated institutions. Many schools that originated in Friends' concern for a "guarded" education (to protect Quaker youth from undue influence by the popular culture) eventually broadened their scope and opened their doors to others who sought the special brand of education that they had developed.

I suggest that there is an intrinsic link between the attractiveness of Quaker schools today and the spiritual values that inspired their creation. I explore this link, beginning with a brief summary of the spiritual insights of seventeenth-century Friends and then detailing some of the pedagogical values that have grown organically out of these spiritual roots. In this brief exploration, I paint with a broad brush. I am deeply indebted to numerous Quaker scholars and others who have developed a much richer account than I am able to give of Quaker schools and the educational perspectives that they have fostered.[6]

The Spiritual Roots

The taproot of Quaker religious thought, the central experience animating the life of George Fox and early Friends, is that "Christ has come to teach his people himself."[7] The living experience of divine power is neither confined to an ancient book nor under exclusive franchise to a select cadre of religious functionaries; rather, it is directly available to everyone, without need for clerical mediation or churchly authorization. Within every person, regardless of formal office or role, nationality or race, religious training or skeptical bent, lies the divine teacher, waiting to be discerned and heeded. Authentic religious conviction entails awakening to this inner authority, which conveys genuine insight and enables us to recognize whatever truth lies in other sources, while exposing that which is false and damaging. By opening our hearts and waiting upon the Spirit, we may directly experience the infusion of God's power and love.

For Fox and the early Quakers, and for most Friends today, the inward Christ is the voice of God as uniquely manifested in the historical Jesus of Nazareth; for contemporary Friends of "universalist" persuasion, the Christ within or "Inner Light" names the deepest intuitive wisdom available to everyone, also found (though differently named) in other religious traditions. For all Friends, the key insight is that we can know directly in our own hearts and souls the truth that matters most; we can recognize that truth in others and, indeed, can learn to read it in the world at large. There is "that of God in every one" (Fox 263); hence, no human being, whether pope or priest, king or magistrate, may claim an authority higher than our own inward teacher.

Yet Quakerism does not sever individuals from the collective wisdom of the seeking community. Each person has a measure of the Light, but we are notoriously fallible in our discernment of truth. How, then, shall we correct false beliefs? Corporate discernment by the gathered Meeting in worship is essential. Traditionally, Friends have also emphasized careful study of scripture, which, while in the absence of personal experience of the Spirit is not itself lifegiving, may nevertheless be used to test the insight of the seeker.

A story from early Quaker history nicely illustrates these themes. The young Margaret Fell, who eventually became the wife of George Fox and is often described as "the mother of Quakerism," recounts the moment when she first became convinced of Fox's insight and spiritual power: In a debate with clerics who were citing Biblical passages to support their claims, Fox retorted, "You will say, Christ saith this, and the apostles say this; but what canst thou say? Art thou a child of Light and hast walked in the Light, and what thou speakest is it inwardly from God?" Fell continues, "This opened me so that it cut me to the heart; and then I saw clearly we were all wrong. So I sat me down in my pew again, and cried bitterly. And I cried in my spirit to the Lord, 'We are all thieves, we are all thieves, we have taken the Scriptures in words and know nothing of them in ourselves'" (Garman et al. 235). To cite Biblical passages without experiencing the living Spirit that animates those passages is to engage in mere word games; it is to be a "thief," claiming authority to which one is not entitled. Hence, religious persuasion should aim not to coerce others by logic, rhetoric, or citation of scripture but to redirect awareness to the source of genuine authority: the inward teacher, the inner light, that of God within.

From this religious epistemology follows a radical egalitarianism. While early Friends accepted the need for legitimate political authority, they insisted by their words and actions upon fidelity to the Spirit as they discerned it. Although a king or magistrate might legitimately exercise the duties of office, that office did not imply superiority in the eyes of God, nor did it entail authority to overrule the Word of God as discerned in the gathered Meeting. As a consequence, early Friends suffered greatly at the hands of incensed political authorities and unruly mobs of common people who took offense at Friends' seemingly impertinent behavior—such as their public ministry, their refusal to swear oaths, their unwillingness to tip their hats to their "betters," and their nonpayment of tithes for support of the Church of England. Viewed as saucy, dangerously wayward, or seditious, large numbers of early Friends were imprisoned, many lost their property, and some even died as a result of persecution.

Fidelity to the inner teacher also entailed for Friends an exceptional commitment to truthfulness, accuracy of speech, and painful self-honesty. Refusal to swear oaths in court reflected Friends' insistence upon a single standard of truth regardless of setting and their commitment to live outwardly in thoroughgoing accord with their inner convictions. Simplicity and brevity of speech were favored over florid, mannered rhetoric.

Friends yearned for an undivided self-resting wholly within the divine light. In Quaker perspective, we can know ourselves truly only as we are deeply known, through radically opening ourselves to the Presence within and giving ourselves up to its searching light. Pride and self-seeking divide our hearts, obscuring our underlying unity: We may heal inner conflict and find true harmony only by "staying low" and ceasing our willful running after this or that attachment. As we "sink down to the Seed" in deep worship, the Word of God may be opened to us and we may recognize "the hidden unity in the Eternal Being" (Fox 28). We come to see that reality is communal: We are all one.

George Fox's great religious awakening—in which he "was immediately taken up in spirit, to see another or more steadfast state than Adam's in innocency, even into a state in Christ Jesus, that should never fall"—assured him that even in this lifetime we may be released from the burden of Adam's transgression, and awaken to a "new creation" in which all is "pureness, and innocency, and righteousness" (27). In this realized eschatology, Fox saw the Kingdom of God breaking through into the present moment and restoring him to a harmonious relationship with the created world. It became possible "to walk cheerfully over the earth, answering that of God in every one" (263).

The conviction that God is present in every person, and, indeed, in all of creation, led early Friends to turn away from war and preparation for war. While they saw that some use of force is necessary to maintain domestic order, Friends declared against armed conflict and reliance upon military power. Commitment to nonviolence did not entail passivity in the face of evil; rather, Friends often felt called to "speak truth to power" in ways that were disquieting or even offensive to others. Friends might speak plainly to awaken others to their own inner guide. But because the spirit of Christ is peace and love rather than strife and hatred and because no individual may claim absolute authority to pronounce upon the heart and actions of another, Friends favored conciliation over contention, love over anger, gentleness over harsh judgment.

By no means have Friends always lived up to these high ideals. Conflict, acrimony, and schism mark various periods of Quaker history, especially during the nineteenth century. Still, most Friends today would probably recognize this brief sketch as more or less faithful to Friends' original insights, aspirations, and values.

Strands of Quaker Pedagogy

The pedagogical implications of these spiritual insights did not spring full-blown at the outset, nor were they derived through theoretical analysis; rather, they became increasingly evident through an organic process over time, as Friends lived out their convictions and thought more deeply about applications to this or that dimension of practice. Among the pedagogical questions raised by Friends' spirituality are these:

- Where is the authority of knowledge to be found?
- What is the connection between classroom learning and the rest of life?
- In particular: If all are given a measure of the Light, and no one can claim absolute authority over the inner life of another, what of the traditional hierarchies of pedagogical authority and power?
- If, indeed, there is "that of God in everyone," what does this realization mean for the relationship of teacher and student?
- If we may regain the harmony between humans and the creation that was lost in Adam's fall, what are the implications for empirical study of the natural world?

Provisional answers to these and other questions have emerged over the intervening centuries and indeed are still evolving, in accord with the Quaker tradition of continuing revelation. There is no final resolution in this ongoing process; just as Friends needed more than a century to find unity regarding the wrongness of human slavery, so the implications of Quaker faith and practice for teaching and learning are themselves a work in progress with no end in sight. With these caveats, we may identify several pedagogical strands growing from the spiritual insights of early Quakers. Those who find the religious lan-

guage of seventeenth-century Quakerism to be archaic may still find power in
the pedagogical ethos, the culture of teaching and learning, that it yields today.

The Priority of Experience

A spirituality that locates authority and truth within rather than in some external voice naturally lends itself to a pedagogy that does the same. From this
perspective, the role of the teacher is not to make deposits of knowledge within
the learner from whence they may be withdrawn in the future.[8] Although the
teacher offers information to invite insight, only when students themselves
awaken to that insight and make it their own has true learning taken place.
Those charged with helping others to learn may not somehow stuff that learning into the craws of their students and expect it to be retained in proper form.
Teaching and learning in Quaker perspective are prefigured by the Platonic
view that all true knowledge is gained through redirecting one's attention. As
Socrates asserts, "Education isn't what some people declare it to be, putting
knowledge into souls that lack it, like putting sight into blind eyes…[rather] the
power to learn is present in everyone's soul…education takes for granted that
sight is there but that it isn't turned the right way or looking where it ought to
look, and it tries to redirect it appropriately" (Plato 518cd, 190).

Sight is already in the soul, but our eyes are turned away from truth. Redirecting our inward vision means awakening more fully to our own experience
and seeing into its meaning. Thus, instruction or education entails skillful questioning that invites us down the path of insight—not simply to a destination
preordained by the questioner but to a deeper intimacy with experienced reality
itself. Education is liberation, an open-ended process in which we grow larger,
see more, and open more fully to the world.

Inspired by Friends' spirituality, Parker Palmer writes, "Only as doctrine
has experiential validity can it be honored at all. The important question is not
what the text says, but what it says that can be validated by you. Whether the
subject is literature or atomic physics, the test is always experiential (or experimental)" (Palmer 1976: 3). Even when the nominal subject of learning is an
external, seemingly inert piece of data, a mathematical formula, a biological
finding, a political trend, still, the central moment of teaching and learning is
not a mechanical transfer of that information from one data bank to another
but a personal, intimate realization of truth, when the light of consciousness
flares and expands in insight, and one can say, "Oh! I see!"

To cultivate these moments of enlightenment, teacher and learner are well served by faith that they are indeed possible, by (in Thoreau's apt phrase) "an infinite expectation of the dawn." If learners have lost this expectation, perhaps through too many experiences of failure, or through harshly coercive prodding, and see education as joyless and irrelevant, it may still be possible for miracles to occur, when they encounter an instructor who believes in their potential for insight, growth, and productivity.

Integrity

Friends' insistence upon lived experience as the fount of true knowledge fostered an uncommon commitment to consistency: living day to day in accord with one's experiential conviction of truth. For teacher and student, the classroom is continuous with the whole of life, and the exercise of our intellects must be situated within the natural environment of our bodily identities, social relationships, and spiritual orientation.

Early Friends refused to swear oaths in court because they saw that to do so implied a double standard of truth: In the courtroom, one was legally bound to more exacting standards than in casual, everyday discourse, where exaggeration, dissembling, and prevarication may be taken for granted. Committed to careful regard for truth throughout all of their lives, early Quakers gained a reputation for exceptional rectitude and reliability.[9]

As in the courtroom, so in the classroom: The pedagogical implications of consistency in word and action are many and profound. In the first instance, responsible teaching and learning require a rigorous discipline of self-examination: Can my claim be validated by what I actually experience? Such care in observation is an essential feature of sound scientific method, but also of the thoughtful study of a literary text, a logical proof, an historical document.

More broadly, the expectation that our behavior be in accord with our convictions speaks to the issue of character and personal integrity: What goes on inside an educational institution should not be divorced from what goes on outside. George Fox challenged his fellow Quakers to "Let your lives speak," and in fact, our lives *do* speak, often more loudly than our words. Responsible pedagogy connects the academic with the rest of life, for example, by bringing a class in environmental issues to the bank of a polluted river, by noting the barrio a few blocks away from a classroom discussion of immigration policy, or by otherwise drawing upon actual, concrete examples from the experience of students to make learning come alive.

When we engage in academic discourse that is untethered from the anchor of our personal experience, our minds are severed from our bodies, our ideas from our actions. Flights of abstract fantasy leave behind the concrete circumstances of our lives. Whatever its diverting attractions, such language opens the door to hypocrisy. Words and symbols are not mere irresponsible diversions, but are themselves forms of behavior; what we say should be rooted in that which we can discern to be appropriate and sound. Truth is not merely something that we know but also something that we do.

The Facts Are Friendly

If Quaker pedagogy invites us into engagement with the world, it also sees that world as approachable and ultimately welcoming. The conception of the natural world as ineluctably "fallen" and shot through with sin, a view attributed to the Genesis account of Adam and Eve's transgression and God's resulting punishment, and elaborated at great length in Calvinist theology, entails a spirituality at odds with the world it surveys. While early Friends certainly were burdened by the sinfulness of their own and others' lives, they also, as shown in Fox's central mystical opening, believed that we may recover in our lifetime an original harmony between God and humans. As Melvin Keiser observes, "Beneath our sinful experience of a distorted world is the illumined experience of the world in its original freshness and power permeated by divine presence" (8). God speaks to us everywhere, calling us to revere and restore the natural world.

Friends' reconnection to a "new creation," their conviction that our original unity with the natural world may be regained and enjoyed, allowed them to enter into scientific studies with a sense of welcoming trust. A respectful empirical observation of the world reveals God's presence, as William Penn declares:

> It were happy if we studied nature more in natural things, and acted according to nature, whose rules are few, plain, and most reasonable....The heavens, earth, and waters with their respective, various, and numerous inhabitants, their productions, nature, seasons, sympathies, and antipathies, their use, benefit and pleasure, would be better understood by us; and an eternal wisdom, power, majesty, and goodness very conspicuous to us through those sensible and passing forms, the world wearing the mark of its

Maker, Whose stamp is everywhere visible and the characters very legible to the children of wisdom. (Penn 19)

Reflecting a "nature-friendly" theology, Friends in the eighteenth and nineteenth centuries were well represented among the ranks of scientific thinkers and within The Royal Society. In the early years of the American colonies, a number of prominent naturalists were Quakers.

Invite All Voices

The radical egalitarianism of early Friends challenged authoritarian hierarchies of all kinds. Themselves excluded and silenced, Friends broke through the repressive hegemony of their time with prophetic power. As Jesus welcomed into his presence the outcasts, the rejected and despised, so early Friends disquieted and transgressed the prevailing social order by a "disorderly" eruption of the Spirit. As it has developed over time, the Quaker testimony of equality is ideally not the assertion of a superficial unity achieved by silencing dissident voices but rather a richer unity in diversity that seeks the fullest presence of all. Such a discovery of deeper unity can arise only when all voices are heard.

Thus, Quaker pedagogy invites all voices into the dialogue, with the conviction that each may bring some measure of light and truth. To notice silent students and pay attention to their nonverbal signals; to communicate appreciation for their presence, and if they gain courage to speak, to welcome their contributions: This respectful, expectant listening mirrors the process of Quaker worship itself. Inwardly, Quaker pedagogy invites all to awaken to their own silenced internal voices, to move toward greater wholeness and an undivided self, thereby awakening to the power of intuitive knowing, to the life within.

If true education awakens, empowers, and liberates, then a teacher's role is to facilitate these processes. Traditional educational agendas have typically functioned to induct students into an approved ideology, thereby subordinating them to existing power structures. At its best, Quaker pedagogy is dangerously unsettling to such agendas, since it posits in each learner a sacredness and potential wisdom to which all should be answerable. Inspired by such a vision, Quaker pedagogy seeks (in Nelle Morton's memorable phrase), to "hear human beings to speech" (128), to invite the awakening of the unique narrative that constitutes the experiential insight of each person.

Friends' treasuring of that of God within every person and their insistence upon hearing every voice have historically been fertile ground for feminist thought. At a time when the very idea of female ministers was cause for ridicule, George Fox, Margaret Fell, and other early Friends insisted that the Spirit is accessible to women and men alike, and that anyone through whom the Spirit moves has a duty to respond, regardless of gender. Four of the five signers of the 1848 Seneca Falls Declaration of Women's Rights were Friends and many of the brightest luminaries of the nineteenth-century women's movement were likewise Friends, including Lucretia Mott, Susan B. Anthony, and Alice Paul, the author of the Equal Rights Amendment (Bacon 1).

Quaker-inspired feminism approaches issues of inclusiveness and gender equality with a straightforward, unapologetic assumption that *of course* equality should be reflected in our words, actions, and policies. Without grounding in the Spirit, the drive for equality too often degenerates into reaction, bitterness, and even violence, whereas a spiritual practice that diminishes fear enables a matter-of-fact assumption of equality that defuses reaction and polarization. The voice of social justice at its best is serene and unapologetic, confronting evil while remaining open and accepting toward the evildoer. Thus, the reality of God within not only confirms the fundamental worth of everyone but also, through its life-giving reassurance of divine power and grace, reduces fear born of perceived weakness, thus enabling one to affirm equality without becoming rancorous or abusive.

What does such spiritually based inclusiveness mean in a classroom? The root assumptions of equality and mutual respect properly set the tone. Those from groups which have historically been marginalized and silenced are assured of full inclusion; those from groups which have historically been privileged find that assumption no longer obtains yet are themselves not demonized or shamed. In actual practice, however, lingering trenchant legacies of racism, sexism, classism, and other forms of oppression distort every educational endeavor to some degree. Friends' spiritual experience does not inoculate against the eruption of these injustices, but at least it provides a vision of equality as well as the insight to claim and live into that vision.

How are these messages of inclusiveness and empowerment to be communicated without inviting a host of abuses? Put simply, how does a teacher make space for "hearing students into speech" without inviting garbage? A "student-centered" classroom can privilege the loudest voices; it can valorize a shallow relativism; it can undermine the natural authority of truth itself.

Patterns of Quaker spirituality are again helpful in addressing these real dangers. As manifested in a gathered Meeting for Worship, Friends value careful listening and encourage speaking from a deeper, reflective place that respects all who are present. Underlying such attitudes is a reverence for truth itself as a reality that makes claims upon us all. As Parker Palmer suggests, Quaker pedagogy is neither teacher- nor student- but subject-centered: teacher and students are jointly engaged in an inquiry into a third "great thing," which "has a presence so real, so vivid, so vocal, that it can hold teacher and students alike accountable for what they say and do" (Palmer 1980: 117). In the person of a sensitive and spiritually aware teacher, such an attitude is infectious and helps to set the tone in all but the most chaotic classrooms. Students themselves yearn for this deeper connection to a larger reality, and when they are assured of respectful and loving support, they are more receptive to hearing its call, not only from the teacher, but also from others and, indeed, from their own hearts.

Thus, Fox's probing query—"What canst thou say?"—is not an invitation to shallow self-absorption, an indulgent shrinking of attention to the small span of one's momentary preoccupations. Rather, it is an unsettling challenge to put ourselves on the line, to say what we know experientially of the larger world. Fox's question to his critics and the pedagogical principle it inspires calls for humble opening to an embracing reality of which we are a part and to which we all must answer whether we like it or not.

Although in most classrooms teachers typically occupy center stage, the symbolism implied by this focus is both seductive and suspect. If teaching is the activity of helping people to learn, then the learners are the focal points of an enlightened educational process. Responsible teachers are attentive to their students, mindful of group dynamics, aware of subtle signals within the classroom, and ready to take into account particular circumstances of their hearers that may affect the learning process. A concept that was originally developed for managerial and business ethics, that of "servant leadership," is useful here. The author of this concept, Robert K. Greenleaf, was himself a Friend and brought his Quaker beliefs to bear upon the analysis of effective leadership. A good leader takes care to make sure that other people's highest priority needs are being served. The best test…is: Do those served grow as persons? Do they *while being served,* become healthier, wiser, freer, more autonomous, more likely themselves to become servants? *And,* what is the effect on the least privileged in society: will they benefit, or, at least, not be further deprived? (Greenleaf 13f)

Greenleaf summarizes a central feature of Quaker pedagogy: The leadership that is teaching serves that of God in the learner, inviting and calling out the best, and supporting the whole person. Pedagogical service does not pander to student self-indulgence but rather invites students themselves to serve others in fuller engagement with their worlds. Such pedagogical service does not preclude firmness, sternness, even anger, if learners do not themselves recognize and honor their own sacredness. But a teacher's firmness should stem not from a bruised ego nor from fear of loss of control but rather from a dedication to the precious potential within the learner that is not being honored.

Nonviolence

Rather than seeing the classroom as battleground or boot camp, Quaker pedagogy takes seriously the invitation of William Penn, "Let us then try what love can do" (87). Various forms of coercion may by themselves secure an external, grudging compliance with a teacher's demands; all too often, however, such pressures elevate fear to the primary pedagogical principle and drive learners away from their own inner teacher. Education becomes no more than a dutiful command performance, backed by threat. Thus, Quaker pedagogy upholds an ideal of nonviolence: a respect for the delicate unfolding consciousness within the learner. Although clear expectations for students are helpful, including an understanding of the consequences of failure, the primary pedagogical tone should be not intimidation but invitation and support, so that with appropriate help students may quicken to the pure joy of seeing and knowing. Classrooms and other learning environments should be safe spaces in which all who are present may drop defenses and open more fully to their shared endeavor.

But what of that most ubiquitous, troublesome feature of educational institutions, grades, and the coercion they imply? How can one reconcile the assignment of grades, with their power to punish or reward, arrogate or humiliate, certify or exclude, with Friends' testimonies of peace and love? An historical reminder may be helpful: As noted previously, early Friends were not anarchists; their disavowal of the use of force was not absolute. While opposing war and preparation for war, they did not advocate the abolition of police, physical restraint, or legal punishment. As George Fox, William Penn, and others asserted, maintenance of good public order requires some use of the sword to punish evildoers (Brock 2730, 322 n. 5). In our efforts to secure safety and good order, we should rely as much as possible upon gentler means and employ forcible restraint, confinement, and other forms of punishment only when genuinely necessary. Even when force is used, every effort should be made lovingly to support the offender in walking a more orderly path.

In pedagogical matters a similar understanding applies. Consistent truthfulness requires that we be prepared to speak not only truth that is pleasant to hear but also, as the blunt, outspoken George Fox himself often displayed, to be truthful in ways that may be needed, if unwelcome and hard to hear. Grades may serve as honest assessment, providing feedback that is truthful if not always flattering. As for the disciplinary function of grades: Brandishing the stick should never be the primary inducement to educational effort. But if all other attempts to reach a wayward student fail, it may be necessary to let the student experience the consequences of unacceptable behavior, whether through poor marks or other forms of discipline.

Actual practice at contemporary Quaker schools provides relevant perspective. A few dispense entirely with grades, relying wholly upon oral and written comments. Most, however, employ grading systems similar to those used in non-Quaker institutions, not solely as final judgments upon students' performance but also to communicate expectations and encourage better work. All have some established means of disciplining students for their own good and for the good of the school. Except as arrayed in an abstract, polarized debate, there is no contradiction between avoiding coercion as much as possible, and employing "tough love" such as low grades or other disciplinary measures as needed.

The theme of nonviolence in Quaker pedagogy can be further clarified by some comparisons and contrasts with the thought of Paulo Freire, whose *Pedagogy of the Oppressed* continues to exercise widespread influence not only upon pedagogical theorists situated within educational institutions but also more broadly among activists for social justice and revolutionary change.

Quaker pedagogy shares with Freire a concern for social justice. Both pedagogies are concerned with the welfare of those who are least privileged; both seek to make the educational process not an induction into traditional power structures but an avenue for social transformation and justice. Both are destabilizing to oppressive power structures: both seek to overcome patterns of dominance, of "power over," and replace them with mutual empowerment under conditions of relative equality and fairness.

Friends' and Freire's pedagogies both invite a fuller consciousness within the learner; both recognize that true education is not so much a process of instilling information as awakening insight. Both are broadly liberatory; education is the cultivation of a natural, healthy state of each human being. Both see education as essentially participatory and dialogic, a process in which sharp separations between subject and object and between subject and subject are softened. Both emphasize that the proper ground for all educational endeavors is love, our underlying connectedness with one another.

However, Freire's philosophical grounding in the dialectical theories of Hegel and Marx inclined him to a different vision of social transformation than is found in Quaker faith and practice. Freire's model of transformation and revolution is oppositional rather than cooperative. He writes that "Freedom is acquired by conquest" (47), and therefore that liberation requires identification with a lower class in conflict with other classes. Because evil is initiated by the oppressors, those who are oppressed may rise up in self-righteous confidence that whatever failings they may find in their own lives are attributable to the inhumane conditions to which they are subjected by those who dominate them.[10] Thus, Freire's model of change is political, based upon class struggle, whereas Friends' model of social change is grounded in a spiritual perspective according to which, beneath class distinctions, we are all, oppressed and oppressor alike, fundamentally equal. Since everyone regardless of social class or political position manifests "that of God," Friends seek to reach out to oppressors and awaken them to the divine presence within themselves, recognizing that they also are children of God.

Likewise, Friends' efforts in teaching and learning do not seek to identify the learner with an oppressed class so as to present a stronger front against the dominant class, but rather to undercut class distinctions altogether by living out the radical vision of an equality in which we are all intimately connected. Likewise, Quaker-inspired "multiculturalism" does not regard differing individuals and groups as thrown together in a "salad mix" of discrete entities but welcomes their diversity while affirming a deeper foundation of unity.

The Spiritual Fruits

Quaker pedagogy is a work in progress; it continues to evolve as Quaker educators realize the deeper implications of their faith and practice, while adapting to ongoing change and shifting circumstance. I have highlighted five strands of Quaker pedagogy:

- **The priority of experience:** Awaken fully to our encounters with the world.
- **Integrity:** Link education consistently with the whole of life.
- **The facts are friendly:** Trust that the creation is welcoming and life-affirming.
- **Invite all voices:** Include all in the community of learning.
- **Nonviolence:** Respect the tender souls of teachers and learners alike.

These do not by any means exhaust the scope of pedagogical principles inspired by Friends' spiritual life. They do, however, provide a preliminary touchstone for self-examination as educators seek to unite professional and personal lives within a larger, encompassing purpose: to support our students and ourselves as all grow stronger, more loving, and more knowing of that which deserves our ultimate attention and care.

Notes

1. For extensive comments on earlier drafts, I am grateful to Langdon Elsbree, Judith Favor, and Paul Lacey.

2. While the term "Quaker" was originally derogatory, it has come to be accepted by most members of the Religious Society of Friends today. I will use "Friend" and "Quaker" interchangeably.

3. The Friends Council on Education lists some ninety Friends' Schools in the United States and abroad. Quaker-related colleges and universities belonging to the Friends Association for Higher Education include Barclay College, Bryn Mawr College, Earlham College, Friends University, Friends World Program of Long Island University, George Fox University, Guilford College, Haverford College, Houston Graduate School of Theology, Malone College, Pendle Hill, Swarthmore College, Whittier College, William Penn University, Wilmington College, and Woodbrooke Quaker Study Centre (in England).

4. During the presidency of Bill Clinton, Chelsea Clinton was enrolled in Sidwell Friends' School in Washington, D.C.

5. In his epistles and other writings, George Fox encouraged the creation of schools for children (both boys and girls) of members of the new Quaker movement. Though no accurate count is available, a number of Meeting and proprietary schools were created in the first fifty years of Quakerism, often attracting as schoolmasters those who before their convincement as Friends had been priests or ministers in other religious traditions. (Paul Lacey, personal communication)

6. See especially Paul A. Lacey, *Growing into Goodness: Essays on Quaker Education* (Wallingford, PA: Pendle Hill Publications, 1998) and *Education and the Inward Teacher,* Pendle Hill Pamphlet #278 (Wallingford, PA: Pendle Hill Publications, 1988); Parker Palmer, *Meeting for Learning: Education in a Quaker Context,* Pendle Hill Bulletin No. 284 (Wallingford, PA: Pendle Hill, 1976), *To Know As We Are Known: A Spirituality of Education* (New York: Harper & Row, 1983), *The Courage to Teach: Exploring the Inner Landscape of a Teacher's Life* (San Francisco: JosseyBass, 1998); Douglas H. Heath, *Schools of Hope: Developing Mind and Character in Today's Youth* (San Francisco: JosseyBass, 1994); Helen Hole, *Things Civil and Useful* (Richmond, IN: Friends United Press, 1978); Kim Hays, *Practicing Virtues: Moral Traditions at Quaker and Military Boarding Schools* (Berkeley: University of California Press, 1994).

7. Variations of this phrase occur throughout Fox's writings; see, for example, Fox 20.

8. I take this "banking" metaphor from Paulo Freire (1989: 72).

9. For similar reasons, Quaker merchants established the practice of single-pricing of merchandise rather than demanding more than they were willing to settle for through haggling with the customer.

10. Freire writes, "Never in history has violence been initiated by the oppressed. How could they be initiators, if they themselves are the result of violence?" (1989: 55).

‍Part Two
Building Community:
Constituting the Classroom

❧ Chapter Two
Liberating Soul Sparks:
Psyche, Classroom, and Community

Mary Watkins

[A Hasidic rabbi tells his son's friend:] A man is born into this world with only a tiny spark of goodness in him. The spark is God, it is the soul: the rest is ugliness and evil, a shell. The spark must be guarded like a treasure, it must be nurtured, it must be fanned into flame. It must learn to seek out other sparks, it must dominate the shell. Anything can be a shell, Reuven. Anything. Indifference, laziness, brutality, and genius. Yes, even a great mind can be a shell and choke the spark.

Chaim Potok, 263

My path/my location: When I was fourteen years old my parents decided to send me to a private school. The only non-boarding option was a nearby Friends' school. They knew very little about Quakerism and certainly did not choose the school on that basis. To their increasing dismay, I discovered a deep resonance with Quaker values of simplicity, silent prayer, and meditation, the following of leadings, nonviolence, and community service. Alongside these interests, my studies of depth psychology, particularly Jungian and archetypal psychology, and liberation psychologies have evolved.

At present, I coordinate community and ecological fieldwork and research within the masters and doctoral programs in depth psychology at Pacifica Graduate Institute and teach courses on the interpenetration of psyche, culture, and spirituality. I think it is less likely that my early exposure to Quakerism *caused* my perception of the interpenetration of these domains and more likely that there are deeply resonant notes in Quakerism, depth psychology, liberation psychologies, and the practices that issue from them: mystical prayer, depth psychotherapy, participatory research, and liberatory education. Depth psychology refers to the various theories and practices that are based on theories of the unconscious, including psychoanalysis, Jungian, Adlerian, Reichian, and Lacanian work.

In my work as a depth psychology educator with adult learners I continue to try to become aware of the pedagogical practices/habits that choke the divine sparks in myself, each student, our classroom learning community, and the work in the wider world that we are each led to. I am in search of practices and theories that—with grace—have a liberating potential for the soul sparks that are gifted to us, that satisfy their desire for the nurture of being caringly fanned into flame. Formal education has too often choked such sparks, isolating the intellect from the heart and the soul, self from other, and self from community. One way I have come to think about my work of reintegrating these domains as a teacher is through the eyes of a creation story that influenced both Hasidism and Quakerism. It has elements familiar to us from Heraclitus, Stoic philosophy, Gnosticism, and Meister Eckhart (see Scholem 1946, 1965).

Howard Brinton (1952) traces Quakers' use of divine or Inward Light imagery but observes that Quakers have not used the image of sparks so familiar to Hasidism. He interprets this as having to do with a sense of the divine as complete in each manifestation, not as shattered or fragmented. "Spark or Sparkle might imply that the Light was divided, a part being in one person and part in another. There was but one Light. The nearer all come to it, the nearer they come to one another, like radii of a circle when they approach the center, to use a figure from Plotinus" (21–22). We do see in Quaker writings, however, a concern with shedding that which hides the light in oneself, and seeking the hidden light in others.

In 1492 the Jews were exiled from Spain. In the aftermath of this tragic dispersion, the kabbalist Isaac Luria (1534–1572), whose family had been forced from Spain to Safed, Palestine, brought forth this creation myth, drawn between the poles of exile and redemption. The German mystic Jacob Boehme (1575–1624) studied and referred to it. George Fox (1624–1691), the founder of Quakerism, read Boehme with great interest. The vision it presents of spiritual life as a process of co-creation with God is deeply resonant with Quaker faith and practice as well as with Quaker imagery of perceiving and liberating the divine light in each and every aspect of creation.

In the Beginning

God was everywhere. It is said that in order to create, God had to contract and concentrate his being, to inhale as it were, so that space for creation could arise. Just as a garden holds the smell of jasmine, even when the plant is removed, this space of potential creation was suffused with the light of God's being. Creation occurred with a series of inhalations and exhalations. The emanations of God's being first created Adam Kadmon, the primordial man. From Adam's eyes, mouth, nostrils, and ears the light of God's being streamed forth. This streaming created vessels of light in which more divine light could be contained and differentiated. Initially this process went well, filling three vessels. But then, as the divine light came from Adam's eyes, it suddenly surged forth with great intensity, breaking the fourth and the earlier vessels, shattering them, and dispersing their light into all corners of the world. Both light and evil were strewn. The shards of light that lodged in each and every being and thing were hidden by shells or husks, *klelippoth,* that must be removed for the light to shine forth.

Quakers experience this divine light or "that of God" within each being. They often speak of this light as a divine seed. In interactions with others, Quakers attempt to orient toward this divinity within the other. George Fox, the founder of Quakerism, instructs, "So feel the seed of God in every particular…and then ye come to be the bone of his bone and flesh of his flesh" (Epistle 99, quoted in Brinton, *Ethical Mysticism* 34). This practice, says Fox, allows us to "answer that of God in every one" (quoted in *Faith and Practice* 66).

Through the eyes of Luria's story we can experience the way in which creation is unfinished and, thus, ongoing. This ongoing work of creation is a work of *restoration,* of liberating the hidden sparks of exiled divine light. Once these sparks are gathered, it is believed that messianic time can begin, a time of peace, plenty, justice, love, and at-home-ness. In other words, creation was not finished by God as imaged in Genesis, with man and woman spoiling it, falling from a paradisiacal state. Creation was seen as continuing, requiring us for its fulfillment in ways particular to each of our beings. The restoration that Luria speaks of is not restoration to the past but toward the deeply desired. Luria's myth works within an interdependent paradigm of the self, where there can be no final coming home for one until the divinity that has been hidden and exiled is liberated in each and gathered together.

In Quakerism this restoration is likened to mending a world that is ripped and refusing to act in ways that further rip the world, such as war and greedful accumulation of resources. William Penn, the Quaker founder of the Pennsylvania colony, put it this way: "True godliness does not turn men out of the world, but enables them to live better in it, and excites their endeavors to mend it" (quoted in Boulding 59).

Holy Converse, Dialogue

In *The Way of Man*, Martin Buber describes the Hasidic understanding that the world is an irradiation of God, with an independence of existence and striving. "It is apt always and everywhere," he says, "to form a crust around itself." In every thing and being beneath this crust or shell lies a divine spark. It is man's task to rejoin each spark with its Origin, a task which is achieved through "holy converse with the thing and using it in a holy manner" (56).

"Holy converse with the thing and using it in a holy manner" entails maintaining an awareness of that spark within each and relating to it in a sacred manner that mitigates against using the other for one's own sake regardless of the negative impact on the other. Quakers aspire to respect the sacred in each human. This has led to testimonies for peace with Native Americans during the colonial period; opposition to slavery, war, and capital punishment; testimonies for prison and mental institution reform; and many initiatives for education. Quakers have a long history of developing dialogical practices that steady interaction in a careful orientation toward the sacred. Notably, Quaker Meetings for Business are approached from this orientation, underscoring the continuity of prayer life with human interactions. Such an attitude has profound implications for dialogue in the classroom, for the dialogical hosting of one's "inner" and imaginal life, and for participatory research and work that fosters cultural and ecological restoration. My life as a teacher feels like a search for an understanding and honoring of these implications, in both the practices I engage in and the theories I work with. First, classroom practice.

When sparks of soul are scattered throughout the classroom, a pedagogy based on *delivering* learning to students, what Paolo Freire calls a "banking model of education," causes further hiding and encasement of the sparks (1989: 72). A teacher who is seeking the sparks in her students must proceed humbly, holding an awareness of how students' projections onto her of greater expertise, intelligence, and value will silence their communion with their own thoughts and experience and their expression of these in the classroom. Creating an undue focus on oneself as the teacher will also result in students turning a deaf ear to each other, falsely believing that fellow students have little of value to offer, a practice that further silences. Teachers are reluctant to yield space to what they cannot control and predict, partly due to their responsibility for the class. But it is only in such yielding that what has been silenced, marginalized, and unseen can venture forth into the community of learning. This does not mean that the teacher has nothing to share from her own years of learning and experience, but that she must take great care that this sharing opens the space for dialogue rather than closes it down. Too often teachers, like some parents, hold a narrow vision of how sparks manifest, subtly steering students into conformity with unspoken and unreflected-upon norms of their disciplines. There must be room made for students who disturb, who are interested in what others judge to be peculiar, who harbor unique perceptions and sensibilities that the classroom often fails to host. To foster a critical approach to the theories and practices within one's discipline is in the Quaker spirit. Quakerism arose as a critical witness to how the institutions and rituals of the Protestant Church at the time were mitigating against direct spiritual experience and the conduct of lives consistent with such experience. It has maintained its critical role within its own practice as well as with regard to society, allowing it to be in fertile dialogue with other spiritual traditions.

I am seeking a space for exploration and learning in which the not-yet-known can arise, where students will experience their thought growing in complexity and depth as they listen in deeply to the multiplicity of viewpoints present in their classroom. I feel the sweetness of satisfaction when I see their sadness at parting from each other, when they reflect on the profound gifts they have received from each other in the course of our learning together. I also feel joy as a teacher when, at the end of the three years of course work in our program, those initially silent, perhaps uncertain about their capacity for thought and expression, have found the area of study and practice they feel called to and have discovered how to lend their voice to it through being carefully listened into expression. I am thrilled to see how those students initially subtly devalued by others have become seen as teachers themselves and exhibit a glow from having their experience, thought, being, and calling recognized and valued. How do we begin to prepare the space for this?

"The thing is to fight with the text, even though loving it, no?"

> I say that reading is not just to walk on the words, and it is not flying over the words either. Reading is rewriting what we are reading. Reading is to discover the connections between the text and the context of the text, and also how to connect the text/context with my context, the context of the reader. But for me, what is indispensable, is to be critical. Criticism creates the necessary intellectual discipline, asking questions to the reading, to the writing, to the book, to the text. We should not submit to the text or be submissive in front of the text. The thing is to fight with the text, even though loving it, no?
>
>   Paulo Freire, *A Pedagogy of Liberation* (1011 cf. qt. on p.29)

Students first formally encounter our class together through the syllabus. They look for the reading and assignments that are due for the first class. They find this passage from Freire, giving a dialogical sense of reading, with the following assignment:

> Begin a reading journal for this class with the following format. This journal will be a place for you to dialogue with aspects of the readings that you find interesting. For each of the authors you read each session (or reading), choose an idea that interests you and write where it leads you in your own thinking (in a page or two). Take Freire's words to heart! Each time we meet copies of this work will be collected at the beginning of class. They may be handwritten. I will not be reading and commenting on each one. The object of this assignment is twofold: to help you work through the readings in a systematic, timely, and thorough manner, and to help you be active in relationship to them—arguing, appreciating, showing the implications (personal and professional), figuring out what exactly rings true or false for you given your own experience, extending a theory into a different domain.

What I look for in the journals is whether a student is engaging the reading. I reflect back to them if they are just listing out the main points or staying on the surface of the reading. I cheer them on as they enter a dialogical back-and-forth with the author and the ideas, as they engage in seeking resonance and discord between their own knowings and experience and what is being presented theoretically.

This practice is resonant with Quakers' insistence that spiritual understanding is not to be accepted on faith from others in roles of authority but is to be sought through one's own direct personal experience. Unprogrammed or silent Meetings for Worship are unencumbered by ritual, sermons, already-written prayers, and gospel interpretations. Rather, a space is made "to wait upon the

Lord and enjoy his Presence" (Whiting, quoted in Brinton, *Ethical Mysticism* 6), to make a clearing in which the sacred can be intimately perceived in one's own experience.

"the creation of a world in which it will be easier to love"

Freire, *Pedagogy of the Oppressed* (24)

My hope is that this initial direction regarding a dialogical stance toward the readings will be extended to students' relations to myself, other students, the ideas we are working with, and the communities where we practice. Sadly, most teachers and students meet together with a history of being wounded by educational practices. There must be room to acknowledge the legacy of our coming together, and to state our intention and our hope to create a safe *and* spirited space in which learning can take root. Despite years of asking for my classroom to be set up in a circle without a podium, this is never done, so I always arrive early and get my aerobic exercise by dragging the podium out of sight. It is as though the very fixtures of the classroom cannot believe that this representation of hierarchical education/knowing is really not needed. Oftentimes I do find the chairs in a circle, but there is the podium stuck in the circle as well!

For my first session with students in the fall I ask that they read about the process of dialogue and council in groups (see Bohm; Zimmerman and Coyle). These processes are similar to Quaker worship, sharing in their focus on deep listening, speaking from the heart, care toward tending the corporate body of the group, and welcoming what freely arises in a nonhierarchical environment of mutual respect and shared attention to the sacred. In worship sharing, a small group gathers to engage in silent Meeting for Worship together. A query is often given to orient reflection and prayer. Opportunity is given for each participant to share the fruit of his/her meditation. In this nonhierarchical fashion insight and inspiration are enjoyed.

In my classes, after some remarks on the practice of dialogue and council, we sit in council for an hour and a half. I stress that we are together not only to express our thoughts and feelings but to learn how to tend the thought of the group (see Bohm). To do this we must allow for ample silence between speakers so that what another has said can deeply enter us and so that we can listen closely to our own evolving thoughts and feelings. To allow for silence in which to metabolize what has been shared makes it more likely that what will be said next will relate to what has come before. I suggest that we need to use discernment regarding when and how much to speak. The group as a whole cannot think well if it does not hear from all of its members.

The challenge for those of us who speak often and amply is to deepen our listening and our capacity for holding the spaciousness of silence. This will create room for voices and images that have a more difficult time emerging within the community. Those of us who tend toward silence must make a special effort to lend our thoughts and feelings to the group. M. Scott Peck says (in Simkinson) that the greatest sin against communication is to speak when you are not moved and to not speak when you are. To create safety so that what has been marginalized and silenced can emerge, the members need to deeply consider issues of confidentiality. They also need to be forewarned about suspending bad habits that mitigate against the deepening of dialogue, such as using the dialogue space to convince or persuade others, to prove oneself worthwhile, to defend one's own point of view, to derogate the other's point of view, to establish a cozy, polite atmosphere that pretends at agreement and suffocates difference, to air personal problems that are not relevant to the inquiry of the group, or to compete.

In council practice, a talking piece is passed around the circle. When it is in your hands, you may share with the group anything you are led to say, briefly and from the heart. You may also pass. When the talking piece is in the hands of others, you listen from the heart. There is no cross dialogue. Each person has a place and a time to share in the circle. A beauty of the dialogue group is that power is de-centered, delivered to the one with the talking piece, and then yielded.

This is their first chance as new graduate students to listen to their fellow students and to bring forth some things about themselves and the beginning of a graduate program that they wish others to know about themselves. Gradually, students begin to share their fears, self-doubts, and hopes for this experience of learning. One person voices years of discrimination as a Mexican American in school settings that sour his hopes and quicken his sense of vigilance. An older woman shares that she never spoke in her college classes years ago and that she holds a deep desire that she can come to value her own thoughts enough to share them. One student confides that she has a propensity to talk too much, particularly when anxious and insecure. She invites the class to gently interrupt her if this begins to get in the way. This taste of council, which most classes decide to continue regularly on their own, is linked with the listening into diverse points of view within the classroom experience about to unfold. Students are cautioned against automatic distancing reactions of disagreement and dismissal and invited instead to draw closer to ideas and experiences they would ordinarily flee from or disparage. They are asked to listen in more closely to these and to treat them as potential teachers of areas they may understand least.

This practice is resonant with Quaker practices of tending corporate worship. Quakers attempt to discern whether their impulse to share in Meeting arises from a leading or not, and whether their sharing serves the larger worship body. Those who are listening do not respond directly to the speaker but hold in their own silence what has been offered. When this rhythmic process of silence, sharing, listening, and silence is sustained, a "gathered" Meeting may be experienced, where there is an experienced unity amidst the diversity present. This has been referred to as group mysticism. Friends are clear that the Meeting for Worship provides a crucial container for individual spiritual experience. The gathered attention and intention of the larger group help to steady the individual in his/her meditation, helping "the way to open," allowing the individual (and at times the group) to become clear about the path to be walked.

Margery Abbott relates that early Friends spoke of being "broken" in worship, meaning "self-will and self-deception were broken down by the work of the Light as they sat in silence. As a result their hearts were made tender toward God and one another." The gathered classroom reveals this tenderness, as students learn to listen each other into speech. It is as though the hard shell of the seed has been softened, allowing the small, green unfurled leaves within the seed to stretch out and begin to become themselves.

Just as I am trying to move the dialogical space from the practice of council into the business of the classroom, Quakers try to move prayerful silence from Meeting for Worship into the corporate handling of the Meeting's affairs. One implication of this is that all perspectives are invited when holding an item of business. Quaker Meetings slowly seek consensus in order to move forward. When there is none, the group continues to listen into the differences that inform it on a particular matter. While this can take great patience, it is a practice that avoids the violence of one point of view usurping another. One holds the conflict until "a way opens."

In the classroom we do not seek consensus, but we do want to hold difference with patience, hoping our careful being with it will allow it to offer its lessons to us. For instance, as we discuss the development of dialogical capacities in human development, we study research that looks at girls and women, boys and men. Pretty soon the distance between the class and the research dissolves, and members are sharing their own experiences of how gender acculturation has impacted dialogue in their lives. As emotions rise, some would like to reduce the complexity of experience to a simplistic formula or to change the subject. But as we allow the heat, we can find ourselves not resting on previous knowledge but actually searching for understandings that are new to us.

As we strengthen our capacities to engage in inner and outer dialogue, students study and engage in practices of appreciative inquiry, public conversation amidst divisive viewpoints, reconciliation work, and community visioning. Such work is aimed at holding a space where deep differences in perspective and experience can be hosted, while respect for common ground and humanity can be quickened. As we know, without careful attention to such divides, others can too easily be negated, leading to psychosocial conflict and violence. As the students relate together over their three years of coursework, experiences within their own group, as well as differences among themselves, can be fertile ground for learning these practices. The microcosm of the classroom contains the same racism, sexism, homophobia, competition between viewpoints, power struggles, and silencing of minority voices present in the larger society. When dialogue is available as a resource, such issues have hope for being brought to awareness and worked through.

The Slow Dilation of the Self: Experiencing the Path between Psyche and Culture

> The ego's firmness has its virtues, but at some point we seek the slow dilation, to use another term of Whitman's, in which the ego enjoys a widening give and take with the world and is finally abandoned in ripeness.
>
> Lewis Hyde (17)

When I was a child there was a "sinkhole" on the edge of our yard. If you put sticks and stones in it one day, you could go back the next day and see that they had disappeared beneath the earth's skin. My mother told me that this would be a good place to dig in order to get to China. As this idea—of going to China—appealed to me, I found myself digging in this hole over years, hoping that eventually I would be able to slip to the other side of the world.

As a Jungian-oriented therapist for over two decades, I witnessed many people slipping down through the hole of depression and other sufferings. Many did pass through the center of being and found the deep connection between so-called "inner work" and the "world work" they felt called to. But I must also share that this was not always the case. More times than I am comfortable with, "inner work" that was initially necessary transformed itself into a defense against deep participation with the world. Some became lost in a cul-de-sac where work with dream, image, and affect became ends in themselves, unrelated to the *anima mundi,* the world soul, of which they are a part. One of the reasons I am drawn to Quakers is the beauty of their rhythmic turning from inward to outward, a rhythm that dissolves these distinctions, allowing the experience of the "Inward Light" to bring them closer to others and the world. Insofar as they experience the Inward Light as one, the closer an individual becomes to it, the closer she becomes to others.

In Luria's creation story, he describes the necessity for two kinds of interrelated work: *tikkun nefresh,* accomplished on a mystical plane through meditation and prayer, and *tikkun olam,* accomplished on a worldly plane through relations with others and nature. *Tikkun olam* can be translated as the restoration of the world. Neither was described as easy, as the sparks of the *anima mundi* are intertwined with and encased in evil. Quakerism recognizes "the *within* that is also the *beyond,*" aspiring to the spiritual marriage Saint Teresa described as the union of pure spirit with the world of life around us (Brinton, *Ethical Mysticism* 36, 10).

I have come to believe that the use of inner work as a defense can sometimes mirror a lack of clarity within the various depth psychologies themselves about how the practice of *tikkun nefresh* and *tikkun olam* are connected. It is this connection that I want my students to experience so that they can feel the way in which "inner" and "outer" work are falsely divided by our Cartesian ways of constructing reality. Brinton suggests that the tension between reflection and action, between being and doing, arises in two strands of Christianity, one reflecting the Greek propensity to seek the Divine in the depths of the soul through contemplation and withdrawal, and the other mirroring the Hebraic tradition's emphasis on action to bring about the kingdom of God on earth. He stresses that Quakerism combines these "two complementary movements, withdrawal to an inward Source of Truth and return to action in the world. Quakerism is both contemplative and active, both metaphysical and ethical" (58). Science rejected the idea and the experience of an ensouled cosmos. Strengthening the divide between internal and external, it banished to the realm of subjectivity all animating sparks. Depth psychology turned its awareness to this interior cosmos, strewn with sparks, voices, symptoms, sub-personalities, and complexes. Whenever these escaped their culturally sanctioned confines of interiority, the task became to "withdraw projections," to restore the sparks of soul to the interior where they now purportedly belonged.

Depth psychology has primarily focused on the inner work of how to with-draw or gather in scattered projections and how to work with multiplicity as it arises in intrapsychic experience. The stance that is taken in Jungian work to achieve the gathering together of what has been shattered and scattered is pre-cisely the attitude that can be cultivated to do the work of *tikkun olam,* the restoration of the world.

James Hillman, the founder of the archetypal school of Jungian and depth psychology, asks us to imagine the *anima mundi* as "neither above the world en-circling it as a divine and remote emanation of spirit, a world of powers, arche-types, and principles transcendent to things, nor within the material world as its unifying pan-psychic life principle" (101). He imagines the *anima mundi* as "that particular soul spark, that seminal image, which offers itself through each thing in its visible form." Through such imagining *anima mundi* indicates the animated possibilities presented not only by each plant and animal but by each event and thing. He asks depth psychology to "break the vessels" that have stored away the sparks of the world within the confines of personal subjectivity:

> Breaking the vessels is the return, the turn again to the world, giving back what we have taken from it by storing inside ourselves its soul. By this return we regard the world anew, having regard for it as it shows its regard for us and to us in its face. We pay re-spect to it simply by looking again, respecting, that second look with the eye of the heart. (129)

Hillman's move, so needed within depth psychology, is prefigured by Hasids and Quakers who never sequestered divinity in a fantasy of personal interiority. Their mysticism oriented them to the world right around them, itself suffused with the sacred. John Woolman (1720–1772) put it this way: "that, as the mind was moved by an inward principle to love God as an invisible, incomprehensible Being, so, by the same principle, it was moved to love him in all his manifestations in the visible world" (8). Woolman argued that it was a contradiction to say we are loving an invisible God, while treating cruelly any creature God kindled life in.

For two decades, while I was intensely involved in doing individual psychotherapy from an intrapsychic and familial perspective, cultural suffering continually bled through in my patients' and my dreams and thoughts. Gradually I began to see that the prevalent paradigm of the self in psychology—an individualistic self—had led to the construction of theories and psychological practice that failed to see how psychological suffering is intimately connected with culture and nature. Thus blinded, psychotherapy often served the inscribing of the status quo cultural arrangements rather than involving itself in an insighting of the cultural changes needed to mitigate psychological suffering.

Nevertheless, the methodologies of depth psychology suggested practices of retrieving what has been marginalized that are as applicable to community and ecological work and to liberatory practices within the classroom as they are to individual healing (see Watkins). What is this depth psychological attitude? Depth psychology is usually defined by its commitment to a theory of the unconscious. In practice this means that due to its partiality we hold as suspect the point of view we are identifying with at any moment. We are aware that to focus our attention entails the falling into the shadows of other aspects of a situation. The process of working depth psychologically has to do with awareness of the multiplicity present in any moment and, further, an effort to retrieve that which has been marginalized by dint of exile or neglect. It is for this reason that the contents of depth psychology can never be fixed, for as we bring one subject matter out of the margin and into focus, another recedes into the shadow.

Given this sensitivity to multiplicity and to the ego's penchant for creating hierarchy out of multiplicity, the process of depth psychology must entail a relativizing of the ego and a honing of its receptive capabilities. The way to gather what has been marginalized is to listen for what has been silenced, to look for what has been pushed aside. This listening which brings the silenced into voice and the extruded into image is the foundation for dialogue. It is through the kind of I-Thou dialogue that Jung describes in his practice of active imagination and which Buber describes in the inter-human and human/nature realms that sparks can be liberated from their shells.

"Motions of Love"

With these thoughts in mind I ask my students to begin or continue a process of self-reflection that includes the following components:

1. Think over dreams you have had and select several that you feel address cultural suffering or cultural and/or ecological issues. Bring one or two of these that you would be willing to share with your classmates. You will not be handing these in to me.

2. Reflect on the issues or suffering in your community or the larger world that have consistently drawn your attention. Have these concerns been present in your dreams and imaginings? How have they lived in your heart and your thoughts? Take notes on this for your own use only.

3. If you do not already do so, begin a journal for dreams and active imagination work. Bring this to class to record your active imaginations around discerning vocation and listening to the call of the world psyche. This will not be collected.

In small groups we share these dreams and then enact them in the large group through a process of dream theater. This enables students to take what they have experienced as most private and intimate and begin to see the way in which it connects them with others, with culture and nature. This practice of sharing dreams with the larger community is well developed in many cultures, though mostly neglected in our own, in which dreams are often derogated as idiosyncratic and merely personal.

We work with Lifton's idea of the double self. There is one part of us that tries to carry on our life, our profession, and our leisures as though unaware of the larger difficulties we face as citizens and planetary creatures. We divorce ourselves from much of what we perceive and know to be true. This process can easily be observed as we read the newspaper, watching where our attention is drawn and where it is difficult to sustain. Part of the process of making the unconscious conscious is to become more focally aware of what we know and to integrate those knowings into our life choices and commitments. As we work on different aspects of psychology, we try to be mindful of things we actually know from our experience but which we do not speak about or act from, silenced by prevalent cultural norms, that may themselves be mirrored by psy-

chological theory. Quaker testimonies of simplicity and integrity have been developed to nurture this process of claiming our knowings and the calls that
arise from them. Care not to over-accumulate material goods and to engage in
simple entertainment is understood to serve the purpose of not diverting one's
attention from that which is sacred and its claims on us as well as encouraging
peace and the right sharing of world resources (*Faith and Practice* 141).

Students are asked to become aware of issues in the world that are trying to
speak to them. Sometimes one notes this by the quickness with which one
turns away from certain topics: the pollution of the ocean, services for battered
women, ecstatic dance. Oftentimes as one becomes familiar with Jung's process
of active imagination, of imaginal dialogue with what arises in the field of consciousness, one becomes more aware of the call of various things in the world:
the silent homeless woman on the curb, the prison one has passed each day for
twenty years, the possibility of nurturing leadership within the gay community,
the abuse of animals, the small flower that offers itself in an abandoned lot.

It is often through our personal history—particularly our personal
wounds—that we hear a particular voice of what has been called the *anima
mundi,* the soul of the world. It is the openness and vulnerability created by our
wound that give us a sensitivity to hear into particular issues in the world, to
bear beauty and to protest what we know is wrong. When this is so, there is no
distinction between "inner" and "outer" work. There may not initially be a conscious link between what has chosen us and our sense of our history and
wound, and yet in time the close intimacy is revealed.

Through the first nine months of our program students listen on this level
as they read the news, participate in the community, and work with dreams and
active imaginations. While listening in this way students also explore their
community and the larger world to learn more about the contexts that are available to their participation. By the first summer each student has allowed a
community or ecological issue or context to choose him or her. Through the
summer each student engages in the activities and work of that site. One engages in a particular way. Rather than entering the fieldwork with heroic ideas
ready to hand as an "expert" from the outside, one is asked to enter in a listening mode. The latter allows the wisdom and the difficulties of the various parts
of the field to emerge. The first summer is seen as practice in being alongside
of, in listening and dialogue, in lending one's hands to what the community is

working on, in bracketing an ego that is heroic or colonizing. The students are extending the space of listening and hosting they have practiced internally and interpersonally within the classroom into their apprenticeship in a community or ecological context.

Early Quakers often spoke of their own attempts to listen for vocational calls, "Divine leadings." Isaac Penington (1617–1679) advised us this way:

> Give over thine own willing, give over thine own desiring to know or to be anything, and sink down to the seed which God sows in thy heart and let that be in thee, and breathe in thee, and act in thee, and thou shalt find by sweet experience that the Lord knows that and loves and owns that, and will lead it to the inheritance of life, which is his portion. (138)

Perhaps no Quaker has written so movingly about the process of waiting for a Divine opening, a leading or leaning, as John Woolman:

> [A]t times this desire arose to a degree of fervent supplication, wherein my soul was so environed with heavenly light and consolation that things were made easy to me which had been otherwise. (1989: 19).

Woolman carefully watched his reactions to slavery and over years tried to keep close to the Divine opening that informed his witness against this oppression. He described this not as an effort of will, but as "a motion of love," "a leaning," "a drawing." He counseled others "to look less at the effects of our labor than at the pure motion and reality of our concern, as it arises from heavenly love" (70). Quakers are noteworthy in their service work for not adopting a stance of superior expertise or of missionary zeal but of trying to place themselves alongside others in a nonhierarchical manner, to work together for desires that are held in common for justice, peace, and liberation.

One cannot restore a world that is not listened to. It is only in sustained, reverential listening that one can hear the exiled—be that endangered species, radioactive waste in the earth, those marginalized by racism, those oppressed by the poverty created by capitalism. In the depth psychology program we ask the students to listen into the world psyche, the *anima mundi*. How does the world present its beauty and its suffering in your dreams? What particular concerns in the world does your psyche resonate with? What is speaking to you? To engage in this one needs to bracket what one thinks one is supposed to be called by as well as the ways that we have each defined our professional identity. Some students initially fear that on opening themselves to this vocational listening process they will be inundated. Fortunately, we are not each called to listen to *all* the sufferings of the world. We are addressed particularly and, I must add, insistently, often over decades. At times we may not be called by things that our expertise has prepared us for and need to have the courage to humbly begin again.

In the second year of coursework, students are introduced to how these attitudes are manifested in dialogical and participatory research, often of a participatory action research nature. Such participatory research carries on the "alongside" quality I have mentioned. It seeks to listen into a field with others, paying attention to what is marginalized within that field. Through dialogue, critical consciousness is developed of what the issues and sufferings are in that field and what actions might be taken to address common concerns. It should be clear that this kind of research and action is not done by an expert *to* others who are in a subordinate position. It strives for full participation through dialogue. Such wide-based dialogue can then as well provide reflection on and critique of any actions taken, providing a reflective loop between consciousness of a difficulty, action to address it, and reflection on the action to refine subsequent interventions. I am describing the kind of education and research done by Paulo Freire, liberation psychologist Martín-Baró, Rajesh Tandon, Myles Horton and his colleagues at the Highlander Center in Appalachia, and feminist researchers such as Lynn Brown, Carol Gilligan, and Mary Belenky. Their research opened out from solely individual work into group and community work, where individuals could seek insight together into the linkages between their psychological difficulties and the cultural context of oppression in which they struggle. Through the development of critical consciousness about the socioeconomic and political structures underlying everyday reality, people could both begin to analyze their situation and begin to dream how change might occur. Participatory modes of research arose that were dedicated to empowering knowledge and action within communities and ending exploitation by academic researchers who wrested knowledge away from communities for their own professional advancement. Instead, research is seen as a tool people can use in collaboratively inquiring into questions of vital interest to their community as well as in studying the effects of joint actions taken with the hope of moving toward mutually desired ends.

For example, Deborah MacWilliams, a public health nurse and policy analyst and graduate student, convened a small group in Bend, Oregon, to study their relation to place. Through site visits, artistic approaches, and dialogue these individuals sought to better understand their accumulated psychic numbing to their environment, built and natural. They struggled to clarify what kinds of places foster human-place relations. What kinds engender numbness and alienation? How might such knowledge inform city planning, urban design, and conservation efforts?

"Hundreds of Ways to Kneel and Kiss the Ground"

> Today, like every other day, we wake up empty
> and frightened. Don't open the door to the study
> and begin reading. Take down the dulcimer.
>
> Let the beauty we love be what we do.
> There are hundreds of ways to kneel and kiss the ground.
>
> Rumi (7)

I did not set out to enact a Quaker pedagogy, nor did I attempt to wrest from the field of psychology that which was "Quakerly." It has not been a matter of causation but of strengthening resonance. I have felt a deep connection between practices of listening and love that have pulled me toward Quaker prayer and service, toward the careful listening in depth psychotherapies, toward participatory modes of community and ecological work and research, and toward the joy of liberatory education. One might argue that the subject matter of my discipline lends itself to these resonances. But I trust that other disciplines and curriculums can similarly yield and am witnessing them do so through the work of students in our program as they pursue their varying professions.

One of our students, Mike Denney, a physician, is reconceiving medical education and practice to include the spirituality that has been severed from it through the secularism of modern science, medicine, and hospitals. Imagine medical students' first human dissection beginning with a meditation that honors the being and soul of the person who has shared their body for others. Another student, Isabel Bradshaw, a mathematician and forest ecologist, practices Zen and is working on preparing a science curriculum and new science practices that begin to include the body and the soul, healing the way they have been stripped from usual ecological monitoring and conservation in environmental sciences. Anne Davin, a project manager for the California Department of Education, brings dialogical practices from the *pueblo* where she lived into the feedback processes between teachers, parents, special education students, state and local administrators. Brent Blair, a professor of community theater, invites the young men in Central Juvenile Hall, Los Angeles, to rewrite and perform myths such as Orpheus, using their experiences on the streets, in their families, and in the underworld of juvenile imprisonment. The young women of Juvenile Hall are invited to rewrite such myths as Amor and Psyche. Through performing their tales and engaging in dialogue with each other, the young people ferret out their own definitions of soul embedded in their life experiences. Lali Mitchell, listening to a nearby valley and mountain slated for industrial development, draws others in her community into dialogical relationship to this place, out of which ecological stewardship and advocacy evolve. In each context the basic attitude of waiting on that of God in each person, place, and thing is possible. The joy released in doing so confirms the practice. While some of these learning sites appear inhospitable scenes for the liberation of soul sparks, the listening and dialoguing of "holy converse" transfigure them.

"But Each Little Spark Has a Shine and a Song"

> When God had made The Man, he made him out of stuff that sung all the time and glittered all over. Then after that some angel got jealous and chopped him into millions of pieces, but still he glittered and hummed. So they beat him down to nothing but sparks but each little spark has a shine and a song. So they covered each one over with mud. And the lonesomeness in the sparks make them hunt for one another, but the mud is deaf and dumb. Like all the other tumbling mudballs, Janie had tried to show her shine.
>
> Zora Neale Hurston (86)

Is not the classroom a place for the dissolving of the mud that Hurston describes here? Is it not a place of retreat where the hum of the song we are each gifted with can begin to be heard? And as its volume increases, is not the world the place to practice this song? The potential community of the classroom has a vital function in our culture now, of being a place of practice for dialogue and critical thought, of the listening for and nurturing of vocation. When this happens in a learning group, it is thrilling and enheartening. A dialogical way of being with each other and with one's gifts sets the stage for this occurring. The rest is grace. As the holy converse of dialogue unfolds within and between, a few of the angels are sure to get jealous about the beauty erupting in our midst.

↯ Chapter Three
"Wait to Be Gathered":
The Classroom as Spiritual Place[1]

Mike Heller

I joked with friends, as I worked on this essay, that a Quaker pedagogy is about being reasonable and sober. As a person who (until recently) has never seen himself as being overly sober, I kidded that I lay awake at night hoping that maybe tomorrow I could finally be reasonable. The joke is useful partly because Quakers sometimes take on a public persona of being somber, overly deliberate, and not very spontaneous, but I doubt that this comical and inaccurate image really defines what it means to be a Quaker.

These essays are important because they attempt to state the usefulness and the limits of bringing spirituality within a Quaker context into our classrooms. Recently, I have come to realize that my teaching has been gradually shaped by my Quaker experience, but it is new for me to acknowledge this influence so directly. Most of what I have to say here is an explanation of how that feels to me in the classroom. But I am not sure that this can be properly called a "Quaker pedagogy." Quakers can claim no ownership of a pedagogy any more than they can own worship in silence. I don't believe we can point to fixed elements and say, "See that over there: That is a Quaker pedagogy." Also, the classroom and the Quaker Meeting for Worship have important differences in purpose. One is a gathering for learning; the other is a form of worship with Christian origins. As we define what we mean by a Quaker pedagogy, it is good for us to question the extent to which spirituality has a place in education. If I raise a note of tentativeness, it is my expression of the humility and carefulness I feel are needed in this complicated business of teaching.

Despite differences between the classroom and the Friends' Meeting, aspects of Quaker faith and practice can enrich our teaching. The Quaker form of worship and the ethics that are derived from this faith have significant parallels with ways of conceptualizing teaching and learning. I suspect that Quakerism has acquired credibility in discussions of teaching because of Friends' beliefs about the importance of the individual and because of the democratic form of Quaker "silent," unprogrammed worship, in which men and women, old and young, are invited to speak. Quakers are also well known for not proselytizing, for respecting multiple points of view and other faiths. Quakers have no creed, no ritual to speak of. They believe that there is "that of God in everyone," often expressed as "the Inward Light." Locating the divine spirit inwardly transcends any single-faith tradition. Quakerism is both Western and Eastern in its beliefs and forms. The practice of valuing the inward life is the great strength of Quakerism.

Quaker practice draws upon metaphors that can be used to express who we are as teachers and students. This idea of pedagogy is more process than static entity, more verb than noun. If we believe that we are spiritual beings, then by the fact of our very presence the classroom will be a spiritual place. The eighteenth-century Quaker antislavery activist and social reformer John Woolman wrote somewhat ironically in his essay "A Plea for the Poor" that "to turn all the treasures we possess into the channel of universal love becomes the business of our lives" (1989: 240). In addressing issues of poverty, Woolman draws ironic attention to the kinds of business we usually value and to which we commit ourselves. I am generally optimistic about this "business of our lives," this business of teaching. The problems and challenges of the classroom as spiritual place involve recognizing the dignity and worth of our students and ourselves.

It is difficult to say these things: our institutionalized language, desire for professionalism, and educational politics work against us, even sometimes defeat us; call it submission to those pressures which call upon us to be reasonable and sober. It is important to try to articulate our vision for what we can become. Ultimately, when we enter into teaching, we are entering "the channel of universal love." It feels as if I am stepping outside of the usual educational politics to risk such a claim.

What It Means to "Wait to Be Gathered" (or a Little Theory)

The concerns and the rewards of the classroom bring me back to our journey as spiritual beings. I take the title for this essay from the poet Charles Wright, who says,

> If we were to walk for a hundred years, we could never take
> One step toward heaven—
> you have to wait to be gathered. (4)

When I first came across Charles Wright's book *Appalachia*, I felt some resonant expression of the concerns and rewards of teaching. Wright's source here is Simone Weil's *Waiting for God*, the title of which might be translated from the French also as "expectation," "hope," or "tarrying for God." By extension, the title is also close to the idea of "service": "waiting upon," and perhaps by further extension, "attending to" or "paying attention to God." We get to where we are going not only by striving, with our nose to the grindstone, not by walking a hundred years, but by waiting to be gathered, an act of coming together with the expectation that something important will happen to us. I hope to walk for a hundred years, and I know that a certain amount of striving is necessary, but in our culture we too often crowd out the essential act of letting go, the surrender to the spirit within. We forget what artists of all kinds have long known, that this posture of letting go of striving creates a readiness for important things to happen. Simone Weil says, "We cannot take a single step toward heaven. It is not in our power to travel in a vertical direction. If however we look heavenward for a long time, God comes and takes us up…the will has no power to bring about salvation" (194–95). In his 1951 introduction to *Waiting for God*, Leslie Fiedler adds, "What we really want is above us, not ahead of us….We are free only to change the direction of our glance; we cannot walk into heaven; we cannot rise without being lifted by grace" (36).

One might wonder what this impulse toward the transcendent has to do with education. Simone Weil writes of the beginning and ending place of education: "the faculty of attention forms the real object and almost the sole interest of studies" (105). Not coincidentally, paying attention to what is outside the self, she writes, is also the essence of prayer and is inseparable from the essence of our humanity. Through this act of attending to the spirit, Simone Weil suggests something about the essence of learning:

We do not obtain the most precious gifts by going in search of them but by waiting for them....In every school exercise there is a special way of waiting upon truth, setting our hearts upon it, yet not allowing ourselves to go out in search of it. There is a way of giving our attention to the data...a way of waiting, when we are writing, for the right word to come of itself. (112, 13)

She says that this way of "paying attention" is at the heart of successful and profound education: "Our first duty toward...students is to make known this method to them, not only in a general way but in the particular form that bears on each exercise" (113). It is interesting that she invokes the word "duty," a term we often mistakenly reserve for a military context. Determining one's duty is a process of locating higher authority. It is intimately tied to one's methods for discerning authority (for Quakers authority is primarily inward, although they have important communal checks on individual discernment) and finding one's proper response to that authority. The older I get, the more I see that duty is an intensely personal issue, and that one's discernment can be greatly aided by one's community.

To "wait in the spirit" and "to be gathered" are historically important metaphors for Quakers. The two metaphors express the active-yet-passive stance of "expectant waiting." Perhaps more than people of other faiths, Quakers have turned to metaphoric language partly because such language fulfills a need in the absence of ritual and partly because these metaphors express the shared experience of the inward spiritual landscape. The readiness of expectant waiting is both individual and corporate, and the language is drawn from Old and New Testament verses: "Wait on the Lord: be of good courage, and he shall strengthen thine heart" (Ps. 27:14). "For where two or three are gathered together in my name there am I in the midst of them" (Matt. 18:20). In one famous passage George Fox writes of his vision climbing Pendle Hill in 1652: "the Lord let me see atop of the hill in what places he had a great people to be gathered" (104). In education, individual readiness is crucial, but the actions of the group are also crucial.

When people refer to "a Quaker-style discussion," I suspect that they sometimes mean a form of brainstorming in which all are invited to speak, an idea which falls short of understanding the dynamic principles behind the Quaker Meeting. The essence of unprogrammed Quaker Meeting is a form of worship in which participants are invited to attend to the life of the spirit within the self. People settle into silence in order "to hear" the life and guidance of the spirit within, and they listen to each other speaking out of that silence in order to deepen that listening. Yet the Meeting for Worship is not inwardly directed only. From the motion of going inward there follows a motion of going outward into the world: Based upon the leadings we have received, we feel moved to speak or to take up some action. Quakers have a long tradition of seeing the inward motion of worship as leading to outward service in the world (see, for example, Olmsted and Christian). Faith in that of the spirit within leads to an ethic based upon simplicity, equality, and nonviolence.

The inward journey is described in archetypal images that speak to us of our personal struggles. One such image is what Northrop Frye, in *The Great Code,* refers to as the U-shaped narrative which runs throughout the Bible and throughout literature. It expresses a movement from apostasy (the feeling of separation from God) to restoration (the journey of return, toward reconnection). It is the narrative of being in exile or bondage (Exodus) and finding one's way home. The U-shaped narrative is the essential plot of the New Testament, the narrative of birth-death-resurrection. This journey also feels like the motion or the process of the classroom as spiritual place. As Steve Smith points out in this volume, redirecting our inward vision invites us to see the value and meaning of our experience, and it often leads to inward awakening. We live a daily process of separation and return. Typically at mid-semester, I feel that we are at the bottom of the U. Around mid-semester, students and I look at each other and know, if not always despair, at least the stare of the banal; we must work together to rise, or be raised, to finish the semester with renewed positive feeling.

Problems

In our world of September elevenths, Columbine High School shootings, Oklahoma City bombings, other acts of terrorism, as well as environmental destruction and a consumer culture in which large numbers of people suffer depression or turn to alcohol and drugs, attention to our inward lives becomes truly an issue of life and death. This attention connects us with our deepest sense of what matters. Lynn Nelson asks, "what are we to do in our schools, schools no longer immune to reflecting the violence of our culture at large?" (2000: 42). It helps me to read the writings of colleagues like Lynn Nelson and Mary Rose O'Reilley who are advocates for changing our schools to address students' inward needs, needs that seem deeper and more important than what is usually measured by standardized test scores. Mary Rose O'Reilley writes in *Radical Presence: Teaching as Contemplative Practice*,

> Theorists...have explored the idea, should a theoretical foundation be needed, that students *have* an inner life and that its authority is central to understanding cognitive development....Some pedagogical practices crush the soul; most of us have suffered their bruising force. Others allow the spirit to come home: to self, to community, and to the revelations of reality. (3)

Our challenge is to find pedagogical practices that honor students' inner lives and that "allow the spirit to come home." Problems arise because it is difficult to find our way, to address these needs in the face of a society that so desperately holds to measures of accountability as a panacea. Reasons, goals, and purposes fail us because logical, positivistic explanations are not subtle enough. We are not merely linear, logical beings. "Waiting for God," waiting to be "gathered," these metaphors for seemingly *not doing anything*, must seem an odd way to talk about educational practice. I imagine the blank looks on my students' faces on the first day of the term, if I say, "We will meet twice each week and wait to be gathered." I imagine the raised eyebrows of members of our board of trustees. To invoke the Columbine High Schools of our society is one step, but it cannot reach everyone. The fact is that too often our schools create environments where students lose their sense of self.

But there are numerous ways for students and ourselves to validate the worth of the self. We and our students are not on entirely different journeys. We are all struggling in our own ways to survive the rush and pressure and violence of the contemporary world. One way I might differ from my students is the extent to which I have thought about how we nurture the self as an agent of social change. Frequently, I feel that my voice has little influence, but I am pretty sure that if I don't speak for making the world (and the classroom) a safer and better place, it is that much harder for students to do so. Vaclav Havel writes that "Consciousness precedes Being....For this reason, the salvation of this human world lies nowhere else than in the human heart, in the human power to reflect, in human modesty, and in human responsibility" (17–18). I have the challenge of inviting students into this largeness. Part of that is the challenge of explaining why I am approaching our work this way, and what I expect to have happen for us.

I try to explain to students, parents, and the powers-that-be what "this business of our lives" is. Some people need more explanation; some may not understand, but many people seem to understand immediately. Why are we doing this? One answer is that creative work is not always linear. Another is that the inward life is more important than we know. Another is that we may not be able "to get there" any other way. The inward is infinitely linked to how we know the outward.

The "whys" spill over into other problems. My expectations sometimes conflict with students' expectations. They bring their confusions to the classroom. I could do all of the talking in class, have them sit in straight rows, and give machine-graded multiple-choice exams, but I cannot totally mask the conflicted realities of the world we live in. It is no wonder that some of the students who are hungry for a clear plan wish that I were more directive. I try to reassure them that I know what I am doing and that I do have a plan. I even hold up a sheet of paper with an outline on it as evidence. Quaker beliefs and practices undermine traditional ideas of authority. Just as early Quakers could not accept the single voice of the ordained clergy in the pulpit, the classroom is a place of multiple valid voices. I do not want to impose my faith upon students. Yet I face the paradox of being the authority in the classroom. I do not want to impose my worldview, but I must make choices about the form of our study. I try to have no theological agenda for the classroom, and I try to honor the students' traditions. I may never fully succeed, but intuition and experience tell me that good teaching emerges by acknowledging the complications and the messiness (of our lives, of the world). For a time, I feared imposing my religious beliefs on my classes, but I now realize that there is little danger of that. I don't have that much influence, and more significantly, I know that my process is not everyone's process. There is always the student in the back of the room who says with his eyes if not his words, "I don't want to do this." I continue to look for helpful, honest responses to such students.

We are teaching or modeling powerful dualities about the self and how we learn. George Fox wrote in his *Journal* of the goal to bring everyone to their Teacher within. He meant that "the true" teacher is "the light and the spirit of Christ in them," "the Seed of Christ in them" (624, 76, 48). I am comfortable not invoking this specifically Christian language, while at the same time believing that we do well to help students see that their best teacher is within themselves. I am also easy with the fact that this is a profoundly subversive move, which decenters the locus of authority, even as George Fox removed himself from the central role of being the teacher. Fox often says something to this effect: "I directed them to their teacher Christ Jesus, and so passed away" (74). Like Fox, our job is to empower others to find their own inward resources and to see and speak for themselves. For those who have no patience with this emphasis on reflection, I would say that this inward awareness of our resources empowers us to do the outward work. The duality within us is the self and not-self. Whether one calls it the divine, the Great Spirit, or a secular term like intuition, the spirit that Quakers refer to as the inward guide is not the ego. Quakers have always struggled to recognize the authentic inward voice, the true inward guide. Similarly, students must learn to discern the inner voices of foolishness and selfishness from those of generosity and wisdom. We are helping our students find the confidence that they can do what is required of them.

Similarly, it seems to me that the Quaker idea of a "gathered Meeting" is not entirely appropriate for the classroom, but this metaphor suggests parallels that are useful. I do not expect us to have an experience in the full meaning of the Quaker phrase, which refers to a heightened, mystical level of "being gathered," but I do want our class to be a small community in which we feel a shared experience and care for each other's welfare. According to one glossary, the "gathered Meeting" means that the group is "united in feeling the movement of the spirit" and that something happens to the group together, expressed by Francis Howgill's statement of 1672: "The Kingdom of God did come upon us and catch us as in a net" (Kimball and Holden 13). When true learning is happening and the class is focused, I want us to be caught up in the inspiring, dizzying subject at hand. Another sense of a "gathered Meeting" suggests that individual personalities vanish in an experience of mystical union. I don't expect mystical union in the classroom, at least not on any given Tuesday right after lunch, nor do I want any of us to vanish, but we can feel a sense of union. At our best, I have felt us under the spell of the muse of learning, when she has caught us in her net.

The paradoxes at work here are at the heart of what it means to be human. The problems of the classroom as spiritual place manifest themselves in these paradoxes. The roles I see myself fulfilling are in tension: I must be a nurturer of students' lives and yet a judge of their work. But my nurturing self does not sit easily with the judgmental self who must evaluate and who must be clear about what is being graded. Peter Elbow has said, "My argument is that good teaching seems a struggle because it calls on skills or mentalities that are actually contrary" (2000: 54, 58). I can accept paradox, I tell myself, but I feel like the boy trying to walk bravely in the thunderstorm.

My friend Ivan Lacore, who is a language arts coordinator for schools in Roswell, New Mexico, talks about advanced work and beginner's work (as Zen masters use the term). We need to know which is which and what we are asking of our students. In my journal, I often feel that I am doing advanced work and beginner's work at the same time. Some days it feels as if the self is a desert of dry sand with no oasis of creativity. Other days it feels as if the creative not-self is walking on water. I am carried, like St. Christopher, on his or her miraculous life of consciousness. On those days, whether I stumble or not, there is no possibility of failure.

Method (or a Few Teaching Practices)

In the classroom, we sit in a circle—I hope a messy circle, which itself becomes a metaphor for how we are working. We keep journals; we write in them in class and out of class; we "publish small writings." I do this work along with students. It is not exactly a daily process, because I don't ask students to write every day, just as I don't write every day. But the process feels as if it has innate affinities with how artists and writers do their best work. The large motion for class assignments is first to go inward and then to go outward. At our best, we are responding to what John Woolman calls a "motion of love" (1989: 23). I am looking for pedagogical practices that, again in Mary Rose O'Reilley's words, do not "crush the soul." In my journal, I listen inwardly and surrender (with some discretion) to whatever words come in. The process for me is circular, as I return in the writing to some "unfinished business"—those things which I am drawn back to think about because there is more work to be done. I think I have said all there is to say, but then more words come in. It is a private-to-public process, beginning with attention to feelings, writing something of how I feel about where I am in relation to things in my life, and then moving some of that writing into a public form.

This seemingly simple motion gives me a new appreciation for the wonder of "making a sentence" (from the Latin *sententia*, thought, meaning, purpose) as a symbol of our humanness. The elementary school distinction of "the declarative sentence" begins to take on large autobiographical significance. It is no accident, as G. Thomas Couser has argued, that the "Declaration of Independence" can be seen as "a form of communal autobiography" (29). The declarative sentence becomes a quintessentially autobiographical act, an assertion of "freedom and the power to remake the world," as James Boyd White said of the American separation from Great Britain (Couser 28). Making a declarative statement is about valuing our ability to say what we see, valuing our own perceptions, and finding the authority to speak. It is about finding and valuing one's dignity and one's voice. The journal work, then, is about much more than a mere listing of daily events. It is about valuing one's inward resources. And the teaching of writing is much more than teaching correctness. We learn best the formal aspects of writing (and probably the discipline of any field) when we value our work and take ownership for it.

The essential journal entry is to record one thing on my mind and how I feel about it, but as Lynn Nelson says in *Writing and Being,* there is no typical entry (20–21, 25). To put it another way, the essential journal entry is to answer the question, "Where are you now?" (28–29). Finding where I am is a matter of geography, of the past and the future, of relationships and the heart. The question, "Where are you now?" is a metaphoric way of asking, "What do you know now?" My directions for the journal go something like this:

> Record in the journal responses to the reading, ideas, feelings, or connections that come to you from your own experience. Record your impressions of this journey of consciousness. But the journal is not only a place to write; it is a process. Each time I open the journal, I begin again, not knowing for sure what words will surface. Often if I leave the journal open, more words will come in. The act of writing draws out ideas that would not have otherwise occurred. Carry the journal with you. Record what you see and feel, not only in this class but in any of your classes as well as in your life outside of class.

It sounds simple enough, but there are large implications here. In this writing, I enter "the river" of my consciousness. As Lynn Nelson says, "the river, remember, is anything, everything: It is our partner, our child, our mother, our father, our school, the house we live in, our job, the tree in our front yard, life itself" (1994: 33). We locate ourselves not only through the linear, logical mind but also by attending to multiple I-thou relationships.

Sometimes, it is not easy to surrender myself to indirection, but it is often humorous and refreshing to make myself vulnerable for my students and, by doing so, modeling this work for them. It is important that I open my journal and write with them. "Open your journal to the next place. Breathe deeply, sit quietly. After a few moments, write something that feels like it needs to be said." I open the journal and I begin again. (In a similar way, I settle into Quaker worship, and I begin again). The journal work is experiential. I do this work with students because I want them to see me valuing the process as worth doing for my own life.

This past year in an upper-level course, one student said that the journal work felt to her like prayer. I had not said this to the class, but I, too, felt it to be like prayer. What she and I felt, I believe, is a quality of focus or attention. To quote Simone Weil again: "prayer consists of attention" (105). As Douglas Steere describes it, "In perpetual prayer, there is something that frames all that we do, something that goes on day and night beneath the stream of our con-sciousness: a gratitude, an adoration, an acknowledgement of creature-liness—of dependence upon God, that we are God's and God made us—a sense of encompassment" (94). The form and processes of the classroom as well as the journal seem to be intrinsically related to the motion of prayer. Regardless of one's faith, the motion of the language of prayer itself transforms us. Perhaps the language of prayer connects with a healing place in our minds and hearts.

The classroom is far from a silent or even a worshipful space—although at times it feels as if we say and feel things that touch on the sacred. There are moments when we feel great respect, even motions of love toward others. I ask students to wonder about what our "real work" is. I ask them to answer for themselves the question, "What matters here?" It is a good question to bring to bear on all of our readings, and I suggest that they ask in all their courses, "What matters here?" The question calls upon us to create priorities. We are learning a body of knowledge, and we are learning to become full human be-ings. The discipline, the subject matter, helps this to happen.

Some time ago, one student said, "I don't want to go inward because I know that what I will find is a terrible void." It does take courage to do this work, but almost invariably I find that what is within is not a void. This fear touches on large mythic issues in our lives. Most of us struggle with inward and outward disasters, our own forms of repentance and deliverance, descent and rise and descent again. The danger seems to me to occur in not doing the process. Peggy came to my office after class and angrily said, "I hate what you are asking me to do." But as we talked more, she confided that she was not writing. She had not yet tried the process. The fear of what we will find within is scary because it is about how we feel about ourselves, and our response requires another kind of faith. I want students to discover a kind of faith with a small "f": faith that what they need for this journey is within themselves, faith that, in the process of surrender, "the way will open." When Peggy began to write, all of her struggles were not resolved, but she did feel a sense of release. I have observed that often the writing moves from negative to positive feelings. Once the negative thing is said, we feel a kind of release that then allows us to move toward positive realizations. My hope is that we are learning to expect and to live a response to something like Woolman's idea of a "motion of love." It is an act of surrender to the mystery of our being, our presence here together. Teaching is not something that just happens. It requires us to be sensitive to and respond to motions of love.

Small Writings, Writing Small

In the journal and the small writings I feel that my class is most like the Quaker Meeting. I have taken the idea of small writings from Lynn Nelson, whose *Writing and Being: Taking Back Our Lives Through the Power of Language* is the best book I know for teaching this approach to writing and the inward-to-outward process, which I have found valuable in Quaker Meetings.

As we write in the journal, shape the small writings, and respond to each other, we enact the idea that "we are the text." It feels as if we find a new urgency in how we interact with the actual texts. There is an interesting unpredictability, a heightened sense of the unexpected in one's own and others' writings. Like in the silence of Quaker worship, I do not know who will speak nor what will be said. Likewise, in the journal I don't know what words will come in even two minutes from now. The experience is something like receiving unexpected (or expected?) gifts; it is really about making ourselves observers, who value the incoming words, the images, and the stuff of consciousness. As Ivan Lacore says, I put my stubby # 2 pencil on the page, often not knowing what I will write, listening for words that are perhaps on the margins of my mind, and welcoming what comes in.

The small writings are much like "messages" one might hear in a Quaker Meeting for Worship. Each of us watches inwardly for leadings for what we might be moved to say. No one else can do this work for us, yet we need the community of the classroom for the work to happen. The small writings are also much like what an artist or a sculptor does when he or she uses the work of art "to make a statement." In this way, small writings take on their significance. We can talk about them as political statements, feminist statements, personal declarations, statements of grief, anger, or happiness.

Although I am emphasizing this reflective work here, it is worth noting that most of the coursework is about reading traditional textbooks and responding to knowledge of the world. Small writings are mostly assigned in addition to our usual class work and discussion. Paradoxically, although they occur on the margins of the course, they become its psychic centerpiece. Often students tell me that small writings are what they value most in the course.

I explain the small writings with a description like this:

> In the small writings you are encouraged to write from your own experience, to try out your "voice," to look for personal connections with the ideas and readings you have encountered. The beginning place for small writings is the work in the journal. I want you to value your own experience as a valid source from which to speak and write—both your inward and outward experiences, the events of your life, your ideas and your feelings, as well as your experience of reading. Bring to the process the beginner's mind of elementary school when you created a picture or wrote a small note to a friend a few rows over, hence the idea of "writing small."

I share with the class what I expect us to experience: "Publishing," that is making copies for a "real audience" of peers, usually makes good things happen. People are often honest and take some pride in small writings. The act of making copies for class raises questions about the importance (or unimportance?) of our feelings, insights, and realizations, as well as questions about content, voice, audience, and composing processes—all of which make for good class discussion: "What can I say? What do I feel I need to say? How do I present my self in writing? And which self do I present?! How can I avoid sounding too timid, too conceited, too preachy? How can I write so that I feel good about what I hand in? How can I write, not just for a good grade but for more important reasons?" Trying to say "something real" returns us to the question, "What matters here?" It is beneficial to value the process, even to talk about process in the writing: "I don't know where to start, but…" "Writing about this is scary for me…" "As I look back over this writing, I feel…" We want to revise and edit for good reasons, primarily to make the writing clear to a reader. As one works with small writings, it is interesting to see how they become a genre, a form, in their own right. A great deal can be expressed in one page. One begins to feel that if he or she can make one page well written and interesting for an audience, then longer papers can be made stronger and more interesting. I want students to have a sense of the choices they make in more formal academic writing, asking themselves what is appropriate and effective in the discourse of a given discipline.

I give students directions like these:

> In the small writings, wonder about things; focus on a key quotation, something that happened in class, or move something out of the journal; improve upon it for "publishing" to the class. When you write about something to which you personally connect, you need not spill your innermost, deepest secrets; discover that you have a wide range of topics and ways to speak about "where you are now."

And I give this kind of guidance for this genre of writing:

> Take us out of the realm of abstraction and generalization, which we often misuse, and connect us to the experience by "putting us there." Try to do more "showing" than "telling" by giving us a filmable scene, a brief moment in time—maybe a half hour of some larger event. Try what Ken Macrorie calls "the secret of 'Once'" (18–20). If you refer to what someone said, put some of it in dialogue form. Maybe at the end tell us what this means to you. Maybe add a p.s. with further thoughts about what this means.

Here are two small writing assignments to which I have returned often (again my thanks to Lynn Nelson):

Assignment 1: Exploring Your Epigraph (A Good First Small Writing)
> An epigraph (not to be confused with an epitaph, words on a gravestone) is a short quotation placed at the beginning of a piece of writing—a book or a chapter or an essay or, in this case, a journal—to set a tone for what will follow….The quotation you select for your epigraph can come from anywhere—the whole world of words is your hunting ground, from the Bible or the Koran or the *Bhagavad Gita* to a song or the label on a soup can. Or a child might utter something that you will recognize as your epigraph….Wonder about how your life feels now and how your epigraph points to some of that feeling….Go over the material you have written in your journal and find something you would like to share with others. Focus on some small, specific thing or a

moment—a memory, a discovery that surprised you, something you struggled with, or an insight you want to share—something you feel would be interesting or valuable or helpful to others.

Work on it further in your journal, or move it onto separate paper or into your word processor, however you work best as you move toward public writing. Do not take on too much material. Think in small, careful terms. Let this small piece grow and emerge, and see what happens. (*Writing and Being* 56–57)

Assignment 2: Tell Me a Story
Tell me a story—a small story, a true story…a story from your heart, a story from your life. Tell me of a time when you were hurt—or afraid—or tell me of a time when you lost something—your keys, your heart, your mind, your mother or father, your way in the world—or tell me about a small joy you had today. ("Warriors with Words" 45)

Solitude of the Soul

Quakers are not entirely humorless. They say, for example, that one should speak in the Quaker Meeting only when one can improve upon the silence. It is difficult to improve upon the silence. Some of my shy students live by this principle. I want to honor the egalitarian ideal that everyone in the class has access to inward truth that can be of value to others; yet at the same time we all are responding to impossibly high standards. The central paradox is that we allow ourselves to have low expectations, low standards, welcoming the words that come to us, and we are surprised to find the wealth of our inward resources. We are learning something of the duality of the self and the not-self, much like what Quakers would distinguish as the self and the spirit. At our best, we find ourselves carried to high places, where the process takes us.

I feel two large impulses in this teaching: the impulse to structure the class so that we express extraordinary respect for each other and the impulse to seek a practice that asks us to think about what matters in our lives. The longer I teach, the more I see that my interactions with students and our best work are guided by our inward lives. I tried teaching a course some years ago in which I did not emphasize the inward work. I felt lost. The readings and coursework failed for me to connect with what matters. Now I see that the inward work is essential for me to feel connected to whatever we are studying. I want students to feel and learn that connectedness. Parker Palmer has said that "we could lift up the value of 'inner work.'"…The key to this form of community involves holding a paradox of having relationships in which we protect each other's aloneness. We must come together in ways that respect the solitude of the soul" (*Let Your Life Speak* 91–92). We are learning to "respect the solitude of the soul" of the other as well as ourselves.

Three Sample Small Writings

There is no typical small writing. I hesitate to include examples for that reason, but examples are useful. Maren's writing below is an elegy for a friend. Kelly's writing is a declaration of how she sees herself changing. And in the third small writing, my own, I provide a sense of how I write and publish small writings along with students, sharing my own vulnerability, which seems important to them and to me.

Maren's Small Writing

> Yesterday is over my shoulder, so I can't look back for too long. There's just too much to see waiting in front of me, and I know that I just can't go wrong. (Jimmy Buffett, "Changes in Latitudes, Changes in Attitudes")

I have a baseball cap, which used to belong to a friend of mine, Brian McDermott. He lent it to me one day when I came to school with a head of greasy hair. He said as he handed me the hat, "You'd better cover that mess." I laughed as I took the hat. Leave it to Brian to give it to me straight. The hat was one of those good "guy" hats—soft, faded, broken in. It smelled like Head and Shoulders and sweat. Brian said with a smile, "That's my favorite hat, so take good care of it." I treated that hat like gold.

Brian graduated and left for college, but he let me keep the hat. "Something to remember me by," he joked. The next time I saw Brian was over Christmas break, when he came home for the holidays. One night, everyone went to a party at our friend Rob's house. Brian said that night, punching me playfully on the arm, "Hey, girl, you gonna ever give me that hat back?" "All you have to do is ask," I replied.

But I never got the chance to give Brian his favorite hat back because Brian died that night. Drunk, he decided to get on top of Aaron's car and "surf." He fell off the roof of the moving car and broke his neck. I remember my brother coming home that night, waking me up, and with tears in his eyes saying, "Mar,

BMcD is dead." Yeah right. Brian's not dead. You're kidding, right? But he wasn't kidding.

I went through that next week in a daze. I held on to Brian's hat like if I let go, I would die, too. I almost wanted to.

Every time I look at that dirty, worn Boston Bruins baseball cap, I think of Brian, his love for life, his crazy personality, his risk-taking attitude. Brian was never afraid. His motto was, "Well, if I die, at least I had fun while I was alive." He did have fun. But he never thought of the consequences of his having fun. I guess that's the way he wanted it. While Brian liked to reminisce with his friends about all the crazy things they used to do, he always said, "Yeah, but just wait for all the crazy shit we still have left to do." Brian was always ready for the next big adventure. He had plans, visions. But he never got to carry them out.

I don't think people have too many regrets for Brian, though, because he lived his life to the fullest and made such an impact on so many people. To Brian, life was twenty years of fun. We often joke that Brian is sitting up in heaven, smoking a joint with Bob Marley and Jimi Hendrix. He's enjoying his eternal life as much as he enjoyed his life on earth.

On the inside brim of Brian's hat, I have written, "God Bless BMcD." Each time I wear it, I feel as though Brian is looking down on me, and it makes me happy. He touches me and makes my life more enjoyable, even though he is no longer here.

Kelly's Small Writing

...you look like a photograph of yourself taken from far, far away and I won't know what to do and I won't know what to say... (Ani Difranco, "Untouchable Face")

So i'm sitting here eating dinner, a peanut butter and banana sandwich and pumpkin pie. It's taken me less than a day to finish the entire thing. i like pumpkin pie. i'm supposed to be on this quasi-diet type thing because my body fat makes up 31.7% of my body composition, which isn't even entirely the point. We need to change things. Shake it up a bit, get people moving. Just because you've been eating pie right and left for so long doesn't mean it's what you should be doing.

But there are things bigger than pie. There are so many people in my life that i wish could read my mind so i wouldn't have to say it aloud. Sure, i talk a lot, but i never say the things i need to say. Those things that matter the most. i really believe it's from reading *Catcher in the Rye* that has made me start thinking so much about people and beliefs that i had put away because i was too busy. What is too busy? Too busy with school and work so that i don't have to have discussions with my parents or my sisters. There are so many things that need to be said that i don't want to say. i mean really, how do you be so open and honest with a person as close to you as your sister without hurting her feelings? i don't think i can. i don't want to hurt anyone's feelings.

And then there are those people that i don't even talk to when i see them on campus anymore. That makes me feel weird. i was once told by this boy that i would forget his name and his face. i told him that i wouldn't. He didn't believe me but the name Andy Genievieves is still in my head, so is his face. There are many people in my life that i wish i could have back, or i wish that i could fix them. That i think is one of my faults. i want people to be easily fixed and that just doesn't happen. We all work on our own levels. We all choose what we want to take with us and what we will leave.

So i have resolved to be the best i know how to be. i have spoken to my little sister more in the past three months than i have in the past three years. She never gave up on me. This means more that i can say. i would have given up on me. i think i am more like myself than i have been in a very long time. When i first came to college i was not so jaded. i was tired of high school but i didn't know that college was just an extension of high school. i felt very out of place. i started dressing like everyone else and i tried to "fit in" but the more i try to fit in the harder it becomes for me to remember who i really am. i decided not to fit in anymore. i really don't mind if people think i'm strange anymore. This sounds strange because i never had anything bad happen to me in my childhood, but i can see parts of myself in Holden Caulfield. His inability to speak the truth and to hold "real" conversations with people. All he wants is to get home to Phoebe and talk. He desperately wants to love and to be loved. i think he wants to be understood without having to say anything. He has people on his mind who preoccupy his thoughts. i think he is ready for a change. Change is good. Even if things are all out of order and chaos is at hand, at least you know you're alive.

My Small Writing

Certain moments in this life cast their influence forward over all the moments that follow. (Scott Russell Sanders)

I remember my first year in graduate school at George Washington University. I was in the army, working and living in Arlington, Virginia. Late afternoons or on Saturdays, I would get in my old red two-door Opal and drive east across the river into D.C.

I took a course from old Dr. A on the American novel, my first summer course. It was Dr. A's last summer before he retired. I went to his office thinking I could impress him. "I like these authors," I said. "I think we can learn a kind of wisdom from these books."

"I don't think you can learn much from these liars," he said. I was discovering that I was not impressing Dr. A. He was sarcastic and mean-spirited. Other students had warned me not to take his class. "He is a mean bastard," someone had told me. I had foolishly thought I could handle any professor. And my writing was not very good.

I remember that Saturday morning when I went to his office to pick up my final paper. He sat behind his desk, a huge unabridged dictionary open on a stand, the city's dusty sunlight coming through the window. I sat on the edge of the wooden chair near his desk. "This is not graduate-level work," he said, sliding my paper across the desk. "But I am not going to fail you," he said.

He said several other things. I left his office, found my way down stairs, and stumbled along the sidewalk, tears welling up in my eyes. I knew that he was right about my writing not being good. I did not know if I could do this graduate school thing.

Now looking back, I see that I felt he had written me off as a human being, that he had failed to see what I was capable of, the potential that I felt in my heart—not my ego but some sense of life within me. I see too what a wimp I was. I wish I had had the courage not to play Dr. A's mind games and the courage to be smart about being loose and creative in the work. But now looking back, I realize that I was struggling with a lot of hidden stuff at that time in my life. I did not know what was happening to me in the army. I did not know where my heart was. I was lost in the dark forest of my life and did not know how to find my way.

The next years were a long journey of finding my way through the dark forest, of finding my heart's direction. It took a long time before I started to feel good about my work. Slowly, I began to feel that I did have some small potential, some heart to bring to this work.

p.s. Now sometimes, I think of Dr. A. I wonder if his meanness shaped his life in retirement. I wish I had said, "Sir, what is wrong with you?" I did learn something from him. I learned how I do not want to be. I learned something about forgiveness, too. I imagine that Dr. A has long since passed away. The fact that Dr. A was a mean bastard wasn't finally important. It was only a sign that he was lost, too.

Note

1. An early version of this paper was presented at the Friends Association for Higher Education annual conference, June 23, 2000, at Earlham College. My thanks to Robert Denham, Newton Garver, and David Scaer for suggestions regarding early versions of this essay. My thanks to Maren and Kelly for allowing me to include their small writings.

✀ Part Three
Extending the Space: Friendly Practices of Composition

CR Chapter Four
A Gathered Presence:
Creating a Community of Conscience
in the Composition Classroom

Richard Johnson

Most instances of language use are acts of human relationship which naturally have moral or ethical dimension. If it is true that on the one hand language enables us to turn human beings into abstractions and to thereby treat them as if they were not human, it is also the case that language enables us to enter imaginatively and sympathetically into the experience of others, to develop complex codes to define and refine moral behavior, and to resolve conflicts through mediation rather than force.

Sheridan Blau

It is a strange thing to be called "professor." I am often startled when someone uses that word to refer to me. Maybe my discomfort is simply a vestige of the old Quakerly distaste for titles. The word catches uneasily in my ears. In part, my discomfort may stem from a haunting feeling that I do not yet know nearly enough to deserve the title, but partly, too, it may grow out of a frustration that I must make daily concessions and compromises contrary to the few things I *do* know. What has sustained me in the profession (apart from the nagging suspicion that I do not know how to do much of anything but go to school) is a memory I treasure of my first teaching job in a small Quaker prep school. Not that it was a perfect place to work—far from it. It was a struggling and imperfect institution peopled with imperfect teachers and perfectly imperfect students. And yet, working there at the very start of my career, I glimpsed a possibility that has sustained me ever since.

What I glimpsed was a year-by-year re-creation of an intentional learning community—not just academic learning, either, but a rich ecology of learning that touched every aspect of life. The headmaster encouraged me to model my classes—at least approximately—after a Quaker Meeting for Business in which I served as the clerk of the Meeting, facilitating students' learning but refusing to fall into the trap of doing their learning *for* them. My professional training had not prepared me for anything like this. In my training to become a public school teacher, I had been trained to make learning as easy as possible for my students. Too easy, perhaps. I had learned to put the food right on their trays in front of them instead of saying, as I learned to do at a Quaker school, "Are you hungry? Let's go on a hunt!" In my training to become a public school teacher, I had been steeped in a model of education as an economic exchange in which students were treated as customers; teaching at a Quaker school, by contrast, encouraged me to think of teaching as a kind of *gifting*. In my training to become a public school teacher, I had learned to use "discipline" as a classroom control technique in order that my students could practice writing, but what I wanted was not for them to *practice* writing but to *do* writing, to do the discipline of writing.

My adaptation to providing a Quaker education required nothing less than a dismantling of the public school hierarchy to which I had previously been accustomed, where students occupy the lowest rank like empty and inert jugs waiting to be filled by their teacher. While my professional training had heavily emphasized the need to seize control in the classroom, as a Quaker educator I learned to decentralize that control, learned to have power *with* my students rather than power *over* them. Nearly a century ago a writer for *The English Journal* commented that "Training in a little autocracy is poor preparation for citizenship in a democracy" (Applebee 64), and that statement rings every bit as true today. Although it was now many years ago, my initial experience of teaching in a Quaker school demanded of me a radical democratization of my classroom, the effects of which still inform my teaching to this day.

I teach now at a community college, but I still feel every bit as committed to providing the best education money can buy to students who could not otherwise buy much. As a Quaker educator working in a public community college, I sometimes feel that I bridge two worlds. I am committed to the ideals of a

Quaker education. And I am committed, as well, to the populist mission of community colleges. I want to provide the best teaching I possibly can to students who could never afford to attend a Quaker college preparatory school, let alone an elite Quaker college like Swarthmore or Bryn Mawr or Haverford. In a way, the two worlds are well suited: The radically democratic practices of Quakers complement the democratic aspirations of the community college movement. My students' lives have been conspicuously short on privilege, but that does not have to mean I cannot offer them the best pedagogy I know of to inspire them as lifelong learners.

One sense of this uncomfortable word *professor*—the sense my employers had in mind when they hired me—refers to one who lays claim to some knowledge and openly shares what he has learned. In that sense, the professor in me knows only a few things about the teaching of writing. I know, for instance, that the best writing grows out of a felt need to express something to a known audience; writing to satisfy a weary English teacher wading through a pile of student papers is a sad substitute. I know that students learn to write best not by learning *about* writing but by *doing* writing; more than that, though, I know they learn best not simply by doing but by doing and then reflecting upon what they have done. I know that the lifelong writing habits a student acquires in a composition course are far more important than the few finished pieces submitted for a grade; a teacher's task is not so much to help students make a few bits of *writing* better but to guide them toward becoming better *writers*. I know that my grading system ought to reflect the kind of learning I purport to value; a process-oriented class in which the grades are still based largely on products is a class still in the process of becoming process oriented. I know that competition for grades undermines the learning community of a classroom. I know how easy it is to fall into the egotistical trap of fostering in students a dependency on the teacher; the more students rely upon a teacher to tell them what quality writing looks like and what difficult texts mean, the more they develop a kind of learned helplessness. And I know that our job as teachers is to help students not need us anymore. In my case this is especially true, since I am almost certainly the last writing teacher my students are likely ever to have.

I know these things, and yet I also know too well the constraints of public institutions and the entrenchments of the teaching profession itself. Hierarchies of all kinds die hard, and the instruction-based, teacher-centered classroom is certainly no exception. Still, some of my efforts to decentralize control in my classroom were very much in synch with certain reforms already under way within the profession, quite apart from Quakerism. Under fire, in particular, was the traditional notion of the teacher as the locus of authority in the first and third of these four areas:

- assigner of topics for composition
- determiner of what traits such essays should exhibit
- writer of formative comments on drafts
- evaluator of how well students' final drafts meet quality standards

I will discuss each of these four loci in turn, with particular consideration given to the parallels between Quakerism and the student-centered reforms in composition pedagogy of the last few decades. Although I must ask readers' indulgence as I trace a bit of history, my primary concern is decidedly forward looking. I will argue that recent reforms have challenged the first and third loci of authority over student learning, but challenges to the second and fourth loci—that is, challenges to the way we evaluate student writing—await us as a kind of next frontier toward a more fully student-centered composition classroom.

Both for the sake of non-Quaker educators and for Quakers who have never quite considered their religious practice in pedagogical terms, permit me to describe briefly the origins of Quakerism *in the language of educators.*

With the translation of the Bible into local languages and with the invention of the printing press, more people could suddenly have direct access to scripture without ordained authorities serving as intermediaries. The locus of authority had shifted. Protestant sects sprang up like flowers in spring, each with its own peculiar hue, some quickly withering but others settling in for the long haul. To describe this revolution in educational terms, instead of religious terms, we might say that the old instruction-based catechism of the Church was replaced by the new Protestants' more self-directed study of scripture.

The emergence of Quakerism ignited yet another profound (though a good deal quieter) revolution, challenging both the need for trained clergy and even the dependence upon received scripture. Recognizing that each seeker must look within for a source of his or her authority, Quakers dedicated themselves to a curriculum of radically independent learning while at the same time appreciating the help that fellow seekers can offer each other along the way. And so Quakers worship together. Silently, but together. And instead of indoctrinating each other with a long catechistic list of answers, we continue today the practice of more clearly articulating the questions we each need to ask ourselves. The catechism (*kata,* off, out + *ēkhein,* to sound) of Quakers is not so much a sounding *off* with dogmatic answers as it is a sounding *out* by the use of an ever evolving series of *queries.* Quaker religious practice, then, is not an authority-centered, instruction-based transmission of doctrine but rather a dialogic encounter, a mutual grappling with questions, a subtle blend of self-directed and peer-assisted cooperative learning. As I hope to show in what follows, my own classroom approach to the teaching of writing attempts in some ways to mirror that spiritual practice.

First Locus of Authority: Gathering to Speak Our Minds

Much of what life offers to teach us is largely relational, it turns out, but learning a communicative act like writing is entirely so. My own education as a young writer fell upon the advent of a struggle between traditional teachers, who retained for themselves full control over the topics students were to write on, and the expressivists, who, in their early enthusiasm, gave students carte blanche to write about whatever they pleased. By the teacher's stepping out of the way—these expressivists believed—students would be freed to write out of their own experience; instead of staged writing that complied (more or less) with the teacher's demands, students were invited to discover for themselves just what they had to say.

My own teaching heart today is deeply expressivist, but even I recognize that a composition course must *unfold* in some way. A course comprising a scattershot assortment of essay assignments—regardless of whether the teacher or the individual students set the topics—is not a *course* at all but just a random bunch of classes. We call a course a *course* because there is some trajectory, some progress down the road. For my composition course, the track upon which we run moves steadily around the triangle of discourse: the earliest, most distinctly expressivist writing finds its home corner in the *self*; subsequent work pushes outward toward some *subject matter* increasingly beyond the writer's private experience; and the final work is most heavily pitched toward an *audience.* So the trajectory begins by helping the writer to "center down," as Quakers say, but then steadily provokes movement outward, away from the self, in what Piaget calls "decentering": from *me* (expressive aim) to *that* (referential aim) to *thee* (persuasive aim). The assignment sequence moves from (1) Remembering and Reflecting to (2) Observing and Reporting, and from (3) Investigating and Explaining to (4) Proposing and Advocating.

Assignment #1: Remembering and Reflecting

In the rush of our lives, we too rarely stand back from the inundation of information and entertainment to gnaw upon our experience for a taste of personal meaning. How much harder must it be for our younger and more stimulus-saturated students to do the same? So we begin the course with an assignment to explore some time of internal struggle or personal suffering in their own lives, from which they have emerged a bit wiser, changed in some obvious or subtle way, never again quite the same person. Because my students do not yet know me well at this point in the term, I can still get away with the somewhat draconian demand that they not write about anything that has happened in the last five years. (Putting one's truck in the ditch last month may prove to be a memorable event—for the writer, at least, if not for the reader!—but only time will tell if it holds the seed of any wisdom). The five-year rule sets their sights on experiences their brains have had time to gnaw upon. A too recent memory will provide plenty of *what happened?* but not nearly enough *so what?* To help students brainstorm for suitable subjects, I ask them to divide the Book of Their Lives into chapters, naming each separate chapter, and then to look closely at the events that mark the end of one chapter and the beginning of the next. Those points of transition are often fertile ground for reflective personal essays.

One of the most important things students need to learn about writing is that it is not only a way to communicate on paper with another person; writing can become for students a way of discovering what they believe—that is, not just a way to say what they mean but a way to find out just what they mean to say. We can use language not only to communicate but also to think, to sort things out, to try to make sense of our experience. When students write for reasons important to themselves rather than just to please an instructor, writing can become a way to develop a sense of self and conviction. I know this; I have seen it work in my own life and in my classroom as we join the ancient and still thriving circle of essayists trying to make meaning from their lives. We get there, slowly, by poking around in the ashes of our experience to find some still warm ember—some memory that haunts us but defies being neatly explained away—and then we let reflection fan that memory until it gives off its light.

A great many composition textbooks on the market today begin with a chapter on personal narrative—and then quickly move on, as if slightly embarrassed to dwell too long on this supposedly nonacademic or simplistic expository mode. So I need to assert that what I am after with this first assignment is something more demanding and worthwhile than teaching narrative structure: more *worthwhile* because telling stories is mostly what we do with language anyway, so students generally have already had plenty of practice before I ever meet them; more *demanding* because what I ask them for is not merely a *story* from their lives. To write, as Thoreau requires, "a simple and sincere account" of even a brief period of one's life is no small task; to teach young people to do so is even more formidable. Without a good deal of coaxing from the teacher (not to mention the occasional shove) students too easily settle for writing that looks more *backward* than *inward*—or if inward, then not *too far* inward, like the snowdrifts poet Robert Bly describes that blow all the way down from Canada but stop short six feet from the house, risking the journey but never quite daring the destination. It is not enough just to tell a true story; I like to see a story that tells some Truth.

So we begin with personal narrative, just as many popular textbooks do, but with this difference: I am interested not so much in covering the expository modes as in opening a way for my students to speak out of their own experience. Precisely because she knows too much about the subject, writing personal narrative forces a student to make decisions about what details to leave out, what order to present it all in, and how to interpret her experience convincingly for a reader. Real growth in writing comes when she learns she need not cling so tightly to what few words she manages to wrestle out onto paper because there is always more where that came from—when she learns, as Jacques Barzun puts it, that she is working not in marble but in clay. Out of the overabundance of memory she must sculpt an unwieldy remembrance in order to give it a narrative shape and to arrive at a version of the past she feels is true. I remind my students it is not how much we cover in the course that matters but how much we *uncover*.

If someone were to ask me what it is about the way I teach writing that is most quintessentially Quaker, I would surely have to answer that it is this early-in-the-term work with remembrance and reflection. I take seriously the etymology of the word *education,* "to draw out," to serve as a midwife drawing out what waits alive but as yet unborn within my students. Teaching writing *as a Quaker* carries with it the special charge of opening my students to the potentials of writing for spiritual growth and reflective, personal insight. Beginning with the earliest Quakers in the seventeenth century and continuing right down to the present day, Quakers have carried on a tradition of writing journals in order to gain some perspective on their own experience. In some cases the journals become for us an archive of precious recollections, offering an insider's view of such historic moments as the struggle to free slaves, the campaign for women's suffrage, famine relief after the Bolshevik Revolution, refugee work with Jews fleeing Nazi Germany (the Quaker school where I first taught served during the war as a refugee hostel), prison sentences for war resistance, and Witness for Peace visits to Central America and the Middle East—not to mention the more mundane struggle to carve a life out of the stubborn Iowa sod. In other cases the journals take a more inward turn, tracing the writers' spiritual paths and providing for us mentors from the past. In most cases, though, the writers scribble away with no thought of ever edifying others; for most, writing is a private place to sort the shards of experience, to introspect, to seek their private and conscientious values, with no greater goal in mind than to sit quietly and to collect themselves, open to such thoughts as happen to arise from the stillness, looking within to see what they find there.

I have risked dwelling too long here on just the first assignment, but I feel called to respond to recent "post-expressivist" reforms pulling the teaching of composition steadily away from having students write personal narratives at all. The personal narrative essay, it seems to me, is a uniquely humanistic activity and part of a long tradition in the liberal arts. Only humans—through oral and written language—can pass on to their descendants the knowledge we have accumulated through our experience; only humans can bring to bear upon remembered experience the transforming power of self-reflection. *Writing* memoir puts life in perspective. *Reading* memoir helps us to pull off the bonds of egocentricity. We can discover through the recorded thoughts of another person that the emotionally complex interior life we carry within us exists as well in other people, even in people seemingly quite unlike us. That seminal discovery is not only a small step out of the isolation of our lives but a giant, transformative leap toward our shared humanity. Telling each other our stories is the glue that forms the bonds of community. If a classroom full of strangers must somehow transform itself into an intentional learning community, telling our stories is an excellent place to begin.

Assignment #2: Observing and Reporting

The second movement along the trajectory of the course involves observing and reporting. Like the first assignment, this second one is centered in the writer's own experience—what she directly observes—but now the subject under study has moved out of the writer's memory and into the present, outer world. Students are instructed to visit a place where people are *struggling* in some way and then to write a profile. Students tend to envision the assignment too narrowly at first but, with the help of some whole-class brainstorming, they soon come to see how very many human endeavors involve struggle: the struggle to release oneself from an outer oppression (an injustice) or from an internal bondage (an affliction); the struggle to free others from oppression or bondage; the struggle to learn and to grow (in knowledge, in skills, in faith); the struggle to survive as a family (or the struggle to break free of family); the struggle to preserve or to improve our communities. As writers, they soon see that they could profile just about any human endeavor, large or small, just so long as their observations reveal the element of struggle.

This second assignment calls upon students to develop a keen eye and a discerning ear; their profiles must be thick with direct observation and specific detail. But if that were all I sought as their teacher, I could just as well send my students out to write profiles of the newest sports bar or of their annoying roommate. I am after something more. What I want—to borrow Quaker educator Paul Lacey's language—is to awaken the moral imagination. If it is true, as we saw in the last century, that imagination can be used in the service of great evil by reducing human beings to abstractions, surely it must also be true that imagination can be used in the service of compassion by awakening us imaginatively and empathetically to the suffering of others. After the first assignment's remembrance of one's own struggle comes this close study of the struggle of another—and perhaps, with a little help from conscience, an empathic projection of oneself into that other's struggle. This is the first step in the awakening of the moral imagination: the movement from a remembrance of one's own struggle to a consideration of how it must also feel for others; one imagines oneself in such a position.

The second step will be not merely to experience empathy with a single, observable instance of another's struggle but, more fully, to immerse oneself in the struggles of the world; it is the movement from imagining "what if that were happening to me?" to imagining "what if we really were all one human family?" This awakening of the moral imagination comprises a kind of hidden curriculum in my classes, but, of course, it is not as though a student must experience empathy in order to receive a good grade on an assignment. Academically, their task is merely to observe and to report. I leave the hidden curriculum to do its own patient work behind the scenes, trusting, as eighteenth-century Quaker abolitionist John Woolman writes in his journal, that "he whose tender mercies are over all his works hath placed a principle in the human mind which incites to exercise goodness toward every living creature; and this being singly attended to, people become tenderhearted and sympathizing" (25).

Assignment #3: Investigating and Explaining

From the primary and directly experiential research involved in observing and reporting for that second essay, students now move into secondary research, one step further removed from the self, reading up on *other* people's observations and making them a part of their own learning. That second essay assignment, with its emphasis on reporting direct observation, is a way station between *me*-centered and *that*-centered writing. This third essay assignment, investigating and explaining, takes students squarely into exposition. The assignment calls for them to explore some struggle in the broader world. I urge students to select a topic for which they feel what Quakers call a *concern*—that is, to choose a struggle that rouses their sense of caring. Recent students have investigated such topics as the struggle of single-income families to make ends meet, sweatshop labor in the Far East, female circumcision in Africa, bride burning in India, and the effects of war in Iraq. Occasionally, a student chooses to investigate a past struggle—women's suffrage, say—but most students select contemporary topics. This is not an opinion paper; students are simply *mapping* a controversy. The task, for now, is to conduct a kind of fact-finding mission, like a Quaker Witness for Peace: What is happening, and how do we know it is true? Whose are the different voices with a stake in one side or another of this struggle, and how do they attempt to speak to each other's concerns? Where do their positions overlap, and where do they diverge? But unlike a Witness for Peace, of course, my students rarely leave the safety and comfort of the library, unless the topic they have chosen to investigate is quite local.

Students' own urge to advocate is often strong, so they must be reminded to maintain a neutral, critical perspective, bridling that urge for now but knowing it will soon find satisfaction in the next assignment. For students, the challenge is to learn that most valuable skill of holding in one's mind what someone else has said, without rebutting it, without championing it, just listening with care. It drives them mad, of course, not to be allowed to race ahead into advocacy. Sometimes the hardest thing in this world is just to learn to listen—really listen—and to wait. The diversity of views in any public controversy is vast, and it is tempting for students—as it is for any of us—to give short shrift to views they do not happen to share. This assignment, then, calls upon students to practice a Quakerly kind of generous listening to all such views—what Peter Elbow has described as "the believing game" (188–189)—and likewise, to play the doubting game against views too easily in sympathy with their own. Though the students soon find they do not agree with every viewpoint, they must try nevertheless to understand the deeply felt concerns out of which such views arise. To successfully complete the assignment, they must learn to step back from judgment and seek only to give each separate voice of the controversy its due respect. At work here is what Quakers call *discernment;* that is, students must bring themselves to a point of understanding the various views, genuinely hearing the concerns of all sides.

While students investigate some suffering or struggle of particular interest to themselves, the class as a whole also investigates and maps a single public controversy. My current class, for example, is focusing on capital punishment, since there have recently been some high-profile executions in this country. For the overt curriculum of studying how argument works, the death penalty has a great deal to offer: Students can examine claims of value ("Is capital punishment immoral?"), claims of fact ("Does capital punishment deter further crime?"), and claims of policy ("Should the electric chair be banned as a method of imposing capital punishment?" or "Should mentally retarded convicts be exempt from capital punishment?"). And unlike some public controversies, this one stubbornly resists attempts to reduce it to simplistic pro/con or left/right dichotomies. For the hidden curriculum of the moral imagination, the death penalty offers something more: an invitation to imagine extending a simultaneous empathy for the family of the criminal as much as for the family of the victims, for the victims themselves as well as for the criminal, for the judge who must uphold the written law, and even (or perhaps especially) for the executioner whose job it is to carry out the judge's orders.

Assignment #4: Proposing and Advocating

Having earlier moved from the *me* corner of the discourse triangle to the *that* corner, the final phase of the course traces the trajectory from *that* to *thee*. In Quaker fashion, the full assignment sequence pushes steadily around the triangle of discourse, beginning with inward reflection, progressing through a period of discernment, and then moving toward outward action. By this fourth assignment, proposing and advocating, students have steeped themselves so thoroughly in public controversies that they are often bursting for a chance to have their own say, a chance finally to join the public conversation, unbridled by my earlier insistence that their writing take a neutral stance. Their task is to propose a solution to a real problem and to advocate for their proposal. Students must pitch their proposals to a specific audience—a *thee*—and so they must consider carefully how to be convincing to that audience. Part of that convincingness, they often discover, hangs upon their ability to practice the old-time Quaker virtue of speaking plainly with an honest voice.

The common sentiment is that Quakers eschew rhetoric, that we have as much disdain for dressed-up language as we have for fancy clothes. We are a plain people, we like to say, and plainspoken as well. That may be true as far as it goes, but it presupposes a somewhat debased notion of rhetoric as fancy and even deceptive language. Composition instructors, though, use the word *rhetoric* to refer to language that calls people to action—and centuries of social action attest to Quakers' considerable rhetorical skill. What distinguishes the subtle rhetoric of Quakers, though, is that we tend (at least in Meeting) to make little use of the language of *entreaty* but, instead, call each other to action by *telling our stories*. Yet it is unlike the merely confessional or even confrontational story-telling of, say, a group therapy session or (God forbid) a daytime talk show. Along the triangle of discourse this represents a movement from *me* to *thee*, but from a *me* that is not only *mine*—from a deeper, inner *me* we all share. This is John Woolman's "principle in the human mind which incites to exercise goodness." Quakers call it the Inward Teacher. Out of the collection of souls in the shared Meeting place—thee and thee and thee—a kind of gathered presence makes itself heard through the spontaneous testimony of one or of just a few, each attempting only to give voice to some subtler level of self that is common to us all and, in so speaking, to encourage that same still, small voice in others. Rather than say Quakers eschew rhetoric, I am more inclined to argue that we practice a sophisticated but peculiar form of it.

For this fourth assignment, proposing and advocating, my students enter fully into the realm of public rhetoric. They have broad discretion to advocate on any public controversy, large or small, local or global, that suits their own passions, but I especially invite them to explore topics related in some way to such broad themes as the search for peace or equality or simplicity or right stewardship of this planet. By directing students toward such traditional Quaker concerns, I suppose I could be accused of presumptuously imposing my religious views in a public institution of learning. But surely these are as much the concerns of a secular ethic as they are those of Quakers. Nurturing in young people an optimism about the ability of compassion to heal the wounds of humanity and encouraging in them the conviction to affirm outwardly what they know inwardly—these are the aspirations of *anyone* answering the high calling of being a teacher. "We teach to change the world," Stephen Brookfield writes. "The hope that undergirds our efforts to help students learn is that doing this will help them act toward each other, and toward their environment, with compassion, understanding, and fairness. [We teach] to increase the amount of love and justice in the world" (1).

Quakers have long been at the forefront of public discourse on issues of peace and justice and equality and environmental responsibility, but that is not to say these are Quaker issues alone. They are humanity's concerns. Both as a Quaker and as a world citizen I have my own preferred views on many such issues, but, of course, I never dictate what positions students ought to hold. I only insist that they find some point of controversy about how the world could become a better place—a more peaceful world, a more just world. To my students, Quakerism has nothing to do with it; their teacher is just a harmless old hippie who still cares about such things and hopes that they will learn to care as well. They play along, many of them acting at first as if they do not really care. But they *do* still care. Beneath the swagger and the well-honed irony, they still

care about this world. They just need the opportunities to decide for themselves what, exactly, they care about without being told at every turn what they
ought to care about, and without being shamed for not caring more.

A single student example may serve to demonstrate the trajectory of this
assignment sequence. Todd (you know Todd, don't you?) decided to make
quick work of the first assignment by remembering and reflecting on the first
time he ever got drunk—in fifth grade. As he worked the piece through successive drafts, though, the bravado of his initial remembrance evolved, through
reflection, into an honest personal confrontation with the true cost of alcohol
in his life. So for his second assignment, he decided to observe and report on a
weekend-long drunk drivers course he had been ordered to attend. Through
careful attention to observed details, Todd was able to convey the pain behind
the faces of the other alcoholic attendees and their bitterness at having been
forced to attend the weekend course. Initially, Todd, too, had thought he was
being subjected to an injustice—thought that the law was picking on him; and
yet, after an entire weekend with these people, Todd began to see their affliction more clearly—and began to see in *their* struggles echoes of his own. This is
the moral imagination beginning to awaken. For his third assignment, Todd
decided to stay with his earlier theme; he researched drinking among underage
college students like himself, both locally and nationally. He gathered statistics
and expert testimony from published sources, and he conducted interviews
with students, bar owners, and police. For his fourth assignment—as much to
his own surprise as to that of his classmates—Todd wrote a letter to the city
council, urging them to make all bars twenty-one-only.

Second Locus of Authority:
Gathering to Determine the Hallmarks of Quality

I never introduce published model essays until my students have already
made a start on their own drafts. My experience has been that students do not
learn well from model essays until they have a felt need; they must struggle a bit
on their own before they are ready to pay serious attention to how the masters
do it. So I wait until students have sketched out a few rough ideas of their own
before we take a look at similar kinds of writing by published professionals.
From our analyses of those published models, we try to identify what works,
and from *that* we phrase queries for ourselves. So for example, through our
study of published proposals to solve some problem, we may notice how the

more effective authors take time to convince their readers that the problem is a serious one worthy of attention. As a class we might compose a query something like, "Do my readers know this problem exists? How can I convince them of the seriousness of this problem?"

Continuing our analysis of the published proposals, we might notice that the better writers often bring up likely objections to their own proposals and then either argue against those objections or amend their own proposals to accommodate the objections. So again, we might write a query like, "Have I anticipated my readers' weighty objections and questions? How can I refute or dismiss their objections without sounding adversarial? Or how can I adapt my proposal to accommodate their objections?" And so on. Instead of *telling* my students textbook fashion what qualities a decent proposal must exhibit, we discover together inductively what seems to have worked for those who have tried this before us. Because we have composed these queries ourselves based upon the strengths we discover among the better writers, the queries do not strike students as merely "canned" questions, such as one might find in a composition workbook. Instead, they are *our* questions. Once we have developed together a set of queries for an assignment, we can use those queries later to focus our workshop discussions.

Third Locus of Authority: Gathering as Resources for One Another

While the blend of self-directed and peer-assisted cooperative learning lies at the heart of Quaker practice and, consequently, at the pedagogical core of Quaker schools, the one place it can most often be found in public schools is the writers' workshop of an English composition class. Central to the development of both Quakerism and the process-oriented, peer-collaborative workshopping movement is a critical shift in the notion of *authority*. In a composition class without workshopping, the students write papers but the teacher is the recognized authority. A workshopping class, by contrast, fundamentally respects the students as birthright authors—new authors, certainly, still wet behind the ears perhaps, but authors nevertheless with sound advice to offer each other and with the developing good sense to take or leave the advice they receive. Participating in a workshop is a kind of service work, I like to think. Sure, students will receive some help from their peers, but the point is not to give only so they can get. The hidden curriculum—at least to my mind—

is that students develop the habit of learning how to serve and not just how to serve themselves.

In my own community college classes, student writers take their drafts through two rounds of peer assistance: On their first draft—a short, tentative draft—they receive a special kind of workshopping; later, on their longer second draft, they receive detailed written feedback from the same classmates.

For the first-draft workshops, I try to model the procedure—as best I can—after the Quaker tradition of the Clearness Committee. Among Quakers, a Clearness Committee is a group of trusted Friends who help a person sort through a difficult decision or delicate personal conflict—not by offering advice but merely by listening and asking open, honest questions. The members of the Clearness Committee seek conscientiously *not* to "fix" the person's problem but, rather, to open a way for the person to hear her own Inward Teacher. "When it is faithful to its foundations," Paul Lacey writes, "Quaker education is neither student centered nor discipline centered; it is inward centered. Quaker education operates from the conviction that there is always one other in the classroom—the Inward Teacher, who waits to be found in every human being. If we appear to be student centered, it is because we know that the student has an inner guide to whom he or she can be led" (*Education and the Inward Teacher* 26).

The goal of workshopping—in *my* classroom—is not to "fix" a student's draft by offering outward advice; instead, we discipline ourselves to asking open, honest questions to help the student writer learn to listen to the voice of her own Inward Teacher. Before attempting this on each other's first drafts, we practice framing nonleading questions—that is, questions to which the asker does not already have an answer in mind—or questions that are not simply thinly veiled advice, such as "Don't you think you should explain a bit more here?" The writer does not necessarily have to answer every question; she can ignore questions she feels are irrelevant, or she can keep some of her answers to herself if she prefers. Throughout the Meeting, workshoppers take turns recording the "minutes"—jotting down all that is said, questions as well as answers—and they give these minutes to the writer at the end of the session. Also, at the end of the session, workshoppers take a few minutes to affirm—as fellow writers—what the writer is trying to achieve in this paper.

Like a Clearness Committee, a workshop group should be small; I like to keep them at around five students apiece. And like a Clearness Committee, a workshop session is only helpful to a writer if she genuinely feels uncertain about her draft. If she already (however mistakenly) feels finished with the assignment, if she thinks she has reached clearness already, the workshop will be at best a waste of everyone's time or, at worst, an exercise in defensiveness. And again, like a Clearness Committee, the other members of the workshop must conscientiously uphold their fellow writer's own authority in matters of improving a draft. We do not presume to know what the writer ought to do to her paper; we just listen carefully and ask the writer open, honest questions. The temptation is strong to leap in and to tell the fellow student where she has gone wrong and what she really ought to do instead; workshopping peers are no less susceptible to this temptation than teachers. I spend many hours each week conferencing with students in our Writing Center, and it has been a difficult lesson for me to accept the fact that I can be a better writing teacher once I stop showing off to students how I could have written their paper better. If a teacher—or a workshop peer—says to the student writer, "Do this, fix this, say this," the writer is soon dispossessed of her authority—indeed, her very authorship. She surrenders her sense of ownership. She receives direct instruction but at the high cost of disempowerment, so that this one specific piece of *writing* may be improved but not this one specific *writer*.

It takes training and practice to be an effective workshopper, just as it does to be a helpful member of a Clearness Committee. A sign of a healthy workshop, as for a healthy Clearness Committee, is a lot more questions being asked than solutions being offered. The workshoppers must constantly bear in mind that it is not their job to fix the draft for this writer nor to tell the writer whether they think it is any good. Workshoppers must learn to refrain from sounding *off* about the *draft* in front of them and, instead, sound *out* the *author* in front of them.

Most students, naturally, suppose that the benefit of workshopping comes when their own draft is under consideration. But I harbor a suspicion that they gain the most from workshopping *other* people's papers because doing so fosters the habit of composing with an eye toward how their writing will be scrutinized by their audience. And as writing teachers know all too well, the deep learning kicks in only when students begin to see their own writing as others will see it.

After the workshop, students come away with all kinds of ideas about their drafts. Most also have garnered a few ideas from informal helpers: roommates, girlfriends, mothers. The next task is to sift through all that to form some kind of revision plan. Teachers who use workshopping in their classes devote a lot of effort to training students to become better responders to each other's drafts; what we need, though, is to focus more on training students to become better users of the responses they get. I invite students to come see me or, if they prefer, another teacher in the Writing Center, where we then engage in something akin to what Quakers call a *threshing session*. In a one-on-one conference I try to help students talk through what they now think should be done with this draft. I never take student papers home to write comments on them. (Well, okay, almost never.) Nor do I sit alone in my office scribbling suggestions for their revision. (Well, not much). As I see it, it is entirely their job to seek out advice for their revision. I am available to them for a conference more hours per week than I care to admit. But they have to want it; they have to come and get it. And it will be *a conversation,* not some scribbled notes from me in the margins of their draft. I am dreadfully slow at reading and marking student papers; I cannot keep the process under twenty minutes per paper. So I spent too many years handing back conscientiously marked papers, having worked as hard on my weekend as during the work week, only to see students stuff my unread comments somewhere in the bottom of those enormous book bags they carry, and I would always think to myself, "There goes another twenty minutes of my life I'll never get back."

Not all students choose to come in for a threshing session, of course, but whether they come or not, they are required—as the next step in the process—to write a long note to me in which they explicitly lay out their plans for revision. In this note they tell me what advice they received, what they agree with or do not agree with, what they think they will do next. The beauty of this step in the process is that, ultimately, it saves them from the awful torment of staring at a computer screen for two hours, wondering how to improve their initial draft. Composing the note forces them to make some decisions in advance, so that when they actually sit down to revise they are merely implementing their revision plan.

Once students have revised their initial draft into a longer second draft, they return again to their workshop mates—only this time in search of *written* feedback. Instead of a Clearness Committee, this second round of peer assistance is modeled after the Quaker tradition of Queries and Advices. Since Quakerism adheres to no set creed, Quakers guide each other's spiritual journeys in part through the use of an ever-unfolding series of provocative questions and friendly counsel. Using the queries we created earlier from our analyses of published essays, students write detailed memos to one another regarding their latest drafts. Sometimes, students who have not yet come to me for a threshing session will decide to do so after receiving back these memos; not all the advice they receive is useful, after all, so the writers have to separate the grain from the straw before they can see clearly what further revisions are called for.

After all such global revisions have been made, we have another class session for editing at the sentence level, and, at last, the students submit their papers for evaluation. At both the revision and editing stages, students do quite a lot of work on papers not their own. Although most of my students' out-of-class work involves their own drafts, *inside* the classroom a great deal of our face-to-face time is devoted to work in service of their classmates. They help each other brainstorm for ideas; they provide each other with extensive written *and* oral suggestions for revising first drafts; they help each other edit the revised drafts for clarity and concision and correctness at the sentence level; and they serve as evaluators of essays submitted by students from other sections of the course. As their teacher I know, of course, that providing all this help *helps them;* in the long run, they learn by helping. But a busy student might well demand to know, in more immediate terms, what is in it for him to spend so much time helping somebody else to improve her writing. He wants his goodwill reflected in his grade. So, to reward students for their generous efforts, I designate a certain percentage of their course grade as service.

Fourth Locus of Authority: Gathering to Measure Our Performance

The first major step toward a more student-centered composition classroom was, as I said earlier, the movement toward student-generated ideas for writing. The second major step followed closely upon the heels of the first as the writing process and collaborative learning movements synergistically came to ascendancy and spread the gospel of workshopping. Within a single generation, two of the traditional four loci of authority had shifted from the teacher to the students. The teaching of writing has indeed come a long way in the past several decades, but few teachers of composition have yet to take the next step: relinquishing control of evaluation.

I remember seeing once a woodpecker that had evidently grown tired of bashing its skull against trees in search of insects. Instead, this woodpecker was browsing from car to car in a parking lot, sampling the bugs right off the grill-work of the cars. My years spent hauling home huge stacks of papers to grade seemed just like bashing my head against a tree, always thinking that if I just bashed myself a little harder, wrote more comments, stayed up later, that some-how my students would become more independent and competent writers. Since I could only assign as much writing as I could possibly read, comment on, and grade, my own inability to handle the paper load became the limiting factor in determining how much work I could assign. Somehow, I had actually be-come the bottleneck in my own classroom. In a constant struggle against the paper load, I began to lose touch with my dream of helping students to become better writers, and I was becoming, instead, an efficiency expert intent on clear-ing off my desk. I entered into a kind of secret competition against my col-leagues: I wanted my students to be impressed by my high standards and by how quickly I could locate the errors in their papers and assign a grade; I took pride in returning papers faster than any teacher they had ever had. I became less concerned about their performance as writers than about their good im-pression of my performance as a teacher. I had been pulled into a cruel vortex, and the harder I tried to swim against it, the faster it pulled me in. I gained for myself the admiration of students and accolades from peers, but the harder I worked the more fraudulent I felt as a teacher. In my heart I knew that I was not so much *teaching* as managing workload. What I needed was not a way to work harder but a way to work smarter. What I needed was not another tech-nique but a transformation.

After more than a decade of following in that same old English teacher tra-dition of grading all the papers myself, I noticed something important: I no-ticed that *I* was getting really quite good at judging student papers. I did not think the papers themselves were getting as good as I might have hoped, but my judging of them was becoming exemplary. That is to say, I was getting quite good at recognizing quality writing when I saw it. My students were not neces-sarily, but I was. One day a colleague of mine, who sometimes had to write grant applications, served as a judge of other people's grant applications. He came back from that experience all excited because he said he now understood exactly what it was that made some applications successful and others less so. His own writing of grant applications had greatly improved as a direct result of having served as a judge himself. Now he knew what his audience was looking for. Now he understood what worked and what did not.

It made perfect sense that grant writers should be chosen to judge grant applications, since who could know better than they, intimately and experientially, just what it took to write a successful one? And it made equally good sense to suppose that serving as a judge would improve one's own ability to write successful grants, since who but a judge could know firsthand where the strong applications shone and the weak ones lacked luster? So I thought, "This is it. This is what I have been missing all along." That was the start of my journey into student peer evaluation, and my teaching has never been the same since.

Peer review is the next frontier toward a more student-centered curriculum. But we have been stalled, in a sense, at the point of "Protestant Reformation," reluctant to lay down our role as ordained clergy in the classroom and more than a little desperate about preaching from our pulpits the scripture of state-approved standards. To justify our resistance to such a drastic change, we haul out all the same excuses we formerly used to defend against the two previous shifts: "students are not sufficiently trained to do the task properly," "it is the blind leading the blind," "it will inevitably lead toward mediocrity." But just as we have found that students should learn how to discover their own topics and should learn how to help each other improve their drafts, so, too, should students be learning to evaluate each other's writing.

They should and they *can!* But recognizing that they can requires a kind of Quakerly trust that students already have burning within them a flame of Truth and Beauty—however dim or obscured that flame may at first appear. This is where a second meaning of that uncomfortable word *professor* comes into play. I am not only a professor in the sense of being *one who lays claim to some knowledge;* I am also a professor in the sense of being *one who affirms a belief*—as in, "He professes that a teacher's task is to help students draw out their own Inward Teacher." So this much I profess: that under our care and guidance as "elders," a classroom community of students can and should put their considerable insights to good use as they work toward a collective understanding of what quality writing looks like.

As a "professor," I am informed as much by what I know (the first sense of the word) as by what beliefs I hold (the second sense). But there is also a third sense of the word, *one who pretends,* as in "He professes to know more than he actually does." For years I pretended to be good at putting a letter grade on student papers. Broad judgments of quality I learned to do reasonably well, as I said earlier. And I learned what kinds of comments on papers were most effective; that, too, I could do, though with painful slowness. But when I say I spent years pretending to be good at grading papers, I am talking about the act of assigning a score. A grade. A percentage. I could, of course, spot an A paper and an F paper on sight; but in between I always felt myself on pretty shaky ground. I was always amazed by my colleagues' eye for fine distinctions: What makes this paper a C+ rather than a B? Or worse, what earns this essay a score of 78 percent rather than 81 percent? I had no idea. Students ask questions like, "How can I bring this paper's grade up three more percentage points?" Goodness knows! I could suggest some ways to improve the paper, of course, but how much improvement would be necessary for those three points I honestly could not say. For a long time I thought it was just me, but when I started working in a Writing Center, I saw papers students had received back from teachers all over the campus. And you know what? Those teachers do not know either. They are just faking it too. I am sure of it. And I daresay the students suspect it as well.

What I *can* do, though, is identify a paper that is finished, is decently written, gets the job done, and I can distinguish it from a paper that strikes me as still needing some work, not quite there, a bit off the mark. In addition, I can identify those rarer papers that absolutely knock my socks off. I can do *that.*

And so can students—especially students who have just spent several weeks writing a paper of their own of the same type, have studied model essays of that type, have identified the hallmarks of quality, and have learned to look for that quality in their peers' and in their own essays. Those students know quite well what it takes to do the assignment with quality. They can spot the slacker papers because they *know.* They do not fall for fluff. They are unimpressed by slapdash.

So I experimented with having my students involved in judging each other's papers. They were apprehensive, of course. But we tried it as an experiment a few times, worked out some of the kinks and tried to resolve some of their lingering concerns. And the results were remarkable. Given just three broad levels of distinction—inadequate, adequate, and exemplary—a group of students making a group decision can score a stack of papers as fairly and as consistently as I can alone and probably more so. In my classes, the three levels of quality are called "Still Needs Work" for papers that have not yet met the expectations of the class, "Ready for Publication" for papers approved for inclusion in the class online magazine, and "Readers' Choice" for the top picks. In the magazine, the words "Readers' Choice" appear alongside the title of the papers so honored.

There is not only good reason to suppose that they *can* learn to evaluate each other's papers, there is also good reason to suppose that they *ought* to be taught to do so. By becoming better evaluators of writing, my students saw what it was they needed to do in their own writing to get those better marks. I did not need to scribble in the margins my guesses about what they needed; instead, they could see it for themselves. Not only that, they felt motivated to do something about it. Since they were no longer just cranking out assignments for some lonely English teacher, with no real concern for communicating to him anything other than that they wanted a decent grade—and since they were, instead, writing papers that would actually be read by their peers—they took a lot more care to make their writing say just what they wanted it to say, to get the message across just the way they hoped. More than that, though, through their new role as evaluators, students in my composition courses were learning to become a discriminating audience—*consumers* of writing, rather than merely the producers. And as consumers, they were developing an eye for quality.

In a traditional class students never see each other's writing (except, perhaps, to cheat), and even in a workshopping classroom students see only the early drafts of just a few peers. In neither case does a student have an opportunity to see how her own final draft holds up beside the rest. Yet how can a student be expected to make her papers more like those of the top students if she never sees any paper but her own? Sure, she reads the model essays in her textbook—Didion, Dillard, Orwell, E. B. White—but how can she be expected to recognize and to respect quality writing if her entire experience in school has been having her own fledgling creations utterly eclipsed by the brilliant pieces anthologized in the textbook? What she needs is to see the creations of students like herself—or rather, students just a bit better than herself. And she needs not merely to glimpse those creations but to consider carefully *in her own mind* what makes them better than her own. If she is only exposed to the kind of writing *her teacher* says deserves merit, her own slavish attempts to please the teacher will lead to little more than meretricious bunk. Instead, the student must conduct her own pursuit of quality; she must *herself* sort out the strong from the mediocre, and she must articulate *for herself* what qualities she values in good writing. This is not to say that a teacher has no role at all in pointing the way toward quality; he patently does. But shining a lantern to point the way does not have to mean dictating the terms or, indeed, doing the work of students' learning *for* them. As retired University of Iowa professor John F. Huntley—an early proponent of peer evaluation—explains, "[E]ducation for a democracy ought to teach the discovery and pursuit of quality by democratic, not by autocratic, means" (293).

What I am proposing is not just a classroom strategy to ease the nasty job of grading a stack of papers every night and two stacks on weekends (though it offers that benefit as well). I see it as a radically democratic shift. Are the students who keep writing C papers doing so because they are C people, or because they have never seen what B and A papers look like? "Too often in American public schools, the difference between C and A is a profound secret," Dennie Wolf rightly protests.

> Too often an A is the private property of those students who happen to be able to perform because of personal grit, or personal skills, or because they get it at the breakfast table. The most fundamental mandate of American public schools ought to be to make that kind of knowledge—knowledge of what it takes to succeed—a common property of every child who crosses their thresholds. (42)

Perhaps the best thing about peer review is that the average-ability writers for the first time have a chance to see what the stronger writers' papers look like, and so they begin to include in their own writing many of the successful strategies they see the stronger writers using.

As students' eye for quality writing improves, their standards continue to shift upward throughout the semester. A teacher's standards of quality tend to remain fixed throughout the semester, signaling to the A paper writer at the beginning of the term that her papers will continue to pull As right to the end without a great deal more effort. But with the students' upward shift of quality standards, the stronger writers—so often not accustomed to having to push themselves very hard to stay near the top—soon discover that they, too, must keep improving just to maintain their high scores, since the midrange writers will soon catch on and imitate whatever they see those better writers doing.

The peer evaluation model offers a better challenge for top-level writers, where quality becomes a continuous pursuit. But the most easily seen improvement comes from students who begin the course writing the lowest-level papers. For the first time ever, they get a chance to see exactly what it is those better writers have been doing all along. They figure out what it is that gives them away as poor writers, and they seek help to correct it. So I found in my little classroom experiments that the low-level papers at the end of the course were not half bad compared to the way those same students wrote on the first assignment. My early experiments worked so well that I soon redesigned my composition courses to make full use of student peer review.

What we do is surprisingly simple. On peer review day I sit with two combined workshop groups—that is, about eight or ten students—and this quality control team spends a double-hour class wading through a stack of an approximately equal number of papers written by students from other sections of the same course. With fewer than six essays, there is no guarantee that students will see sufficient range of quality to score the papers reliably; with more than ten essays to read, their brains begin to have trouble remembering which was which. Eight seems optimal. But I like to throw in a ringer sometimes—an outstanding or oddly inventive or just downright controversial paper from a past semester—just to see what conversation will come of it. The conversations *themselves* are enough reason to do peer evaluation.

We keep reading and swapping the papers around. After a person reads a paper, she jots down a few notes to herself: What are this paper's greatest strengths? What in this paper still needs some attention? What level of quality do I think it is currently at: still needs work? ready for publication? readers' choice? No one will see these notes but the person writing them; their only purpose is to help the evaluator recall a few things to say about each essay and to keep straight which paper is which.

Once everyone has read every paper, the evaluation session truly begins. For this we need to appoint, after the manner of Quaker Business Meetings, a "clerk" and a "recorder"—that is to say, a facilitator and a scribe. The clerk's task will be to walk us through a discussion of each essay; from the comments made in discussion, the clerk must glean a few helpful and supportive comments to be forwarded to the writer of that essay—something she did well, something she could still do to improve it. With the advice and consent of the other evaluators, the recorder writes those comments on the student's essay. At that point, the clerk must ask for the consensus of the group: is this paper ready for publication in the class's online magazine, or does it still need more work? After a bit more discussion the recorder indicates on the student's essay the sense of the group. Students whose papers are not yet considered "up to spec" deserve to be told by the group *specifically* what they might do to improve their papers' chances of passing muster, and every student, regardless of the consensus score, deserves a few words from the group on what she did particularly well and what she might still do were she to try to improve the essay further.

I myself serve as a member of these peer review groups, modeling for them the ways I write comments and the kinds of things I think are important in a quality piece of writing. But my goal, always, is to wean them from me. I speak up less and less in the group as I witness them internalizing the standards of quality writing. My job, as I see it, is to get out of the way as much as possible once I see my students engaging with the material and, ultimately, to make myself unnecessary. So the act of evaluating, instead of being just another out-of-class chore for the teacher, becomes an in-class learning opportunity for students.

These peer review sessions are yet another example of the use of a Quaker practice in my classroom. In Quaker Meetings for Business there are a number of ways to make one's disagreement known, depending upon the dissenter's depth of feeling. One might simply "stand aside," allowing the general consensus of the Meeting to prevail. Or, if one objects more strongly, one might ask to have one's objections "minuted," even though one is still willing to allow the general consensus to prevail. Or, if one objects so strongly that one simply cannot sit by and watch the rest of the Meeting stumble into madness and error, one can even singlehandedly block consensus.

In the peer review sessions of my composition classroom, we employ the same spectrum of dissent. After we have all read the same stack of student writing, we attempt to reach consensus on how we judge the quality of each essay. In most cases, the sense of the group is clear—especially after they have practiced peer review a few times. But not infrequently a couple of students will have a somewhat different notion of the quality of an essay. Generally, they stand aside once they have talked it through with the group. Occasionally, though not at all often, a single student insists upon minuting her dissent from the rest of the group; we record her dissent and deliver it to the author of the essay along with the group's consensus score. On rare occasions someone will object so strongly that she simply cannot allow the group's general consensus to stand. A lone student—or the lone teacher—might be the only one to grasp the sheer brilliance of the piece, and so the group is blocked from assigning a score to that piece. It rarely happens; but when it does, it *needs to.*

I have yet to see a team fail to come to consensus over a lousy paper. Everyone recognizes, it seems, when an essay is lazy or thin or dishonest. The strong dissent—on those rare occasions when it happens at all—nearly always centers around an essay that is so creative, so wacky, so wonderfully unexpected a response to the assignment, that the peer reviewers just cannot figure out what to make of it. Typically, the weaker and the average writers on the team will dislike the paper and insist it fails to meet the goals of the assignment, while the better writers on the team—the closet poets—will argue it is the best piece they have seen in a good long while. The group's consensus is blocked, as well it should be, and they send the essay back to me to deal with separately. Very much like what happens in Quaker Meetings, the wisdom of that consensus-blocker is often not understood until quite later. Though the process of coming to consensus is sometimes frustratingly slow, one of the greatest strengths of Quaker practice is that dissent is seen as a potentially healthy thing; we are careful never simply to dismiss it in favor of the will of the majority.

So the clerk of the evaluation session must manage the discussion and ascertain the sense of the group. It is a formidable leadership task and one that ideally every student ought to have an opportunity to undertake. At the end of the evaluation session, the clerk leads the group through a debriefing; the recorder, meanwhile, takes notes to be written up later as the minutes of the session. Under the clerk's leadership, the group attempts to articulate in its minutes exactly what qualities they tended to prefer in the better essays and what qualities they were put off by in the weaker ones. Certain questions invariably arise: How should they respond to a student whose paper was solid but short? How should the group score a brilliantly conceived paper with a lot of surface errors still plaguing it—or, just the opposite, a grammatically and mechanically flawless piece of fluff?

These minutes bring up interesting issues to discuss with the whole class at a later time, and they are often (no surprise) the very concerns that haunt teachers grading a stack of student papers. The recorder preserves these moments for later consideration. Additionally, the recorder makes notes about how effectively the session moved along, how easily consensus was or was not reached, how many participants spoke up repeatedly, and how many seemed too passive. This is prime learning time because students take a few moments to consider *for themselves* what seemed to work well and what did not, to articulate it, to identify examples of it—and so to be in a much better position to incorporate *their own* advice in their own next assignment. They begin to view their subsequent papers the way they think their readers will see them—and *that,* as every writing teacher knows, is half the battle.

Later, back in my office, I look back over the peer reviewers' decisions to reassure myself that the standards from one team to the next are pretty much the same. Although I have been using peer evaluation for nine years now, I still second-guess the process sometimes. If I doubt a team's decision on a paper, I simply toss it into a pile for another class to read and see if they come up with the same score. If they do, then I consider the possibility that *I* may be misreading the essay. After all, I know the writers, so I may be prejudiced one way or another: demanding much more out of a strong student I know can do better or, conversely, presupposing that a strong writer will have written a better paper than she actually has done. Likewise, I may overrate a paper written by a weak student just because I am overjoyed to see any serious attempt at all. It is too tempting for me to grade, unconsciously, on how hard I think the student worked on a paper, or on how well I am accustomed to the student performing on other papers. So if two independent teams both agree upon a score different from one I might give, I generally go with the teams' score. But if, as more often happens, the second group's score confirms my earlier suspicions, I will discard the first group's score and use the second group's.

On the whole, though, there is surprisingly little disagreement, either among the groups or between the groups and me—especially after the teams have been through the process a few times. With a little practice, they become quite adept at recognizing quality writing when they see it, just as we all had to do when we first became English teachers and faced our first mountains of papers to grade. The best-kept secret in academia is that most of us learn best by getting a chance to teach others. Why not tap that power? Why not—in

Quaker language—awaken students' own Inward Teacher? Why not let every student have a chance to sit at the big desk? Just as the Quakers have long asserted that everyone, regardless of station, should have the opportunity to minister, so, too, should every student have the opportunity to teach—to offer advice to other student writers, to judge their efforts, to discover experientially what quality looks like.

For all my proud progressivist talk, though, my community college students are every bit as grade addicted as students anywhere. I would probably have a mutiny on my hands were it not for this: I welcome endless rewrites. "Still needs work" does not mean F; it means the student still needs to work on this piece; it means the essay just is not yet finished. Peers are not so much putting a grade on a paper as they are *vetting* it. We publish an online magazine for the course, and students' essays must pass a peer review before being posted (just as *this* essay must be vetted by professional peers before being published). Student writers are invited (after a mandatory conference with me) to revise their paper in accordance with the feedback the evaluators gave them, and then they may resubmit the paper for another evaluation by me. This does not mean they can simply resubmit the very same essay as if I were a Court of Appeals; they must significantly revise the paper first, taking into consideration the kinds of remarks the team made about their paper. But at least they know they are not stuck with the grade their peers from another class gave them; just knowing that seems to allay most of their initial fears. From *my* perspective, as the teacher, the option to revise and resubmit drives the fear out of students' creative risk-taking. Since I know that learning entails taking risks and making mistakes in a climate of trust, I am always pleased to find a few students willing to break out of their school-sanctioned, safe, pedestrian writing. The option to resubmit frees such students to experiment with writing in ways they never before felt permitted—or at least never felt permitted to do for school.

And if the open invitation to revise and resubmit does not allay their initial fears about peer evaluation, this does: In the full scheme of my semester's grade book, the peer-generated scores on their final drafts play a relatively small part. Without getting too far into the details of how I determine course grades, I can at least offer a few suggestions for teachers interested in trying student peer review. We may be required, like it or not, to assign letter grades to *students* at the end of every term, but at most schools no one requires us to assign letter grades to every *paper* students write. "Still needs work," "ready for publication," and "readers' choice" may be all the judgment we need to make on students' essays. Why do we need to make finer distinctions on their final *products* if, as we claim, we are mainly concerned with their writing *process?* If we value the process of writing as much as we claim to do, then most of the marks in our gradebooks ought to reflect that.

My own gradebook is largely ones and zeroes: credit if a student meets a deadline, no credit if she does not; a mark if she participates in her workshop, no mark if she is absent or underprepared. Part of my gradebook records service, as I mentioned earlier. *Service* includes any work they do on behalf of the class but not directly for the sake of their own essays: writing responses to peers' drafts, workshopping, serving as an evaluator. Another part of the gradebook records what I call *professionalism:* Meeting deadlines, mostly. *Practice* covers a variety of short exercises and sentence skills work. Under *process* I reward students for demonstrating that they are developing useful habits as writers; this is where I credit them for trying new invention strategies and for doing substantial exploratory writing, for showing evidence of significant revision, and for writing an "afterthoughts" reflection on their learning when an assignment is finally completed. Under *product* I record peer review scores. Taken all in all, a student who manages (eventually) to prepare every essay for publication *and* who garners *all* her other marks receives a course grade of B. The lower grades go to students whose poor habits or erratic attendance erodes their grade through missed workshops and the like—or, of course, to students who simply never manage to bring all their essays up to par. An A, in my grade book, requires that at least some (though not all) of their essays receive a mark of "readers' choice." From an A student, I want to see writing that at least occasionally knocks their peers' socks off.

What I have found, using peer evaluation, is that some students begin the course concerned about whether their papers will be graded fairly by other students, but they leave the course saying they felt the grades were *more* fair than if a single person—even an English teacher—had done the grading alone. The peer review score is, after all, a consensus score. Most of the students I get from the high schools nowadays are already accustomed to group workshopping, collaborative projects, peer editing, and so on, so my use of peer review just seems like the natural extension of that—which, indeed, it is. That does not mean they rejoice at the scores their peers give them! They still like to think this is Lake Wobegone, where they are all above average, and they resent being told otherwise—by their peers as much as by their teacher. So, yes, of course, they complain, especially at first. But what has changed is *my role* when they complain. I never let myself get caught up in defending a peer review's consensus score, though the owner of the paper may try very hard to enlist me in that fight. Instead, I talk with the writer about *why* her paper might have received the score it did and what she thinks she might do now to remedy the problem. It changes my role for the better; rather than a defender of the score, I become an interpreter of the score and an "elder" (in the Quaker sense of the word) to the student who seeks to improve it. I no longer have to defend the score because it did not come from me—or at least not from me alone. As a member of the scoring groups, I still read all the papers, offer my comments, and decide on a score for the paper; the only difference is, now I am no longer the *only* voice arguing for what score a paper should be given. And more important, now I am not the only person in the class learning what quality writing looks like. And is that not, after all, what we want students to learn?

The Role of Professor

Like most teachers I know, I am sometimes haunted by my own sense of professional fraudulence. It is that third meaning of the word *professor* rearing its head again: *one who pretends*. That familiar doubting voice snarls at me for professing to uphold high standards of quality while, at the same time, leaving greenhorn students to evaluate each other's papers. It is a feeling that seems to come on most strongly during those moments when the students are so engaged they do not need me; I could leave the room and not even be missed. I start to worry, in such moments, just what they are paying me to do here. What exactly am I *teaching*?

But what I do, when that feeling gets too strong, is simply *remember and listen*. I remember the words of some of my teacher heroes, such as Parker Palmer, saying,

> I have no question that students who learn, not professors who perform, is what teaching is all about: students who learn are the finest fruit of teachers who teach. [T]eachers possess the power to create conditions that can help students learn a great deal. Teaching is the intentional act of creating those conditions. (1998: 6)

My role as the professor is to help create the conditions in which the gathered wisdom of the classroom community can make its presence known. As Paul Lacey writes, the good teacher

> seeks to make himself transparent, so that the teaching itself stands clear. The good teacher tries hard to be available to students' needs without making them dependent; he or she does not want personal disciples....The outward teacher is most effective when he or she is, in Kierkegaard's words, "a witness, never a teacher." (1998: 31–32)

I *remember* the words of these teachers of mine and hold them close to my heart.

And I *listen* to the caliber of my students' talk. I am convinced these consensus-seeking discussions are, in themselves, the most educational part of the whole course. Where else can one find one's students engaged in a fertile debate over what constitutes quality writing? They talk, and they figure it out—not by being *taught* but by dialoguing toward discovery. Instead of filling up the classroom with my own hard-earned omniscience, I am opening a community in which students can engage with the subject and with each other. Rather than use the classroom space "to tell my students everything practitioners know about the subject—information they will neither retain nor know how to use—I need to bring them into the circle of practice in that field, into its version of the community of truth" (Palmer, 1998: 122).

In other words, my role as teacher is not to teach students what writers think but to teach them to think like writers—to *do* the discipline of writing rather than to learn *about* it. Every paper I ever marked up for a student to fix according to my specifications taught that student little more than how to lip synch the words the way I wanted them sung. For me to write all over their drafts, telling them everything I think they should do, would be like giving a hungry person a fish instead of teaching her to fish for herself. Sure, I could probably turn her draft into a swell essay; I could do the work *for* her. But all she would leave the course with is a few swell final drafts; she would not be taking away any lifelong habits to see her through future writing tasks. She would have missed out on the opportunity to learn to do her own fishing. And fish she must, because after me she will in all likelihood have no more English teachers.

To do the discipline of writing requires that students do what authors have always done: struggle to find their own words, try those words out on a trusted circle of fellow writers, struggle again to get it right, and send those words off into the world to see what the audience thinks of it. There is no fraud in that. But it involves seeing my role as *professor* in a whole new way. It requires a great transformative leap from seeing myself as hired to teach writing to seeing myself as hired to help students learn to write. The difference is not merely semantic; it is the difference between enabling students' learned helplessness and helping them to learn. It is the difference between holding forth as the authority and sending forth a new generation of *authors*.

CR Chapter Five
The AmerIcan Essay:
Where Spirit and Silence Meet

Barbara Mallonee

And because something of the Divine is implanted at birth in every human being, Friends strive to release the potential in all people.

Leonard S. Kenworthy, Quaker Education: A Source Book (107)

"What *is* the essay?" I look at my students and they look back at me, and I realize it isn't silence in the classroom that I value. *Mayday!* I think, my mind casting about, desperate to cut through a silence that is a dead silence—not productive, fruitful, fertile. Born to Methodist stock in the Midwest at the start of World War II, I wince at any sign that I am a backsliding Quaker—though, in fact, today *is* May Day, and in Baltimore on the first of May, the air in the room is warm and thick. Those students gathered before me are uncomfortable with silence. I can be comfortable with silence, but I also like buzz and hum, so I plunge on. "What *is* the essay? Well, among other things…" In my classroom, I like imparting knowledge, hearing voices process it, hearing voices question it. I like to listen to my students read aloud their own work and that of others. I like the rustle of paper, the scratch of pencils, the squeak of chalk on the board. All in all, I love the sounds of language, the noise of business and busyness, the crunch and bite and slither and drum of words.

If my classroom does not feel like Parker Palmer's Meeting for Worship with a concern for learning, that is not because I teach in a Catholic institution. Education at Loyola College, as at a Friends' School, celebrates the glory of God, and many of my Jesuit colleagues begin classes with a period of reflection they call the *examen:* long stretches of silence in which to examine moments of consolation and desolation in daily life. Though I often begin my classes with journal writing or quasi-spiritual exercises and then speak to students out of silence, there is an alternate experience that my students and I share that comes much closer to the self-conscious experience of Friends worshipping together. Musing on Palmer's *The Courage to Teach,* I do think I could call the shepherding of students through essays a Meeting for Worship with a concern for writing: there, in that shared writing enterprise, silence, as Friends know silence, is genuinely the theme. My students write essays in silence; I read their essays in silence; when we meet in class or conference to discuss those essays, long pauses for reflection frame our verbal interchange. In those soundless stages of producing *the essay,* we watch rings of meaning ripple across a vast pool of possibility.

The essay is a genre that simulates Meeting for Worship as George Fox and his band of Seekers conceived it on Pendle Hill in 1652. To teach writing in a Catholic institution as the intersection of spirit and silence is, I think, not to be unduly subversive nor to inappropriately overlay my curriculum with a Quaker gloss. Rather, as a Friend, I find teaching the essay an opportunity for outreach within an institution that values diversity and service.

> **Essay** [Ofr.*essayer,* LL. *exagiare* < L.*exagium,* a weight, weighing < *ex* out of + *agere,* to do, drive] **v.t.** 1. To test the quality of; try out. 2. To try; attempt. **n.** 1. *a)* a trying or testing. *b)* an attempt; trial. 2. A short literary composition dealing with a single subject, usually from a personal point of view and without attempting completeness. **SYN.** see **try.**

Sailing in a sea of silence, the essay is an adventuresome form of literature. The form originated, as did Friends, on the other side of the ocean, and when it crossed the waters to take up residence here, it changed and flourished—as did we. The personal essay, an exercise in self-realization, is well suited to a nation that, because it was dedicated to liberty for all, opened its arms to a religious group, fleeing from England, that believed that "there is that of God in each person." The form can be traced all the way back to the ancients (to Seneca, Plutarch, Plato, Herodotus), although it is often credited to the Frenchman Michel de Montaigne (1533–1592), who wrote *of* books and *of* smells and *on* innumerable topics like friendship and heroes, producing a total of three books of essays in all. The essay flourished in Europe, in China and Japan, and in the

United States in the eighteenth and nineteenth centuries before retreating to the fringes of literature in the twentieth. In a piece on the essay written in 1976, Edward Hoagland lamented the second-rate status of the essay. Twenty-three years later, as guest editor of *The Best American Essays 1999,* he was able to report a great resurgence of interest in the essay:

> Essays are reappearing in unexpected places, in *National Geographic* as well as *The New Yorker,* and on the airwaves and in newspapers, as corrective colloquy or amusing "occasionals." Paralleling the flood of memoirs that are coming out, the essay form is in revival. (xviii)

The New Yorker, Atlantic Monthly, Harper's Magazine, Orion, The New York Times Magazine—all speak to the growing popularity of the essay as a locus for contemporary thought. More to the point for educators are the continually updated anthologies of essays, drawn from magazines, literary journals, and newspapers, that are published for use in freshman writing classes. Particular praise might go to Robert Atwan, the man responsible for the annual *Best American Essays,* a series that began in 1986 with Elizabeth Hardwick as its first guest editor. Robert Atwan also edits three teaching anthologies I find invaluable because of their contemporary edge: *Ten on Ten, The Writer's Presence* (edited with Donald McQuade), and a college edition of *The Best American Essays.*

I feel confident teaching the essay in my classroom as a living literary form. I am also struck by the close match of the formal properties of the essay to those formal Quaker principles that shape my spiritual life. The essay has distinguishing characteristics that have been well documented by those who write essays—all of whom seem eventually driven to write an essay about the essay! My intention in this essay-on-the-essay is to lay out the full array of those characteristics in the order in which I teach them, and to show that they parallel fundamental Quaker principles articulated and practiced across two hundred years. The five points, in sequence, shape my syllabus each semester, and each semester I choose appropriate essays to illustrate them.

Point One: Individual and Idiosyncratic

> The essayist is a self-liberated man, sustained by the childish belief that everything he thinks about, everything that happens to him, is of general interest. He is a fellow who thoroughly enjoys his work, just as people who take bird walks enjoy theirs. Each new

excursion of the essayist, each new "attempt," differs from the last and takes him into new country. This delights him. Only a person who is congenitally self-centered has the effrontery and the stamina to write essays.

> E. B. White, "The Essayist and the Essay," *In Depth* (728)

The fundamental principle which Friends stress, that in every person there is something of God capable of receiving direct illumination from God, must apply equally to children as to adults, and must therefore set the tone for the whole life of the school.

> *Christian Faith and Practice in the Experience of the Society of Friends* (452)

The essay, I tell my students, is a distinct genre. It isn't storytelling (though it may contain narrative). It isn't journalism (though it gathers fact). It isn't a sermon (though it has a point). It isn't an argument (though it is reasoned). It isn't a poem (though it lavishes care on economy in language). It has its own formal properties, and the first of these is its reliance on its writer's happy sense of his or her own distinct personality. The essay is not autobiography. Rather, it is a construct that maps human thought. Edward Hoagland, in "What I Think, What I Am," says that "a personal essay is like the human voice talking, its order the mind's natural flow, instead of a systematized outline of ideas" (362). If the goal of education for Quakers is to awaken each person's own measure of the divine, then the essay is a window to an emergent inner **I**.

It is hard to get freshmen, who have been cautioned in secondary school never to use the first person and whose success as writers has been measured in factual reports and term papers and "objective" literary analyses, to shift attention from the material under discussion to their own impressions and preferences in exploring the material. They have been reared to give voice to the work of others. Hoping to liberate through models, teachers of freshman writing use anthologies filled with clamorous distinctive voices—George Orwell, Virginia Woolf, Henry David Thoreau, Zora Neale Hurston, Annie Dillard, James Baldwin, Shelby Steele, Joan Didion. In sound and style and structure and subject matter, these professional essayists are self-indulgent. As Meeting for Worship invites a roomful of Friends to let their minds roll, so, too, does the essay. Says Hoagland, "Through its tone and tumbling progression, it conveys the quality of the author's mind" (363).

"I can use the word *I?*" my students ask.

"You can!" May. Should.

Suggested Essays: Annie Dillard, "Living Like Weasels"
Lucy Grealy, "Mirrorings"
Zora Neale Hurston, "How It Feels to Be Colored Me"
Brent Staples, "Just Walk on By: A Black Man Ponders His Power to Alter Public Space"
E. B. White, "Once More to the Lake"

Point Two: Inspired

The theme of the essay can be anything under the sun, however trivial (the smell of sweat) or crushing (the thought that we must die).
Cynthia Ozick, "She: Portrait of the Essay as a Warm Body," *The Atlantic Monthly,* September 1998

If we are faithful to our measure of Light, we shall be guided up toward God, and up to a greater measure of Truth. To go beyond our measure and imitate persons who have a greater measure than we have, is to be deceitful and to represent ourselves as something more than we are.
Howard Brinton, *Friends for 300 Years* (28)

The essay is nonfiction, rooted in the stuff of the world and affirming that all of God's creation is important. Whatever the essayist fancies worth talking about and feels able to write about is appropriate subject matter. In Meeting, as we wait in expectation for thought to begin, we let images and feelings and memories scroll across our minds until something snags, reverberates, makes us stall and contemplate. We breathe in—and then begin.

"I've been thinking about lilacs," says an older woman.

"Yesterday we marched at the Pentagon," says a young man.

"Have you ever heard a player piano?" asks a visitor.

"My house was robbed."

In Meeting, we hear how messages begin, and by the same token, when we read essays, we can almost hear, somewhere in the essay, the gasp of hilarity, of horror, of joy or amazement or epiphany or anger that was the actual starting point of the essay. Scholars search for enlightenment; Friends seek Light; it is with small sparks that illumination begins. With Dagoberto Gilb, working at a construction site in L.A., catching a glimpse of Victoria Principal on a scorching summer day. With an overweight, badly scarred, thirty-year-old Natalie

Kusz, celebrating tenure at a midwestern college by piercing her nose. With Lars Eighner, scavenging in dumpsters. With a young Ian Frazier, just fooling around as a barefoot boy in the woods. My students are accustomed to over-generalizing about Capital Punishment or Sexism or Prejudice or the Environment or Love or Drugs or Animal Rights. To write about the death of a well-treated pig or a haircut in the kitchen or fireflies on a summer night seems an invitation to triviality. But in the mind of the essayist, as in the mind of a practiced Friend sitting in silence on Sunday morning, no subject is too small or insignificant to invite significant thought. "I think I'll write about showers!" says a young man to his classmates. "I played ball in Camden Yards," says another. Scooters, jeans, sunglasses, *Friends,* genealogy, the band Good Charlotte—this year my students have had a lively spring.

Suggested Essays: Joan Didion, "On Keeping a Notebook"
                      Ann Hodgman, "No Wonder They Call Me a Bitch"
                      John McPhee, "Silk Parachute"
                      George Orwell, "An Episode of Bedwetting"
                      Cynthia Ozick, "The Shock of Teapots"

Point Three: Informed by Inquiry

> What I do know is that the world is too rich, too various, too multifaceted and many-layered for a fellow incapable of an hour's sustained thought to hope to comprehend it. Still, through the personal essay, I can take up one or another of its oddities, unresolved questions, or occasional larger subjects, hoping against hope to chip away at true knowledge by obtaining some modicum of self-knowledge.
>
> Joseph Epstein, *The Norton Book of Personal Essays,* (22–23)

'Tis the gift to be simple, 'tis the gift to be free
'Tis the gift to come down where you ought to be
And when we find ourselves in the place just right,
'Twill be in the valley of love and delight

When true simplicity is gained,
To bow and to bend we shan't be ashamed
To turn, turn 'twill be our delight
'Til by turning, turning we come 'round right.
Old Shaker Hymn

"Though more wayward or informal than an article or treatise, somewhere it contains a point which is its real center truthful point," writes Edward Hoagland of the essay ("What I Think" 362). No matter its subject, large or small, the writer of an essay pursues truth—and truth is always a subset of Truth. Friends use queries to probe their inner and outer state. For the essayist, the gasp or groan or smile that an event occasions translates into puzzlement—and then into a question that prompts a quest for insight. Alice Walker wonders why world-famous Bob Marley would ask to be buried at Nine Miles, the impoverished place on Jamaica that he sought to leave. George Orwell ponders why he shot an elephant in Burma he knew full well he should not have shot. Sally Tisdale asks why women worry about their weight. Joyce Carol Oates, remembering a deserted house, considers domestic abuse.

Friends speak of "centering," and the first step for the essayist as for the worshipper is to focus attention on a particular topic (the color mauve, lemon pie, Rosa Parks, dolphins, a whisk, the Bible, astronauts) or question (what is a moment? why is the sky blue? why does race matter?). Then the intellect gets to work to pursue an answer or insight. *Discernment* is an important concept for both the Society of Friends and the Jesuit order of the Catholic Church. In the essay, discerning "true knowledge" materializes as a rich and diversified goal.

Suggested Essays: James Baldwin, "If Black English Isn't a Language, Then Tell Me, What Is?"
Amy Cunningham, "Why Women Smile"
Debra Dickerson, "Who Shot Johnny?"
Vicki Hearn, "What's Wrong with Animal Rights"

i: Inquiry: Kinds of Truth

Scientific inquiry is a spiritual activity, not possible for things and animals, only possible for rational persons. Science is itself the standing disproof of materialism, the clear evidence of the truth of Sir Thomas Browne's description of man as the great amphibium, a creature designed to live in two worlds, the physical and the spiritual, the natural and the supernatural.

William Wood, *Christian Faith and Practice in the Experience of the Society of Friends* (138)

Obviously, the first person doesn't guarantee honesty. Just because they are committing words to paper does not mean that writers stop telling themselves the lies that they've invented for getting through the night. Not everyone has Montaigne's gift for candor.
                    Tracy Kidder, Introduction, *The Best American Essays 1994* (xii)

While in the academic sphere different disciplines focus on different kinds of truth (truth in history is different from truth in chemistry), in the essay all breeds of truth are honored. John McPhee's essays are objective. JoAnn Beard's are subjective. Diane Ackerman works from the five senses. Thomas Jefferson lays out good sense. Benjamin Franklin lays out common sense. Claims in essays can range from abstract to concrete, from general to specific. In the essay, a composite can be as compelling as an actual factual person. Some essays are whimsical. Others have the hard edge of a documentary. Story can be as convincing as history. The bed of knowledge in an essay might include not only proven fact and hard information but also imagination, feelings, intuitions, intimations, leadings. Like a Friend, the essayist is disposed to give greater weight to the experimental. "This I knew experientially," said George Fox. The essayist is free to mix truth up.

Suggested Essays: Gretel Ehrlich, "Spring"
                    Stephen Jay Gould, "The Dinosaur Rip-Off," "The Streak of Streaks"
                    Lewis Thomas, "The Tucson Zoo"

ii: Inquiry: Strategies for Investigation

The essay is a notoriously flexible and adaptable form. It possesses the freedom to move anywhere, in all directions. It acts as if all objects were equally near the center and as if "all subjects are linked to each other" (Montaigne) by free association. This freedom can be daunting, not only for the novice essayist confronting such latitude but for the critic attempting to pin down its formal properties. The essay challenges formal analysis by what Walter Pater called its "unmethodical method," open to digression and progressive meandering. Dr. Johnson described the essay as "a loose sally of the mind" and "an irregular, undigested piece."
                    Phillip Lopate, *The Art of the Personal Essay* (xxxvii)

Understanding cannot come through a narrow approach to knowledge but the emphasis will vary from person to person. It must not be thought of as necessarily only intellectual. For some it will come through a feeling for imaginative and artistic expression;

for some through the inheritance of a traditional standard of craftsmanship. For others, and perhaps in a measure for all, it should come through training in the knowledge and skills necessary for homemaking and the care of children.

Christian Faith and Practice in the Experience of the Society of Friends (449)

Each discipline has its own array of strategies for arriving at the truth. Biologists use the scientific method. Social scientists employ both abstract statistics and oral history. Psychologists give credence to memory. Mathematicians use deduction. For the theologian, Biblical concordance convinces. The historian seeks patterns of cause and effect. Literary scholars study word etymology, scansion, and critical theory. Those in education use standardized testing. Business and law schools use case studies.

John Dewey differentiated between formal and commonsense inquiry. In using commonsense inquiry, the essayist is electing a broader and more difficult framework for truth than what takes place in the disciplines. The essayist might employ any available strategy to discern truth, nor is there a rigid protocol for employing any combination of strategies for assembling information and arguments. With my freshmen, I begin the task of establishing credibility in an essay by inviting them to access their own experiences, current and remembered; I encourage them to trust their own impresssions and observations. We read Annie Dillard's essay "Total Eclipse" or E. B. White's "Once More to the Lake." They write their first essays on any topic they choose, letting the power of personal experience and the force of language convince.

In preparation for their second essay, we move in our reading to essays that range more widely in the world, watching how essayists gather up material to inspire thinking but also to authenticate thinking. In one of my favorite examples, "A Biological Homage to Mickey Mouse," Stephen Jay Gould builds an explanation for the appeal of Mickey Mouse that begins with his own experience with Mickey Mouse, makes use of his perspective as an evolutionary biologist, but also rambles through a broad landscape of material: He incorporates a reference to Florence Nightingale, an account of an anniversary screening of *Steamboat Willie* (1928), actual measurements with dial calipers of Mickey Mouse's head over a fifty-year span, the research of Konrad Lorenz and Charles Darwin, his own knowledge of neoteny, and comparisons with other Disney characters.

In another essay I admire, written to herald Mickey's sixty-fifth birthday, John Updike discusses the power of Mickey as a cultural icon; it is no surprise that a writer's revelation should turn on the definition of the word *genius;* he, too, confesses his personal affection for Mickey, and, like Gould, he studies the oddity of Mickey's ears, but the rest of his evidence, though as varied as Gould's, is utterly different in kind.

I am especially struck, in reading essays, by how seriously their readers and writers take imaginings, projections, and feelings. That openness in essayists to whatever "speaks to my condition" seems a Friendly trait to me. Within the Society of Friends, as we worship together, as we study together, as we transact business together, we accept a wide range of evidence as support for the building of a sense of the Meeting that we can accept as sound. Recently, our Executive Secretary, in the course of discussion, said, "All those statistics are compelling, but I just feel that." The Meeting listened, concurred. William Penn wrote,

> We judged not after the sight of the eye, or after the hearing of the ear, but according to the Light and sense this blessed principle gave us; we judged and acted in reference to things and persons, ourselves and others, yea, towards God our Maker. For being quickened by it in our inward man, we could easily discern the difference of things, and feel what was right and what was wrong and what was fit and what not, both in reference to religion and civil concerns. (*Christian Faith and Practice* 38)

My students write their second essay on any topic they choose. They are required to range far and wide as they explore that topic; they must include experiences of others, statistics, a relevant news article, an interview with an expert, five references to literature or film or works of art, a picture. The assignment is artificial. To use a wide range of material is not necessarily preferable to using a narrow range of references. Writers do both. They choose. To know to choose is important.

Suggested Essays: Marcia Aldrich, "Hair"
                                   Annie Dillard, "Stalking"
                                   Stephen Jay Gould, "The Median Isn't the Message"
                                   Diane Kappel-Smith, "Salt"
                                   Richard Selzer, "What I Saw at the Abortion"

iii: Inquiry: Shapes

The shape of the essay reflects this free choice of strategy. The freshman essay at Loyola College is no five-paragraph theme. Discursive thought is the primary organizing principle for the essay, and often its pattern is explicit; even when the essayist follows a chronological order in its presentation of idea and information, the trail of thought rises above and is the primary cognitive trail a reader follows. Abstracts rather than outlines are useful tools for studying the structure of the essay. As one moves through the essay, one hears the interplay of question and answer, of statement and elaboration, of qualification or contradiction, of accumulation of supportive fact, all building to an intellectually and emotionally satisfying resolution at the end. Often visual design enhances the presentation of thought. One looks in the essay for ample use of white spaces, of numbers or interruptive devices that break an essay into sections in order to make a complex of thought more clear. One listens for cadences, the rise and fall of prose rhythms; unlike term papers, essays are fun to read aloud!

As in a message in Meeting, in the essay one is expectant that through indirection direction will become clear. Hoagland hears in the essay "a solo voice welling up from self-generating sources, or what Thoreau once called an 'artesian life'" (*Best American Essays 1999* xviii). The shape of the essay is free form. "How long should my essays be?" my students ask. The length of an essay is not to be prescribed, though its outer limits can be set. How much thought do we want to cut off? How much elaboration can we do? In the essay, as in Meeting, there is no required length for a message. Even in a Quaker Meeting, we may "minute" things, but no "minute" lasts exactly a minute.

Suggested Essays: Judy Ruiz, "Oranges and Sweet Sister Boy"
Alice Walker, "Beauty: When the Other Dancer is the Self"

iv: Inquiry: Insight/Ideas

The essayist does what we do with our lives; the essayist thinks about actual things. He can make sense of them analytically or artistically. In either case, he renders the real world coherent and even meaningful, even if only bits of it, and even if that coherence and meaning reside only inside small texts.

Annie Dillard, Prologue, *The Best American Essays* (19)

I am not going to wait until I have fathomed all mysteries and secret lore before I begin to live.

> Francis H. Knight, *Christian Faith and Practice in the Experience of the Society of Friends* (107)

As Quaker messages shape thought, so does the essay offer to its readers a finished and shapely idea. The Book of Discipline is filled with pronouncements and testimonies that are significant outcomes of discernment, general and abstract, intended to influence lives. The essay, too, evolved to crystallize thought. "In the old distinction between teaching and storytelling," writes Hoagland, "the essayist, however cleverly he camouflages his intentions, is a bit of a teacher or reformer, and an essay is intended to convey the same point to each of us" ("What I Think" 363). An exercise in "mind speaking to mind," the essay makes a point, and in the essay the reader can find that point. Some essays are powerfully didactic, but most are revelatory, each offering an idea that is refined and with sufficient nuance that it teaches the reader rather than preaching or reiterating a cliché. The hallmark of the essay is that, with rare exception, the idea of the essay can be found in a single sentence or two paired sentences. E. B. White speaks of "the sanctity of the English sentence," and in the written sentence, as in a sentence spoken in Meeting, the point of the essay becomes luminous.

The following are significant ideas, generated within an essay, capable of standing outside the essay as coherent and significant thought:

1. Sin was not necessarily something that you did: it might be something that happened to you.
    George Orwell, "An Episode of Bedwetting," *Ten on Ten*

2. All people who work with their hands are partly invisible, and the more important the work they do, the less visible they are.
    George Orwell, "Marrakech," *In Depth*

3. This is a personal story of statistics, properly interpreted, as profoundly nurturant and life-giving. It declares holy war on the downgrading of intellect by telling a small story about the utility of dry, academic knowledge about science.
    Stephen Jay Gould, "The Median Isn't the Message," *Ten on Ten*

4. The Napo River: it is not out of the way. It is *in* the way, catching sunlight the way a cup catches poured water; it is a bowl of sweet air, a basin of greenness, and of grace, and, it would seem, of peace.

        Annie Dillard, "In the Jungle," *Ten on Ten*

5. The swan song sounded by the wilderness grows fainter, even more constricted, until only sharp ears can catch it at all. It fades to a nearly inaudible level, and yet there never is going to be any one time when we can say right *now* it is gone.

        Edward Hoagland, "Hailing the Elusive Mountain Lion,"
        The Norton Book of Nature Writing

6. Books fill vacant spaces better than other collectibles, because they represent a different order of plenitude—they occupy not only the morocco-bound spine span on the shelf but the ampler stretches, the camel caravans of thought-bearing time required to read them through.

        Nicholson Baker, "Books as Furniture,"
        The Best American Essays 1996

7. The loss we felt was not the loss of ham but the loss of pig.

        E. B. White, "Death of a Pig," *Ten on Ten*

Some ideas are enormous in scope. Many ideas in Quaker literature elaborate on such broad themes as harmony, equality, community, and simplicity. When George Orwell, pondering why "imperialism was an evil thing," writes in "Shooting an Elephant" that "I perceived in this moment that when the white man turns tyrant it is his own freedom that he destroys"(99), he lays out a major idea, as does E. B. White when he writes, "Science is preoccupied with an atom, not an atoll"(222). Students assume they too must write Big Ideas. Studying the essay, they discover that essays also give full respect to small ideas if they are authentic and well built. Friends have "books of discipline" full of insights of great reach and power, but Friends also admire texts like Robert Lawrence Smith's *The Book of Quaker Wisdom* with its more homely, local observations. In Meeting for Worship on most Sunday mornings, we are apt to hear smaller moments of discernment. Friends tend to be both eclectic and egalitarian. Any idea, if its ethical resonance is right, is worthwhile. In my classroom, too, originality and ingenuity, not scope, are the measure of an idea.

Point Four: Infinite

> That blessed principle the Eternal Word by which all things were at first made and man
> enlightened to salvation is Pythagoras' great light and salt of ages; Anaxagoras' divine
> mind; Socrates' good spirit; Timaeus' unbegotten principle and author of all light;
> Hieron's truth; Zeno's maker and father of all; Plotinus' root of the soul; the divine
> power and reason, the infallible, immortal law in the minds of men, says Philo; the law
> and living rule of the mind, the interior guide of the soul and everlasting foundation of
> virtue, says Plutarch.
>
> Howard Brinton, *Friends for 300 Years* (37)

> Essays came into my life as a precocious, passionate reader as naturally as did poems
> and stories and novels. There was Emerson as well as Poe, Shaw's prefaces as well as
> Shaw's plays….An essay could be as much an event, a transforming event, as a novel or
> poem. You finished an essay by Lionel Trilling or Harold Rosenberg…to mention only
> some American names, and you thought and felt forever differently.

> Essays of the reach and eloquence I am describing are part of a literary culture. And a
> literary culture—that is, a community of readers and writers with a curious, passionate
> relation to the literature of the past—is just what one cannot take for granted now. The
> essayist is more likely a superior ironist or gadfly than a sage.
>
> Susan Sontag, Introduction, *The Best American Essays 1992* (xiii)

There is that sense that even well-conceived big ideas, though powerful and effective and enduring, are impermanent. On the one hand, the essay is defined as writing that culminates in a point. On the other hand, it is defined as "not attempting completion." Essays are a written record of the ongoing evolution of human thought. Meeting for Worship allows two planes of query: Each individual seeks inner light, and, through its shared spoken messages, the Meeting as a whole seeks a gathered moment that advances an evolving truth that we are building across broad stretches of time and space. As Meetings create a record that spans centuries on broad common issues—human rights, equal rights, violence, diversity, stewardship of the earth, sexuality, the arts—so, too, do essays become part of the vast human endeavor to map in writing the contours of the universe in which, for millions of years, we have lived.

Our ideas, laid out one by one in the context of the personal essay, often seem small and insignificant, so small and fleeting, wrote Emily Dickinson in 1878, that we need to snatch them while we can:

Your thoughts don't have words every day
They come a single time
Like signal esoteric sips
Of the communion Wine
Which while you taste so native seems
So easy so to be
You cannot comprehend its price
Nor its infrequency

As manifestations of the divine, our ideas resonate in ways we will only discover as we explore and amplify them and then give them wider exposure. Essayists give us many signals that we are part of a greater conversation. They quote others, refer to others, make allusions. They use epigraphs. They revisit topics (thirty-four years after Virginia Woolf wrote "The Death of the Moth," Annie Dillard wrote "The Death of a Moth"). Essayists use the second-person pronoun (and Friends the familiar second-person pronoun) to enhance the sense of actual interchange. Though essays, as messages, are at first located in a particular time and space, the inevitable universality of topic and the very medium of language make them transcend. When they are grouped in anthologies, their larger reach becomes even more apparent.

Suggested Essays: Anwar F. Accawi, "The Telephone"
Barry Lopez, "The Stone Horse"
Walker Percy, "The Loss of the Creature"
Scott Russell Sanders, "An Inheritance of Tools"

Point Five: Integral

This is the word of the Lord God to you all and a charge to you all in the presence of the living God: be patterns, be examples in all countries, places, islands, nations, wherever you come; that your carriage and life may preach among all sorts of people, and to them; then you will come to walk cheerfully over the world, answering that of God in every one.

Howard Brinton, *Friends for 300 Years* (29)

Each human mind has two personalities, one on the surface, one deeper down. The upper personality has a name. It is called S.T. Coleridge, or William Shakespeare, or Mrs. Humphrey Ward. It is conscious and alert, it does things like dining out, answering letters, etc., and it differs vividly and amusingly from other personalities. The lower personality is a queer affair unless a man dips a bucket down into it occasionally, he cannot produce first-class work. There is something general about it. Although it is inside S. T. Coleridge, it cannot be labelled with his name. It has something in common with all other deeper personalities, and the mystic will assert that the common quality is God, and that here, in the obscure recesses of our being, we near the gates of the Divine. It is in any case the force that makes for anonymity. As it came from the depths, so it soars to the heights, out of local questionings; as it is general to all men, so the works it inspires have something general about them, namely beauty. The poet wrote the poem, no doubt, but he forgot himself while he wrote it, and we forget him while we read. What is so wonderful about great literature is that it transforms the man who reads it towards the condition of the man who wrote, and brings to birth in us also the creative impulse. Lost in the beauty where he was lost, we find more than we ever threw away, we reach what seems to be our spiritual home, and remember that it was not the speaker who was in the beginning but the Word.

E. M. Forster, "Anonymity: An Enquiry," *In Depth*, 266–67

The essayist Lewis Thomas suggests in *Lives of a Cell* that perhaps our role as a species is to communicate. We were created in order that we might, in turn, create information and ideas that lead us to understand our place in the universe. There is no writing that is not creative writing, but it is also true that the literary genres especially invite us to know the creative pulse and impulse of original thought, divinely inspired. While early Friends were suspicious of the creative arts, wary of what seemed a seductive power, encouraging the profligate and the ornate, Friends now celebrate any artist's rich and powerful gift. If we are in God's image, then creation by us is good. Simplicity, Friends are told,

does not mean that life is to be poor and bare, destitute of joy and beauty. All that promises fullness of life and aids in service for Christ is to be accepted with thanksgiving. Simplicity, when it removes encumbering details, makes for beauty in music, in art, and in living. It clears the springs of life and permits wholesome mirth and gladness to bubble up; it cleans the windows of life and lets joy radiate. (*Christian Faith and Practice* 434)

In creating works of art, we find an aesthetic pulse. Even when the topic is as prosaic as a game of marbles or a migraine headache or a common toad or as awful as discrimination or war, in making art of it, we participate in activity that is constructive and thereby good. The essay enacts the Quaker assumption that "the way will open," that "the way will clear." There is an optimism to the essay, and an ambition. Essayists—even young essayists—believe that revelation is possible.

Suggested Essays: Annie Dillard, "The Stunt Pilot"

Edward Hoagland, "Heaven and Nature"

Maxine Hong Kingston, "No Name Woman"

Lewis Thomas, "The World's Biggest Membrane"

Alice Walker, "In Search of Our Mother's Gardens"

If we are to educate people **for** democracy we must educate people **in** democracy. And this is not so much a matter of encouraging self-government in schools, and substituting self-discipline for external authority and punishments, valuable as such experiments may be. It is primarily a matter of developing and training those qualities—at once intellectual and moral—which made for a democratic attitude toward life. The capacity to weigh up facts and theories in the kind of temper that is impartial without being indifferent, the capacity to argue without scoring off opponents and to listen sympathetically without contempt, the capacity to get beneath the skin of the other man and to appreciate other points of view—these qualities, so simple, so obvious and yet so rare, are the fruits of a democratic education.

> *Christian Faith and Practice in the Experience of the Society of Friends* (443)

The richness of the black writer's experience in the South can be remarkable, though some people might not think so. Once, while in college, I told a white middle-aged Northerner that I hoped to be a poet. In the nicest possible language, which still made me as mad as I've ever been, he suggested that a "farmer's daughter" might not be the stuff of which poets are made. On one level, of course, he had a point. A shack with only a dozen or so books is an unlikely place to discover a young Keats. But it is narrow thinking, indeed, to believe that a Keats is the only kind of poet one would want to grow up to be.

> Alice Walker, "The Black Writer and the Southern Experience," *In Depth*, (691–92)

To teach the essay is to roam the fertile fields of the academy and to cross back and forth between church and state. When I ask my students at the beginning of a semester, "What *is* the essay?" I expect that across fifteen weeks they will learn from me its salient characteristics: that it is individual and idiosyncratic, that it is inspired, that it is informed by inquiry that takes shape as an idea, that it is infinite in reach and impact, and that it is integral activity. I believe that my students will come to appreciate the essay as a significant genre in the canon of American prose literature, but I most hope that they will come to understand that the essay stands on our national landscape as a sacred spot, a place to hear that "still small voice" that, nurtured by silence, begins to speak out.

As I read my students' essays in the quiet of a Saturday afternoon, one by one they seem to rise and speak. The questions are provocative, the ramble through ideas and information an excursion into territory I've not explored before. The voice of each writer seems genuine; the point of each essay insightful and satisfying. Some days, as beyond the window a breeze blows or rain falls or autumn leaves or snow, the afternoon's reading even has the feel of a gathered Meeting, one essay bouncing off another.

The pace of the day is slow. There is ample time for silence between the essays though never complete silence. As I read, I hear a faint murmur, for although the essays arose first in solitude and silence, usually they have been workshopped in class or in my office, an occasion for the writer, before a message is "published," to engage in dialogue with other voices that become part of an inner thought process in which images and ideas float in and out.

Workshopping is a reminder that while fanning the light within is solitary activity, writing is communal. Paul Lacey writes in *Growing into Goodness: Essays on Quaker Education*

> A commitment to holistic education announces that the institution not only values the development of body and mind, feelings and intellect, psyche and soul, but is committed to offering programs and activities which allow each aspect of the self, and of every self—faculty and administrators as well as students—and the self in community, to be nourished. It is a commitment to encouraging the smudging and crossing of lines....It is a commitment to making connections, making contacts, encouraging risks and experimentation, becoming interrelated, intimately "involved" together as companions in learning, reducing the prompts in the name of greater independence and autonomy for students, integrating thought with action and ethical convictions with ethical behavior. (258)

Writing the essay is a liberal art. It is liberating for the young writer, and it is also a step toward feeling the power of a political liberty conceived in a land dedicated to religious freedom in order that a broad-based spiritual life be a national resource. When I walk into my freshman writing class on any Tuesday or Thursday morning, bearing the essays I have read, I greet a new generation of young people at the start of a new century in the United States of America. In this country, the young are often disregarded as an intellectual and ethical force. It is true that within the disciplines in which they will major, much preparatory learning will have to be done before students can perform at the level of their professors, but in a class in which they are writing the personal essay, young people can feel early on in their college career a sense of empowerment that adults enjoy.

In the middle of the word "American" is the expression **I CAN**, which has long been a popular rallying cry in this country. As successive generations of young people once crossed mountains, woods, and open plains in pursuit of better lives, so my students can move out across the empty page, carving new paths across the landscape of American thought.

The essay invites American enterprise. It is, not surprisingly, multicultural, politically in tune, sweeping into its fold whites and blacks, indigenous peoples and immigrants, city dwellers and country folk, more than two political parties, gays and lesbians, rich and poor, young and old, Protestants and Catholics, Buddhists and Jews, men and women. And the essay is contemporary. The writers we study are continuing human conversation as we speak—and in my noisy classroom we *are* speaking. Even as we discuss his essay "Beauty," Scott Russell Sanders could be writing in the silence of his study yet another essay for *Orion.* Jamaica Kincaid could be at work on another essay on gardens for *The New Yorker.* Edward Hoagland, who wrote an essay on natural light for *Harper's Magazine,* could now be writing, as did Henry Beston in 1928, on darkness. Is Michael Pollan railing yet again against grass? Will Cornel West be in the *New York Times Magazine* on Sunday? Joyce Carol Oates in *The Georgia Review?* Garrison Keillor on the last page of *Time Magazine?* It's as much fun to wonder about essayists as to wonder who will speak in Meeting on Sunday next.

And, in late spring, as the semester ends, it is fun, too, to wonder about my students. After our long months together, I hope that they see themselves as a new generation of young American writers. As they put down their pens and pack up their books, I know that they have known the power of writing to make sense, both spiritual and intellectual, within a frame of silence. For the last time, I watch them go. As they walk out into an academic discipline and then a lifelong career, I hope that they seek often a circle of stillness—and heed what I pray is a persistent hum: *One day, speaking from the Light within, one day, soon again, it could be I.*

⚄ Part Four
Continuing Exploration: Personal Journeys into Quaker Pedagogy

○3 Chapter Six
Teaching from the Spiritual Center

Barbara Dixson

This week, June of 2001, I completed 25 years of teaching. I'm fifty-one so that's about half my life. As I look around the teaching communities to which I belong, I feel a great deal of commonality with others who, like me, care deeply about good teaching and have followed an erratic path to become the teachers they are. Their stories, which I've read in books and journals, talked with them about in classrooms and along sidewalks, and e-mailed about all over the country, have amused, comforted, and enlightened me through the years. I hope it is useful for others to hear my story, finding in it a way to see their own lives more clearly. My own pathway took a turn for the better when I chanced upon Quakers fifteen years ago, in due time becoming a member of my local Friends Meeting. I found in Quakers a group of people with values and practice which lend themselves to deepening commitment and growth in all of myself, including myself as a teacher.

A brand new graduate student at a large southern land grant university, I began teaching with fear, excitement, hope, and the values given me by my life thus far. I had the good-girl values of my Methodist family, opened wide by my habit of reading every book that came my way, then shaken and shifted by the social-activist, stylishly radical atmosphere of my liberal arts undergraduate college, and finally sobered and tempered by several years of working with Georgia's poorest families. I had those values, and many questions. As a requirement for my Introduction to Graduate Studies course, aimed at teaching research skills but also offering survival techniques to a group of young men and women thrown with no preparation into teaching, I kept a daily writing teacher's journal for my first month of teaching. Going back and rereading that journal, I find that I began my teaching career with my directions and questions clearly in place. For example, I felt from the beginning fiercely responsible to my students, to give them the best that I had and all that they needed from me. None of my early positions have been abandoned, but all of them have evolved. Not just experience but also reflection grounded in Quaker values and carried out in Quaker practice has nurtured the growth of my understanding of and approach to teaching.

The longer I stayed at the large university where I earned my Ph.D. and taught for nine years, as teaching assistant and then instructor, the more its hierarchical social structures seemed ethically untenable to me. In 1985, my family and I moved to the Upper Midwest where I had been offered the job I still have, at one of the four-year campuses of the University of Wisconsin. Stevens Point is a small city in a rural area of a state where the Republicans are more progressive than the Democrats back home in Alabama, where prosperity and at least surface equality rule, and where instead of talking about fraternities, students talk about the environment. My new life roused new hope, new intensity, and new questions.

Seeking answers to my questions or at least a way to approach them, I found the Quakers. First, it was the people who felt right to me; the small Meeting included women and men I admired from my community, who discarded pretense and form for form's sake and who worked for what they believed in rather than for approval or success. Next, it was the practice which drew me: choosing a chair from the circle, sitting, settling into silence, giving my inner self the opportunity to come into the light and stretch, hearing from time to time the words one of these Friends I respected felt led to speak into the silence, feeling the connection and trust among us, I felt as if my long-hidden inner self, the one who remained passionately, gawkily determined to be good and to do good (though not in the way the Methodist minister or any other authority said she must) had come home at last. Finally, starting to put down roots as a Quaker, I began to read what Quakers have been writing over the past 350 years. Quakers frame their values as advices, testimonies, and queries, rather than as catechism, acknowledging that what we know emerges from our life position and experience and that what we know will continue to grow over the years of our lives as individuals and as a community of seekers. This stance matched my own lifetime stance, and the articulated Quaker values, such things as peace, equality, simplicity, and truth, affirmed my own.

As a Quaker, I have had regular opportunities to hear my questions, to consider my values, to listen for answers. Each week, in my inner space, I bring my students and colleagues to Meeting. Each week, I take my inner, ongoing Meeting to my students and colleagues. In that centered place together, we continue the journey.

Truth

Be honest with yourself. What unpalatable truths might you be evading? When you recognise your shortcomings, do not let that discourage you. 1.02 11

Are you honest and truthful in all you say and do? 1.02 37 (*Quaker Faith and Practice, Britain Yearly Meeting, Advices and Queries,* 1995)

In one of my earliest memories, I learned my mother's views on truth and lies. It was spring, and I'd adventured far from home (into the neighbor's yard), finding treasures, and returned clutching a fistful of daffodils and tulips. Dreamlike, the next sequence I recall is my mother advancing on me, asking menacingly, "Did you? Did you pick Mrs. Holland's flowers?"

"No, Mama, no"—and I retreated to the corner, counterbalanced, sat back suddenly on the white enamel kitchen garbage can with the foot-levered lid.

A spank, and "Don't you ever lie to me again!"

Next sequence: Alone, I rang the doorbell of Mrs. Holland's house, reached for resolve, and said, "I'm sorry I picked your flowers."

"That's okay, honey. You can have them," she told me, sweetly, with a compassion I can still feel today.

In the years that followed, I learned the ambiguities of truth-telling. In my mother's view, *I* should always tell *her* the truth. On the other hand, when my father spoke yet another unwelcome truth to his boss, she would say, "Why can't you learn some tact?" My father's uncensored honesty proved a block to his advancement in the militarily organized bureaucracy in which he worked.

By the time I arrived at graduate school and my first freshman English class, I had become as ferocious a truth-teller as my dad yet with a defensive edge. My third journal entry, on the day I returned marked papers to my students for the first time, reflects on honesty. My students "didn't like my criticism of their writing; the faces were no longer smiling, and most of the eyes avoided mine as they walked out of the room," I wrote. I wondered if I should have been less forthright in my criticism. Considering also the pedagogy I was reading which addressed the topic of honesty, both in writing and in responding to student writing, I concluded, "Clearly, for me, being as honest as I can manage in both my living and my writing is worth its cost. The occasional immediate pain saves me the long-term confusion and the unmistakable sense of being off balance" (9-29-76).

With my students, I learned to temper my criticisms by balancing them with an equal or greater amount of honest praise. It took me longer to learn to apply this gentle approach to authorities of whom I was critical. When the professor who had assigned the journal gave a homework assignment which I found wasteful, I wrote about it scathingly, calling it "my old enemy busy work," and beginning sentences like this: "I began to feel restless...I was disgusted...And it was certainly in an excess of conscientiousness...." I went on to talk about the other useful and desirable things I might have done had I not been forced to do the assignment, remarked that what I had learned was surely not what the professor intended, and ended with a sarcastic comment: "I am reminded that I should feel rather certain of what it is my students are likely to learn from the work I assign to them." The gracious man who read this journal did not respond at all to this passage or to others where I inveighed against the invasion of privacy represented by the journal assignment itself. Instead, he let silence reply to my anger, limiting his comments to tiny marginal notes and to brief, positive overall remarks.

Daisy Newman begins her history of Quakers in America, *A Procession of Friends*, with a story that my father would surely have appreciated. When violence against Jews intensified in Germany, several American Friends "decided to make a direct appeal to Hitler." They quietly got ready and sailed for Germany, because, as Daisy Newman puts it, "Friends never were afraid to 'speak truth to power'"(23). These Friends made it all the way into Gestapo headquarters, where they received permission to implement a plan for food relief and emigration of persecuted peoples.

The difference between this sort of truth-speaking and the kind I learned at home is the approach one takes to power. Friends approach authorities as they would approach other Friends or the homeless or their own family, with kindness and respect as well as truth. It's this kind of truth I've been learning in the twenty-five years between the reflections cited above and now. I've continued to tell students truly their weaknesses but also their strengths. I've learned to write recommendation letters that present as positively as is true my evaluation of a student. And with colleagues and administrators, I've learned to speak positive truths freely and to speak critical truths gently but clearly.

What has turned out to be more difficult has been knowing how to speak truth in my work with student teachers. As their university supervisor, I am privileged with their miseries and complaints, while as colleague to my students' high school cooperating teachers, I am also privileged with their views and emotions, third party to the oddly intimate relationship of veteran to apprentice teacher which they have with my students. What to do when I have been entrusted with sensitive knowledge?

Part of what I have learned as a Quaker is to trust the process of experience plus reflection, especially when the experience is one of failure. Quakerism's founder, George Fox, knew his Bible but saw it as an aid to spiritual knowledge rather than a holy text; he rejected outright those posing as spiritual authorities, and when he had his great revelation of the Christ within, the inner light, he affirmed it thus: "And this I knew experientally" (11). Quakers rely on written texts (but no one sacred book), the support and vision of the community, and most of all, the understanding given to the individual in silent, receptive waiting.

That Quaker process saw me through one of my failures with truth.

A number of years ago, halfway through a semester, one of my student teachers called me, frantic, saying she could not get on for another day with her cooperating teacher. The teacher criticized her unjustly, gave her incomprehensible directions, and interfered in her interactions with her students. But I must not tell the cooperating teacher any of this: My student teacher, an extremely introverted person, could not bear to discuss any of this emotionally laden material with the veteran teacher.

When I spoke with the veteran teacher, she told me how inadequate were the student's responses to class preparation and to classroom management challenges. I must not speak to the student of any of this, she enjoined; the student was so sensitive that any criticism upset her dreadfully.

Both grew increasingly distressed. I solved the problem by locating a different placement for the student, with a teacher who had a special understanding of this shy student and who did indeed prove a supportive, nonthreatening, and effective mentor to her. I danced around the truth, saying to the first cooperating teacher that my student wanted to move to this friendly placement (about 20 percent of the truth), saying to my student that the cooperating teacher did not think she had learned enough yet to be certified (about 20 percent of the truth). The results were disastrous. The student, though she succeeded in her second placement, grew increasingly distrustful of me and was angry not to have had the opportunity to complete further work she'd hoped to have time for. The teacher, too, had diminished respect for me. As I reflected on this experience, seeking to understand how to be truthful while refraining from giving hurt to anyone, I found Quaker writings helpful.

Several of the testimonies from Britain Yearly Meeting's Faith and Practice speak to this dilemma of telling other people's truths:

> The Quaker testimony to truthfulness is central to the practice of its faith….From time to time…adherence to factual truth can give rise to profound dilemmas for Quaker Peace and Service workers if they are in possession of information which could be used to endanger people's lives or give rise to the abuse of fundamental human rights….Some of us are clear that in certain difficult circumstances we may still uphold our testimony to truthfulness while at the same time declining to disclose confidences which we have properly accepted. Such withholding of the whole truth is not an option to be undertaken lightly as a convenient way out of a dilemma. (20.45 Quaker Peace and Service, 1992)

Another testimony explains, "Integrity is a condition in which a person's response to a total situation can be trusted: the opposite of a condition in which he would be moved by opportunist or self-seeking impulses breaking up his unity as a whole being" (20.44 Kenneth C. Barnes, 1972). Barnes goes on to point to the exemplary integrity of Dutch Friends, who lied to save Jews from the Gestapo.

Such reflecting on my experience and on Quaker testimonies led to a shift in my approach. Clearly, the situations in which I found myself did not threaten "fundamental human rights." Without formulating principles or rules, I have nonetheless found ways to tell the truth fully and clearly and in the best interests of all concerned. Recently, I had a student about whom I had concerns for months in advance. He did not get on well with his classmates, seemed extremely shy, and had trouble completing projects for class. Nonetheless, I found the student a placement and committed myself to his support. When he immediately began to have difficulties, I coached him on class preparation and classroom management as well as relationships with colleagues. In conferences with him and his cooperating teachers, I spoke and wrote everyone's concerns, even the ones that had been spoken to me alone for fear of giving offense, first letting each person know that this openness was my intention. When it became clear that the student could not succeed, I told him directly that it was time for him to stop student teaching, also told him all the positive things I'd observed as he made his way through a very difficult process, and helped him extricate himself from the tangles of the university bureaucracy. This work took huge amounts of time, thought, prayer, and energy, and it took a great deal of trust in the three other people who were also closely involved: my student and his two cooperating teachers. Though everyone felt this drain on energy, all of us were affirmed by the process: the teachers for their mentoring, the student for finding a new way that will work better for his life, and me for staying with my truth and light at every step.

With another student this semester, I found my job to be relaying to him the criticisms he was not hearing from the two women who were his cooperating teachers. "I don't understand why they don't just tell me straight out," he complained.

"You need to listen for tactful suggestions," I told him. "Lots of women have trouble with being really direct."

He looked at me, shook his head, smiled, and said, "You don't seem to have any trouble with that."

I've known this student for years, and so I heard the remark as rueful affection and laughed.

Respect: Equality

And this is the word of the Lord God to you all, and a charge to you all in the presence of the living God, be patterns, be examples in all countries, places, islands, nations wherever you come; that your carriage and life may preach among all sorts of people, and to them. Then you will come to walk cheerfully over the world, answering that of God in every one. (*The Journal of George Fox*, 263)

Do you respect that of God in everyone though it may be expressed in unfamiliar ways
or be difficult to discern? (*Quaker Faith and Practice, Britain Yearly Meeting,* Advices and
Queries, 1.02 17)

The South I was born into in 1950 was stratified in many ways, by race,
class, age, religion, and birthplace. It wasn't until I hit my teens that I attained
the perspective necessary to question this system, nor was it till then that I became aware of the ugliness with which many white people approached those of
different races. From my own white, middle-class family, I learned that the
same sort of respect which goes from young to old and vice versa, goes among
races, classes, and people of different nations and religions. My father's kind
and formal manners applied equally to the retired missionary lady who lived
across the street, the black men who worked in my grandfather's water-tower
painting crew, the German woman who moved in several houses down, and the
working class mechanic, articulate only with his hands, who worked on the
family cars.

As a teacher of teachers, I find that respect is a principle which all my pre-
service teachers hold sacred. When they write and talk about the sort of classroom community they intend to establish, respect is the one quality they are
certain they will have, respect between themselves and their students, respect
among their students. When I ask them how they plan to accomplish this, they
become much less certain.

Like my own beginning students, I brought to my first teaching assignment
a fierce determination to establish respect as the basic tone of the class, and,
like them, I moved tentatively toward implementing this principle. First, I called
my students "Mr." and "Miss," so that even in my journal notes about them, an
odd air of formality prevails:

Miss Skutack sits in the front seat on the far left and watches the class with detachment,
generally. At the times I feel most inspired she seems to be agreeing with me by suddenly turning on her attention. The day I read well the opening poem of the *Tao Te
Ching* I got from her steady intense watching, eyes wide open, a flicker of a smile at the
end. Then she went away again. (10-6-76)

The formality of the address subliminally suggested the respect with which I
centered teacher/student relationships.

Next, I learned to communicate to my students that I valued their opinions, even if unorthodox. My first animated discussion occurred when students discovered I would let them express both positive and negative views about the assigned reading: "Finding that I would allow censuring of Beardsley's long-windedness was the catalyst that precipitated general excitement" (10-1-76). Experience, even a little, revealed that this sort of openness to diverse opinions was harder than anticipated, and by the time I wrote my summary remarks for my journal, I was more tentative than at the beginning: "I think I can refrain from judging them if their opinions offend me," I reflected.

Most pervasively, my commitment to respect flamed up into a blaze of responsibility. Prior to beginning to teach, I'd considered sick leave a mental health necessity of the jobs I held and freely took days for resting. A couple of weeks into teaching, I came down with a flu one day at work, couldn't find anyone to take my class for me, and so turned up at the appointed time, shaking and semidelirious with fever. Luckily, a kind professor rescued me and sent me home to recover. My journal recounts this story and then comments, "Reading back over this, I'm not sure if it's clear that what I'm attempting to say is how responsible I feel to my students. I have been working since I was seventeen and have never before had a job I would have gone to feeling that bad" (9-8-76). This sense of responsibility extended into the twenty-two hours a week I spent that first quarter on my one class, into the meticulous way I responded to each paper, and into the way I talked teaching day and night.

My informal midwestern students, who knew each other primarily by the names I called them, soon talked me out of "Mr." and "Miss." "How can I call her up and say, 'Miss Koziczkowski, would you like to go out?'" one young man pleaded, and so won his case. But the devotion to respect remained.

The problem I've discovered is that, while respect is essential, it reaches its limits with certain nonconforming, weak, or troubled students. Here are some examples of what I mean:

- Two students taking a class which was required for their major, who saw no value in the class material, were not able to read well enough to succeed in the class, and wanted only to get past this barrier to their goal.
- A student who had extremely poor social skills in a class which frequently used small-group activities.
- A sweet, deeply introverted man who thought a teaching license would be a sensible career move, but dressed in sweats and was too shy to chat with students.

- A young woman who had outbursts in class when frustrated, railing against the class, the work, the professor.
- A young man whose freshman year found him unfocused and uncommitted and who found it easy to procrastinate and prevaricate about late assignments.
- A young man who arrived at a point in his life where school and life itself seemed pointless.

It's where the ethical, rational, democratic principle of respect reaches its limits that the Quaker testimony to equality, and to that of God in everyone, steadies me and shows me the way. With all the students mentioned above, respect, the sort of respect which is an ethical principle based on a set of ideas, would acknowledge their right to be who they are, offer them polite treatment, but judge them as inadequate and, more or less, dismiss them. With the two young men mentioned in the first example, I did just that, with the result that they channeled their disappointment into anger and began a campaign of harassing and threatening phone calls in those pre-caller-ID days. My conscience was clear, so that I felt not only frightened but also unjustly treated. From my perspective now as a convinced Friend (and a much more experienced teacher), I suspect that I could have helped these young men discern their own responsibilities in a way that would have led to a better outcome for all of us, had I moved beyond the ethical version of respect to that fuller version which focuses beyond justice issues towards that of God in each person.

In his overview of Quaker history, *Friends for 300 Years,* Howard Brinton explains:

> Equality was the earliest Quaker social testimony....The Quaker doctrine of equality does not mean equality of ability, economic resources or social status. It means equality of respect and the resulting absence of all words and behavior based on class, racial or social distinctions....Within the Meeting equality appears in the equal opportunity for all to take part, regardless of age, sex or ability. (131–132)

Even at a time when society was rigidly hierarchical, when, for example, anywhere but in a Quaker Meeting it was unthinkable for a woman to speak in public, Quakers chose radical equality, a testimony they have held to through the ensuing centuries.

George Fox in his journal and in his letters to Quaker Meetings around England spoke often of the "inner light," the "seed," the "inner Christ." His admonition that we must walk cheerfully over the earth, answering that of God in everyone, is a precept familiar to every Quaker I know. In a recent article in *Friends Journal,* William Edgerton says, "What gives Quakerism its only real claim to distinction is the doctrine of the Inner Light. If there is a spark of God in every single human being on earth, the implications of that are breathtaking" (7).

For me, absorption of this view meant a paradigm shift. Beyond seeing my students and colleagues as reasonable, ethical beings, I now also see them as spiritual beings. When I focus on a person, I focus towards what I see as central, "that of God" in the person. It's like looking into someone's eyes, rather than only at their lips or gestures as they speak. I expect people to respond from this central, spiritual place, from this source of loving energy. Because my perceptions and expectations have changed, my interactions with others have also changed.

Here's what happened with the last of the situations mentioned above: Five or six years ago, I was teaching a class I still remember as an all-time favorite. The particular literary topic interests me intently; the students were reading diligently and coming to class faithfully; and in class, conversation was lively, and students participated energetically in the activities I suggested, such as small discussion groups, a graphics exercise, and a dramatic rendition of a scene. A number of those students went on to study teaching methods with me and to student teach under my supervision, and several of them remain in close communication, several years into their professional careers.

One student, however, attended only sporadically and produced sketchy work when he turned up. I asked him to come to my office and discuss his work with me, as he was failing, and he seemed to me quite capable. He turned up, looking sulky, and burst forth, "The trouble is, I hate the way you teach the class! I'm bored. I can't stand to be there."

An earlier version of myself would have said—politely, perhaps circuitously, but definitely—"Tough! Straighten up or fail." This more recent version of myself, though, instead of being offended or judgmental, was interested. I looked at the young man's troubled manner; I wondered what prompted words so clearly not in his own self-interest; I said "hmm" and listened until his words ran into silence. We sat in silence together. Into the silence came a thought, and I made a suggestion: "Do you think you could get the work done on your own?" Yes, he thought he could. I formulated a plan for a sort of independent study and he accepted, not gracefully. From time to time, I would find written work in my box, and enough of it accumulated that he passed the class quite successfully.

A couple of years later, this young man turned up in my office for advising, having decided to become an English teacher. We looked at his progress report together, and he acknowledged that he'd gotten very depressed the semester we'd worked together, with some poor grades as a consequence. I had serious doubts about the sort of teacher he would make, doubts which I continued to consider with his subsequent ups and downs in early fieldwork and methods. By the end of the methods class, though, he had gotten his balance, and he proved himself a stellar student teacher, going to great lengths to write the most effective lesson plans, and devoted to his students.

All this time, this young man had never referred directly to what had passed between us during his difficult semester. One day in student-teaching seminar, though, another student teacher asked him where he got the amazing energy to continue doggedly to support and help a promising but impossible adolescent, a girl with years of trouble behind her. "I had a terrible semester once," he replied. "And some people"—he glanced at me and met my eye for a long moment—"believed in me and stood behind me. And it meant a lot to me. I want to pass that on."

Presence

It definitely wasn't in childhood that I learned about presence. On the contrary, I learned what modern Quaker scholar and mystic Thomas Kelly calls

> the ordinary experience of time....In this process, time spreads itself out like a ribbon, stretching away from the now into the past, and forward from the now into the future....In this ribbon of time we live, anxiously surveying the past in order to learn how to manage the most important part of the ribbon, the future. The now is merely an incidental dividing point, unstable, non-important. (68–69)

School life reinforced this sense of time, with anxiety about work undone as a constant theme.

In fact, the first time I realized there are other possible approaches was in an undergraduate class I took, on the vague recommendation of friends, called Gestalt and Existential Psychology. Looking back at Fritz Perls' *In and Out the Garbage Pail* and Barry Stevens's *Don't Push the River*, I recall my sense of absolute revelation in reading Perls' "theory that everything is awareness" (unpaginated) and trying out Fritz Perls' exercises that Barry Stevens was reporting on, "saying 'Now I am aware of…' 'Now I am aware of …' and so on"(118). Of course, Perls' abandonment of commitment, ethics, and metaphysics, along with projection, planning, and agonizing over the past, turns out to be at least as inconvenient as his dismissal of writing conventions such as pagination. Nonetheless, my inner life was permanently changed by the beginnings of my awareness of it in the present moment and by my occasional choice of silence so that I might hear my inner voices. Still, this experience of presence remained only a possibility, an approach I turned to when I had time away from life's urgent realities, time to try a shaky new possibility.

When I began teaching, I brought with me the linear, controlling approach to time which had proved itself so effective in prior academic success. Not only did I have more to do in any given week than I could well accomplish, but, also, I felt responsible for cramming a prescribed amount of writing skill into the ten-week package of the quarter: "I have occasional feelings of panic. The quarter is two weeks gone, one fifth over, and I have only begun to attempt to teach my freshmen to write" (10-6-76). And silence in the classroom, the silence which is necessary to attend to the present moment, scared me. My journal notes a day when, despite my carefully prepared lesson, "My students watched me as if I had broken into an obscure dialect of Italian, took close notes presumably on my bizarre behavior, and pretended not to know their own names." I concluded, "my students feel vulnerable making statements of any sort and so will remain silent unless they feel particularly confident; whereas I feel threatened when nothingness begins to fill the classroom and so will say something unless something else is happening" (10-4-76).

My student teachers seem to have the same need to control time and the same fear of silence with which I began. As their university supervisor, I observe their classes at least monthly. One of the most common weaknesses of a beginning teacher is the inability to lead a good discussion. Typically, the new teacher feels a need to "cover" certain questions and concepts and cannot tolerate even ten consecutive seconds of silence. As a result, the new teacher speaks; some students listen; many students do not listen; and while some information may be taught, thinking habits of analysis and synthesis are not.

Of course, a future-oriented sense of time has advantages: order and accomplishment. It's helpful to know what day the midterm project is due, and it's necessary to get classes prepared and papers read. But the disadvantages are powerful, too: a teacher-dominated classroom, pervasive anxiety, and a loss of joy in the process of planning, teaching, and grading.

Because I continued to read up on contemporary theories of psychology and also occasionally dabbled in meditation, first encountered in another college class, I carried with me through the early years of teaching a sense that there were other possibilities. When I started to attend Quaker Meeting, I felt an immediate sense of rightness. *Friends for 300 Years* explains that from the beginning, "The small group which met in silence to 'wait upon the Lord' was the dynamo which generated light and power in the Quaker movement" (Brinton 6).

Brinton includes reports from the earliest Quaker Meetings on "the way in which Truth first came to that community." Here is a typical description: A group "'met together, when but five or six in number, to wait upon God in silence and the Lord blessed us with his presence and gave us the spirit of discerning'" (5). Contemporary Quakers, as Patricia Loring explains in *Listening Spirituality,* come to Meeting with a wide variety of understandings about the process, from seeing it as a practice gratefully free of the elements of the religion in which they grew up, to a gathering of like-minded people to right social injustices, to a "kind of undisciplined Zen meditation hall" (11–12). But the heart of Quaker worship, Loring argues, is still the "'Holy Expectancy'" with which the early Friends gathered:

> The inner stillness is a mode of listening, of reverent anticipation that does not prescribe the way in which God may speak to us....We rest from our own work and wait on what will be given to or done in us. Sometimes it is a blessed stillness, a peace literally beyond understanding....We may find some of our bothers returned to us shorn of their compulsive force....The grace to deal with our lives and our human condition as gifts and opportunities for spiritual growth—rather than to be possessed by them—is just one dimension of the work of God within us. (18)

Spending an hour each week in this sort of still presence first made me deeply aware of the angry buzz of anxiety generated by my sixty-hour-a-week job and gradually opened me to ways to make changes.

Thomas Kelly, who points out the future orientation of the ordinary experience of time, also speaks eloquently of the "Eternal Now." This is an experience of the present moment as sacramental (another idea dear to Quakers—that every moment is indeed a holy time):

> The present Now is not something from which we hurriedly escape, toward what is hoped will be a better future. Instead of anxiety lest the future never yield all we have hoped, lest we fail to contribute our full stint before the shadows of the evening fall upon our lives, we only breathe a quiet prayer to the Now and say, "Stay, thou art so sweet." Instead of anxiety lest our past, our past defects, our longstanding deficiencies blight our well-intentioned future efforts, all our past sense of weakness falls away and we stand erect, in this holy Now, joyous, serene, assured, unafraid....In the Now we are home at last. (71)

From the first time I read Kelly's words, they seemed to me to articulate a truth I'd been reaching toward. Still, it's difficult to see how to move from concept to application. Some practical Quaker approaches have helped me to do this. First, I read about the Listening Project, an undertaking by North Carolina Friends to reconcile differences among the different branches of Quakers there who held opposite views on the question of abortion. A group of Friends set out to listen well, to listen completely, to listen without refuting the point of view of the person to whom they were listening. Next, at a regional Quaker gathering, my family and I attended a workshop on family peacemaking. In this workshop, we did listening exercises. It seemed so obvious and simple for us to fill in the blanks in sentences like "I feel frightened when you _____" and to listen quietly, attentively, supportively, yet it turned out that we had never really heard each other say these things before.

Then, two years ago, my husband and I attended a couples workshop led by Peg and Nils Pearson. I had read about the concepts of active listening before; in fact, I even sometimes teach an essay by Carl Rogers in which he lays out these principles. But to spend a weekend serenely, attentively listening to what my husband had to say, then rephrasing it till he felt clear that I understood his meaning, and then being heard in the same way—that proved immensely powerful. And thus I've edged toward a practical implementation of my growing sense of presence.

Over the years that I have been thinking about and revising my sense of time, my teaching has grown. I am still extremely well organized, with a syllabus that delineates each of the semester's assignments. I still consult my calendar often and make it to my many appointments on time. I still—a solution I worked out on that anxiously quiet class day in October of 1976—find ways to encourage my students to read and think about the reading before I ask them to discuss it. But, with all that taken care of, I find myself most of the time centered and aware in the present moment. Discussions, which in the beginning worried me so, now glow as a steady source of pleasure through the semester. In my American literature survey class this semester, I went in with a plan each day, and I used many of the approaches I've learned over the years, including asking open questions, asking questions which connect the reading to students' lives, getting students to ask the questions, and moving to activities from time to time such as choral readings, art responses, even musical responses. What I brought from my sense of presence, from my work on active listening, was my habit of noticing how students were responding. That kind of attention to the in-class moment helped me know when to ask follow-up questions, when to throw away my plan and try something else, when to ask students to talk to their neighbors rather than to the whole group, and when to provide for all of us lovely chunks of silence, where students might write or simply think about their responses before returning to conversation.

Mary Rose O'Reilley, in *The Peaceable Classroom,* tells of her own growth as a teacher, learning to trust herself to use silence, to be less directive, to invite students' inner growth. She supports the sort of presence I've been discussing:

> I'm suggesting that we shift our sense of ourselves as successful teachers away from the quality of our corrections and toward the quality of our mindfulness. I do not know why the act of paying acute attention changes the dynamics of a situation, but I can say without reservation that it does. (49)

Gradually, O'Reilley learns to see teaching as an aspect of her spiritual practice. In *Radical Presence,* she asks us to consider "what might happen if we try to frame the central questions of our discipline as spiritual questions, and to deal with them in the light of our spiritual understanding" (2). She applies this approach not only in the classroom but also in advising, and in that most trying of a writing teacher's jobs, grading papers:

> When I started to look at grading papers as an aspect of spiritual practice, one of the first things I noticed was how much unacknowledged physical tension I was bringing to

the task. What I am now trying to cultivate—and with by no means perfect success—is an attitude of friendly visiting as though the student were present with all her life and concerns spread out, as though I had nothing else in the world to do than to talk with her. (*Peaceable* 75)

I, too, have been applying my sense of presence, my desire to listen with "acute attention" but, like O'Reilley, "with by no means perfect success." For example, too busy and lulled by many years of successful work groups in my classes, I did not register the early sounds of a dysfunctional group this year. When I do remember to stay centered, things go better for me and for my students. I advise about thirty students, and I've learned in an advising session to listen, to ask questions, to make notes, never to hurry the conversation. In this way, the questions students felt too dumb to ask will emerge, or their need to talk about their life's direction will venture forth. Even more, in working with student and cooperating teachers, active listening is essential. Both the student and the veteran teacher in this situation frequently feel painfully inadequate. Each is sure she should know what to do yet has no idea, yet would feel foolish if caught out asking. My job—as with a student afraid to ask her cooperating teacher for more responsibility this semester, or a cooperating teacher misjudging a diligent student as lazy—is to listen, check my understanding, and then pass my understanding on, checking again to be sure we're all clear. Besides becoming a better teacher through this approach, I bring into each day the sense that this day counts, that on this day, moment by moment, I am present to my life and doing the work—both the professional work and the inner work—that I am called to do.

Seeking

Revelations through the Spirit are progressive in scope according to man's ability to receive them. (Brinton, *Friends for 300 Years*, 32)

The spirit of seeking is still the prevailing one in our faith, which for that reason is not embodied in any creed or formula. (*Quaker Faith and Practice of Britain Yearly Meeting*, 26.16, Arthur S. Eddington, 1929)

Take heed, dear Friends, to the promptings of love and truth in your hearts. Trust them as the leadings of God whose Light shows us our darkness and brings us to new life. (*Quaker Faith and Practice of Britain Yearly Meeting,, Advices and Queries*, 1.02 1)

I suppose I've always been a seeker, and thus a Quaker before I knew it. I was a religious child whose adolescent disappointment in the dogma (which seemed to me untrue) and the practice (which seemed to me empty) of the church in which I was brought up led me to an equally fervent period of atheism. With maturity came questioning, then openness, then some experimentation with religion, and finally the discovery of Friends faith (which seems to me to state precisely what its adherents see as true) and practice (which nurtures my life).

The academic life has its own assortment of dogmas, to which I've also brought my skepticism and seeking. When I began teaching, I began by believing that I knew how to write, and my job was to pour this knowledge into my students. Reading a book which suggested that teachers should trust their students to discover their own writing strengths and values, I was both attracted and somewhat shocked. "I don't see how my students will learn to use logical development, varied sentence structures, specific nouns and verbs, and their dictionaries unless I tell them how to do these things and point out when each of these activities might be helpful," I protested. The next day, still assimilating these new possibilities, I concluded that it might be possible to work some of these approaches into my own "more traditionally directive teaching mode"(10-9 and 10-10-76).

With literature, I dutifully wrote down my professors' views, most of them gleaned from criticism, and I listened politely when my major professor told me, "I am not a writer. I am a literary critic."

All the while, I also acknowledged, "I have an arrogance in me that tells me I must think, decide, judge for myself" (10-9-76). This trust in my own perceptions and responses grew all through graduate school. In one of my last classes, I wrote a paper on Jane Austen's portrayal of marriage and was furious when the professor, offering no counter evidence, graded me down for my views. As I came to trust my own understanding more completely, so I offered the same liberty to my students.

Now, when I teach writing, I do still teach skills and techniques, and I ask students to think about rhetorical concepts like audience, purpose, and voice. But I teach the skills with the detachment of someone discussing the arbitrary though necessary rules to a game, and I assume that students already know a great deal about writing and about the rhetorical concepts which increase its effectiveness. I also assume that they are perfectly capable of deciding for themselves what makes good writing. This semester, I chose a Wisconsin classic to read with my second semester freshman English class, Aldo Leopold's *A Sand County Almanac.* A number of my students were forestry or wildlife majors, so I thought they'd appreciate this environmental pioneer's homey little sermons on conservation. Instead, quite a lot of students found him needlessly long winded, and a vocal minority took umbrage with a stance they perceived as that of the snobbish insider. I was startled—only asked them questions, though—and by the next week, most of them had talked themselves around into enjoying the outdoor details and the insights which are still informing environmental policy-making. As they wrote their own research papers, they were able to connect the values they'd clarified in this discussion with the choices they themselves were making as writers.

In teaching literature, I find that I am teaching faith and practice, not dogma. My faith is that reading is a source of joy and a way to figure out how to live. My practice points in that direction, as I ask students questions about meaning and values as they emerge in the reading, coach them on finding supporting evidence, and build in some individual choices in reading selections. Sometimes, I offer the views of critics but as the voices of members of the reading community rather than as the dogma of the literature class. One of the classes I teach is required for students who hope to become elementary teachers. Over the years, I've discovered that a substantial number of these students have reading difficulties or a history of painful reading. Finding themselves members of a community seeking truth together, these students begin to see reading as something not merely required of them but also of value to them. This semester, I had a severely dyslexic student in this class, someone who, in order to get the reading done, scanned it into his computer and then listened to the voice reader read the text to him. He began the class with trepidation, but he soon relaxed, proved himself capable, and took his rightful place as a person with valuable insights (and funny stories) to offer the community. At the end, he told me he'd expected to suffer through the class but instead had loved it.

Over my twenty-five years of teaching, my purposes have shifted. I hope my students will love both reading and writing. I hope they will know whatever they need to know to be competent and effective in the things they take from my classes. I hope they will have the experience of being in a community of people seeking truth together, valuing and listening to and respecting each other, and that they will therefore have the chance to take this approach to learning, to being with others, into their subsequent lives.

The Practical, Humble, Constant Practice of Prayer

Like many people, I had given up the practice of prayer as I had learned it when young, for it seemed to me at best a convention, at worst a superstition. It was George Garman, in *The Amazing Fact of Quaker Worship,* who helped me to see that I do, in fact, pray:

> When I go up to kiss my sleeping children and linger with them, in quietness and love, that is prayer. There is a wordless unity of God, myself, my children, a sense of gratitude and reverence, awareness of my need for strength, shame for my failings, a promise to try again. Exercise is good for us; prayer is the right kind for the spirit. (*Quaker Faith and Practice for Britain Yearly Meeting,* 20.12, Anne Hosking, 1984)

When I began teaching, I certainly cared. Again and again, my journal returned to my desire to do well for my students, to my sense of responsibility for them, to what I noticed and hoped for individual ones among them. One entry responded to a writer's comment that the attitude most professors held towards teaching was "somewhat interested." I was amazed, noting that I'd been teaching, writing about teaching, and talking about teaching all that day, and that the professors in my department seemed to me to have a "lively interest" in teaching as well (10-13-76).

I certainly would not have labeled any of this commitment or reflection "prayer." One of my early steps away from my home church came at age ten, when the minister talking with me at church camp proved himself incapable of explaining what prayer is or how to do it effectively. I decided he didn't know, and that if he didn't know, who would?

The first time in my adulthood I consciously chose an attitude of prayer came at a moment of dire emotional need and with a preamble something like this: "I don't think you're there, God, but if you are, I desperately need your help." Encouraged by the results of this attempt, I moved on to further experimentation.

Here's how George Fox described his sense of the presence of God in the universe: "I saw also that there was an ocean of darkness and death, but an infinite ocean of light and love, which flowed over the ocean of darkness. And in that also I saw the infinite love of God" (19). It's towards this light and love that prayer reaches. Luckily for someone with as many intellectual doubts as I have about any religious doctrine, there's no necessity for a more specific definition of God. The direct experience of this infinite love, an experience fostered by the practice of silent waiting and inward listening, is enough.

These days, strengthened and directed by the words of Friends like Jan Wood, who talked to me about her own practice of prayer, and by the writings of Friends like Thomas Kelly, who writes with passionate devotion of the "life of prayer without ceasing" (11), I find my own prayer practice woven into all the dimensions of my life. Including, of course, teaching. Prayer can mean for me a direct, conversational appeal to God, or it can mean a wordless "centering down," as Quakers say, into a still, luminous central place of my being. Years of practice, practice of silencing the clamorous inner voices, of stilling my restless body, of letting go of fears and angers, of attending to the sensory input of the particular moment, and of listening inwardly, have made it possible to move in a moment into this still, radiant place. It's like stepping into an inner bubble of quiet at the center of activity. Time slows, giving way to the immediacy of the moment and of an immense, loving presence. Returning to activity half a second later, the loving presence has infused itself into activity. In this new light, the next right step shines out clearly, with a whiff of joy drifting through the process.

As I'm running, driving, standing in my office before class, or pausing in front of the blackboard, I center down in this way, or I ask God's help in working with a student, or—very often—I hold my students in the Light, an inner visualization in which I imagine the student surrounded, protected, illuminated with radiant love. I hope this practice is good for my students. Each new article I read in *Prevention* magazine on the efficacy of prayer gives me new heart. What I know for certain is that it is good for me. Asking for patience, asking for courage, asking for more love, I receive these blessings of the spirit, blessings which are the seed and rain and soil of good teaching.

Last Thoughts

For a Quaker, religion is not an external activity, concerning a special "holy" part of the self. It is an openness to the world in the here and now with the whole of the self. If this is not simply a pious commonplace, it must take into account the whole of our humanity: our attitudes to other human beings in our most intimate as well as social and political relationships...there is no part of ourselves and of our relationships where God is not present. (*Quaker Faith and Practice of Britain Yearly Meeting*, 20.20, Harvey Gillman, 1988)

Early in graduate school, I learned academia's view of the spiritual life. We were studying T. S. Eliot, and the professor remarked contemptuously that Eliot had been corrupted by the need to conform; thus, he said, *The Four Quartets*, infused with the mysticism Eliot found in the Anglican church, were a terrible comedown from *The Waste Land*, which questions all values and belief. Later, I learned the lesson more personally. I wrote my dissertation on Doris Lessing's science fiction series, *Canopus in Argos*. Lessing's work is informed with her interest in religion and mysticism. The first novel in this series, for example, offers a science fiction explanation for such Biblical events as the destruction of Sodom and Gomorrah, and Sufi teaching tales precede some sections of the books. As a result, I spent a good deal of time researching and writing about these religious elements. When the manuscript was rejected for publication, the anonymous reviewer scathingly pointed out that a very promising manuscript was marred by a silly interest in the metaphysical. Her suggestion was that I drop such distractions and join the serious academic community.

Arriving in the Midwest, I discovered that serious people said in public that they had a religious affiliation—a distinct change from my previous department. But it wasn't until I first attended a conference of Friends Association for Higher Education (FAHE) that I met people who consciously and openly took their spirituality into their professional lives. I still recall vividly my first FAHE conference and the presentation given by Michele Tarter, in which she spoke of her powerful sense of being spiritually led to begin a particular research project. Michele studies women's journals, consulting primary sources, and her work has led to publication of studies and of lost journals of great value. From this research, she was further led to take her knowledge of women's journals into women's prisons, volunteering to read and write with these incarcerated women. From a later conference, I recall seeing Sterling Olmsted, a John Woolman scholar, respond with loving presence to a member of the audience who asked persistently unfriendly questions. Sterling's response transformed the questioner, and gave me a new look at my teaching.

At yet another FAHE conference, Mike Heller used writing in a workshop presentation in a way that modeled perfectly the way I'd like to use writing with my students, and Paul Niebanck used queries to help teachers talk about teaching, an approach I've taken into my Methods of Teaching class. Recently, Steve Smith gave a presentation on teaching as clerking the classroom. In a Quaker Meeting for Worship with Attention to Business, the role of the clerk is to set the agenda, to help those present speak their truths and hear each other, and to help the group arrive together at a loving, Spirit-informed understanding and sense of direction. It's a revealing way to speak of the life of the teacher.

These examples and many others over the last decade have made it possible for me to become conscious of my desire to, as Mary Rose O'Reilley puts it, approach the central questions of our discipline "in the light of our spiritual understanding," and have the sort of classroom that "will allow students freedom to nourish an inner life" (*Radical Presence* 23). Twenty-five years into teaching, I want to study and write and attend committee meetings as a spiritual practice; I want to e-mail and interview candidates as a spiritual practice; and I want to visit my student teachers and lead discussion and grade papers as a spiritual practice. When, joyfully, things come into focus and I am able to teach from my spiritual center, bringing all the levels and parts of myself to the present moment, that's when I do my best at teaching and living both.

CS Chapter Seven
Teaching as Listening:
Silence as Heart Knowledge

Stanford J. Searl, Jr.

When I was growing up in the woolen mill town of Ludlow, Vermont, in the 1950s, our home seemed to be inordinately noisy and busy. In part, I suppose it reflected the fact that my grandmother (who raised me) came from a family of thirteen children, with eight sisters. Usually, of course, they didn't all show up at once; however, when one or more of the sisters visited, they strutted about, as loud, brazen, pushy women, simply full of the devil in a fun-loving manner. All this part of my upbringing, with the various great-aunts cavorting around the kitchen, dancing, singing, drinking, full of loud talk, funny stories, and expressively good times—at least on the surface—couldn't be any further from Quaker spirituality and its related pedagogical practices.

At times, in the midst of the busy chaos, as these sisters would flaunt themselves, my grandfather would get sick of it, and citing a phrase from the 1930s radio program, "Burns and Allen," would cry out, "Quiet down there, Gracie!" Momentarily, then, the hubbub would cease; then, all too soon, the sisters would start up again.

Looking back, remembering, reflecting about how I have come to engage quite fully in what I have come to name as "Quaker pedagogy," I do think that one basis for these practices remains relatively simple: I wished to find various ways for myself to quiet down, to take the learning process itself to more settled, I would say "centered," places, cultivating the kinds of knowing and learning that can only occur when what the Buddhists might call the "monkey mind" is stilled. In too many ways, I had become a rather complete product of this loud, physically and sexually aggressive upbringing, enjoying a little too much noise, too much shouting, a certain kind of exuberance that tended to go too far, upsetting others as well as myself. Put simply, it meant that underneath whatever pedagogical theories were connected to stillness and listening, I had my own issues in the discipline of quieting down, of an engagement in a kind of centered listening.

This upbringing, with its emphasis upon somewhat combative, definitely competitive socialization carried over into my role as college teacher, of course. In fact, in rather revealing ways, as a doctoral student I had found that the work of the intellectual historian Perry Miller appealed to me, in part because of its fiercely combative individualism and self-styled lone wolf identification of scholarly identity. However, when I became a core professor at the Union for Experimenting Colleges and Universities (now the Union Institute and University), an innovative, learner-centered, self-directed, and interdisciplinary doctoral program, I found that my pedagogical identity began to shift. Concomitant with a more scholarly interest in contemporary worship in the manner of silent Meeting Quakers, I imbibed the ethos of feminist caring, social action and student-centered learning. Also, my identity as a teacher shifted from a lecturer/speaker to an individual mentor, guide, supporter, and critic. In part, I think that the shift from a competitive pedagogy to one that valued listening and the kind of learning that issued from an open, inward approach to knowledge originated in my growing identity as a Quaker scholar; at the same time, little by little, I began to develop or discover a different voice, an alternative role to the teacher/scholar as lone wolf (Crowell and Searl 1-14). In this newly emergent guise, my interest in teaching represented a shift from a primary emphasis upon speaking and proclaiming words to a role as a teacher who attempted to deepen and develop a discipline of listening, an alternative, more inwardly centered way of learning and knowing.

Hence, when I did engage in traditional teaching through various five-day, intensive doctoral seminars as part of the university's limited residency requirements, these shifts started to happen. In part, I found myself wanting to shout, along with my Vermont grandfather, "Now, quiet down there, Gracie!" Alas, I had become discouraged with adult, experienced, ostensibly mature independent doctoral learners who were so "full" of themselves and carried forth, not dancing and singing, but in long, extended monologues of angst, pain, despair, and anger in the midst of my seminars. Besides, given my own education in competition, parts of me took this as a personal challenge, upsetting and nasty in that I needed to talk back and join the choral responses. It seemed like a litany of despair in one particular way: The participants (only a few) who acted out appeared to cry, "Listen to me; pay attention to me; see and hear me!"

Usually, aside from these upsetting seminars, I did not "teach" in this rather traditional manner, because students (we name them as "learners") engage in doctoral work through relatively independent ways, set out their programs at a distance, and come together for seminars on a relatively limited basis. For the most part, whatever "teaching" I did revolved around more individualized, tutorial aspects, a series of conversations and connections in the form of consultation, feedback, and related forms of advice about the doctoral work, quite individual and at a distance. However, at least once a year, I remained obligated to teach at least one five-day, intensive, residential seminar. Participants came from all manner of fields, ranging from business to psychology to writing, to meet one of the "residential" requirements of our interdisciplinary doctoral program. In the past, I had offered a variety of different seminars, such as one that investigated aspects of feminist research and another that examined nonfiction writing.

However, no matter what the topic, I continued to be personally and professionally upset by some of the dramatic, personal, difficult tensions at these residential events. Doctoral learners came from all over the United States as well as areas such as the United Kingdom, Africa, Israel, and countries in the Caribbean. People came from very different fields of study and with a multiplicity of personal and academic needs. Yet in nearly all of these seminars (before I instituted versions of Quaker pedagogy), too many incidents happened that became upsetting, difficult, even intolerable for me.

As a teacher, facilitator, guide, I had to learn to deal with conflict, of course, and, typically, I didn't have a good handle, didn't do a good job of conflict management. Variations on a theme occurred again and again in my seminars: Adult doctoral learners would arrive for the five-day residential experience and by the end of the first day, I felt exhausted, disgusted, upset, usually because one or two of the participants had acted out, dominated the group, expressed deep, sometimes really contradictory needs, mostly around the anger and frustration felt by them. It seemed as if their doctoral program, maybe even life itself, the rest of us, had become barriers to learning and life. In fact, it had become so bad for me that—even though it remained a contractual obliga-tion—I simply didn't present any seminars at all for a couple of years, because I felt so unsettled, upset, and frustrated by people's disruptive behavior, their personal antics, the acting out, the anger and domination. As my grandfather had said from time to time in the family, usually in the midst of kitchen revels, mostly to the raucous sisters, "Quiet down there, Gracie!"

Theory and Context

During this same period of time, I had begun to reinvent myself as a scholar, researcher, and person by engaging in a qualitative research project about the spiritual practices of Quakers in worship. Furthermore, as a faculty mentor and advisor in the doctoral program, I had found myself engaging in doctoral work that explored how to incorporate aspects of feminist research, person-centered learning, and spirituality into my own scholarly work. So, in some ways, I felt primed to explore the possible uses of Quaker spiritual prac-tices and related pedagogy to my teaching in these residential, now painful, seminars.

I started with a key, rather practical question of curriculum: How could I provide a structure and learning process that encouraged quieting down, leaving out some of the busy-ness and noise of the world in order to settle in more deeply as one might do in Quaker silent worship? Could I find a Quaker ap-proach to learning that would encourage—in a systematic, structural manner—a more deeply thoughtful, reflective approach to learning? Most of all, in a rather immediate, practical way, could this use of a Quaker pedagogy, whatever it really meant, calm the anger and hostility of these adult doctoral learners? And what about my own intense, upset responses? Please God, I prayed, allow the way in this to be open to me.

At the same time, since this was supposed to be (and I took this very seri-ously) a genuine seminar in doctoral education, I had to ensure that it explored, again in serious ways, matters of theory. What might this aspect of theory really mean? I asked myself.

In my own research about the devotional practices of Quakers within the setting of silent worship, it struck me that effective Quaker spiritual practices engaged participants in the form of what I have come to name as a "heart knowledge," or what George Kalamaras has called a "non-conceptual (or non-categorical) awareness" (64), a form of tacit knowledge, an epistemology that could emerge out of the silent Meeting and the waiting together. From Kalamaras's revealing book, *Reclaiming the Tacit Dimension: Symbolic Form in the Rhetoric of Silence*, I learned that one could conceptualize this alternative epistemology in rather exciting ways, keeping a focus upon the kind of knowing that has more in common with being: bringing a certain kind of open attention to a unified, holistic response that could emerge out of being quiet, waiting together in the silence of the worship process. Even though Kalamaras did not draw upon Quaker texts, I thought that his focus upon tacit knowledge and nonconceptual awareness explained some of the findings from my own research. Kalamaras described what he identified as

> a concept of a *practice of silence*. What I mean by this, in the most general sense, is any technique of meditation aimed at having a direct and sustained experience of consciousness. In particular…practices of silence as various techniques that evoke an awareness of what Fritjof Capra in *The Tao of Physics* calls, "the intuitive mode of consciousness." (17)

The theoretical or epistemological framework articulated by Kalamaras helped me to interpret some of my own research and connected with my interest in alternative ways of knowing in feminist research. It seemed to me that the text by Kalamaras could provide one useful study in connection with a seminar that tried to provide both a theoretical and practical view of silence as a way of knowing.

Citing various mystics and scholars of mysticism, including the Quaker writer Evelyn Underhill, Kalamaras summed up his viewpoint about silence as an alternative way of knowing:

> The unity that the practice of silence yields is, quite paradoxically, multidimensional, diverse, and random. The experience carries a perception of the limited individual self as completely identified with the limitless, expansive Self and thus no longer bound to the more narrow definitions of conceptual consciousness….In other words, the practice of silence is meaningful in at least two ways. First, the awareness the practice yields is meaningful as a way of informing and thus expanding one's conceptual sensibilities. And second, the awareness the practice yields is meaningful in itself in that it grants the meditator knowledge of, or direct access to, the transactional process of the universe. (84, 123)

I wanted to infuse this seminar with some of the theory connected to the uses of Quaker silence; reflecting upon these ideas about nonconceptual awareness, a unified sense about an epistemology of the silence, a way of knowing that originated as some inner part of consciousness, reaching at times to the unconscious through dreams and other images, I hoped that seminar participants might start to cultivate alternative ways to create knowledge. I thought that a focus upon silence as a way of knowing, as expressed by Kalamaras, had potential as one pedagogical key to the possible seminar. However, based upon my own personal experience and research findings, as well as other studies such as the 1992 Swarthmore Lecture by Brenda Clifft Heales and Chris Cook, *Images and Silence,* (15–25) I knew how the problem of the ego—and its discontents—loomed large in this work of teaching and learning.

I thought if I could find multiple ways to incorporate the uses of silence and centered listening into the curriculum of my teaching, some of such approaches might serve to quiet my own ego. In my research into the devotional practices of Quaker silent worship, I had discovered that Quakers understood silence as a powerful metaphor about how to transcend one's ordinary thoughts (Searl 8). I wanted to find ways to incorporate such contemplative practices into my own teaching, while trying to maintain an intellectual and experiential rigor. I hoped that by introducing a form of silent waiting into the structure of my teaching, I could still the ego—both others' and mine.

Drawing from my own analysis about Quaker worship, I noted that other Quakers had similar concerns. In my own research findings, other Quakers wondered how to put their own ego and its sorry, whining voices aside and become open to other emergent voices. Since my research participants had defined this as an issue, it was a simple leap to apply this problem of the ego and its discontents to my previous doctoral seminars. That's precisely what upset me the most: A few, somewhat disturbed, certainly disruptive participants had entered the seminar experience with their egos in the highest gear, wrapped in the assertive, angry, difficult parts of themselves, shouting for recognition. I tried to draw upon my experiences in Quaker scholarship to help me identify this concern. Of course, given my upbringing and temperament, I knew from firsthand experience about the assertive, contradictory and self-destructive aspects of the ego. It could be dangerous for me as a teacher to engage in the combat among various assertive egos.

I wondered: In this secular but real "alternative" context of learning, would it be possible to create a learning environment that would be infused with spiritual practices, with a purpose not so much about worship or devotion as ways to come to the divine but to still the mind, allowing a certain heart knowledge to enter? Indeed, I had become intrigued with the work of a few colleagues in Friends Association for Higher Education, particularly with Mike Heller's unpublished but wonderful paper about the potential for a curriculum in silence.

In Heller's sensitive portrayal of how he proposed to integrate the spiritual practices of silence and contemplation into his own teaching, he commented,

> My own best work comes from listening to that within me but not my ego. I try to leave my ego at the door. This too is part of surrendering to the spirit: the awareness on a daily basis—in conversation, in writing, in teaching, in Meetings, in dreaming and visioning where we might go next—that I step aside to let the Other lead my thoughts forward. (7)

In effect, I supposed that—as part of this spiritually informed education—such a learning process might be structured to promote leaving the ego out. I wondered if I could construct a large cardboard box, with a slit in the top, the sides of the box labeled in large, scrawling Magic Marker black: "Place Your Ego Here," with an arrow pointing to the open slit in the top of the box. Then, in some liturgical manner, as doctoral learners entered the space of the seminar, there could be gestures (with pieces of paper?) that enacted the dropping off of the ego. Of course, I would need to take the lead and do the initial dumping of my own ego into the box.

Mike Heller's work helped me to formulate a more spiritually centered version of my own teaching. It was his focus upon listening, that inclination to be more receptive as a teacher, that struck some sympathy within me. Also, I responded to the pedagogical attention to a certain kind of inwardness that emphasized waiting and letting go, being present, and made sense to me, and I wished to try it out for myself within the seminars that I taught at the Union Institute and University Graduate College.

Mike Heller's quiet assurance offered me more confidence about my own role as a teacher in a common, contemplative, enterprise. I loved his comment: "For the teacher to become quiet is to elevate the ideal that one's best teacher is within the self" (12). Heller's wry, wise call for a contemplative curriculum had some resonance for me in my struggle to bring silence and listening into my own teaching. I heard an emphasis upon listening as a spiritual and an academic practice. Why couldn't I join artists of the contemplative in a quest to establish practices of centered listening as one of the major themes of such a curriculum? I wanted to be open, in the sense that I had discovered in some of the poetry of Walt Whitman (who I considered to be a "Quaker" poet), in ways that defined my role as a teacher in an absorptive mode.

In his "Preface" to the 1855 edition of his poems, Whitman describes how one of his complex roles is to become a "free channel of himself" (717). Of course, much of the time, it's a challenge to understand the various dimensions of the poet's identity because of Whitman's expansive vision. Yet I understand the poet's absorptive mode when he presents himself as a channel, vehicle, and conduit; these metaphors express the poet's interest in becoming a listener at times, in an imaginative sense. In the original "Preface," Whitman uses phrases about this prophetic role in such terms as the poet's "spirit responds to his country's spirit" (711). For example, the poet "incarnates" the people and geography of America (711); his poetic voice can enter "the essences of the real things and past and present events....On him rise solid growths" (711). The poet has become a mythic figure who can be a vehicle for his celebratory muse. Intuitively, I felt drawn to explore what it might mean for a doctoral seminar to become an occasion for a creative, mutual construction of spirituality and its meanings, with myself as teacher in the role of this sort of conduit and vehicle. Whitman's poetic roles inspired me in coming to this work.

In addition to this influence of Whitman and the moving work of Mike Heller, I received help and direction from other Quakers, particularly from people who talked and wrote about the application of Quaker spiritual practices and the uses of silence in their teaching. In inspirational ways, I learned so much from attending conferences sponsored by Friends Association for Higher Education. At one of these conferences, I heard Mary Rose O'Reilley talk about the uses of silence and contemplation in her teaching. Afterwards, I read her books, including *The Peaceable Classroom, Radical Presence: Teaching as Contemplative Practice,* and *The Barn at the End of the World.* When I heard her speak, I had the feeling that she embodied a certain kind of stillness, a contemplative posture that drew me towards her ideas through some creative, poetic process, and not through the typical, highly developed arguments of academic life.

With some fondness, I can remember sitting in a session with her in the Stout Meeting House at Earlham College. I remember my delight, listening to her meditative voice with one ear and a songbird's trilling with the other ear and feeling drawn to the potential of a curriculum of listening, of paying attention, thinking more seriously about these ideas in my role as professor. Later, *Radical Presence* seemed to open up these ideas more for me. In "An Experiment in Friendship," Mary Rose O'Reilley wrote,

> Attention: deep listening. People are dying in spirit for lack of it. In academic culture most listening is critical listening. We tend to pay attention only long enough to develop a counterargument; we critique the student's or the colleague's ideas; we mentally grade and pigeonhole each other. In society at large, people often listen with an agenda, to sell or petition or seduce. Seldom is there a deep, openhearted, un-judging reception of the other. And so we all talk louder and more stridently and with a terrible desperation. By contrast, if someone truly listens to me, my spirit begins to expand. (19)

I craved the kind of expansion illustrated by Mary Rose O'Reilley's words and her presence. After all, because of my family and community upbringing, I knew what it was like to be competitive, to shout my way through an argument. My research about Quaker worship had continued to challenge these assumptions about my own identity, in ways that shifted my attention from the values of the ego to those associated with waiting on the Spirit, with listening, with letting go the need to compete in everything. These ideas—coming from a variety of sources—felt particularly challenging.

I also had the chance to meet with Parker Palmer after one of his workshops in upstate New York. In preparation for this meeting (really a short consultation), I had read his book, *The Courage to Teach: Exploring the Inner Landscape of a Teacher's Life*. I wanted advice about my difficulties in attempting to present the "results" of my research on Quaker spiritual practices. Parker Palmer said that I should read poets such as Emily Dickinson and noted that when it came to Friends' devotional life, it might turn out that indirection, subtlety, delicacy of approach—in short, a poetic approach—would be the most suitable approach.

As I listened to this wonderfully centered advice about poetry and indirection, I felt encouraged in many ways to explore what I had come to understand as the rather different kind of knowing that can originate within communal silent worship, a sort of "heart" knowledge. As I understood it in terms of per-

sonal, expressive experience of worship (others in my research had testified to
something similar), it had become possible to speak—or testify—out of silence
in ways that allowed an emergent, clarified voice to appear, not simply the old,
tired voice of the ego. The search for such an emergent voice seemed to be
paradoxical, in the sense that this alternative voice—or identity—came forward
through an attentive kind of listening, a contemplative stilling of ordinary consciousness. It felt quite true that poetry, indirection, and dream provided the
best ways to write about such experiences.

In *The Courage to Teach,* Palmer called upon readers to embrace "paradoxical
thinking" (66) that faces up to what he later named as one's "divided" life (167).
Instead of living in the tension of such a divided life, between the head and
heart, facts and feelings, theory and practice, Palmer urged us—as teachers—to
actually embrace learning that can transform us: "What I want is a richer, more
paradoxical model of teaching and learning than binary thought allows, a model
that reveals how the paradox of thinking and feeling are joined—whether we
are comfortable with paradox or not" (64).

Palmer made the point that in education, particularly in teaching, it's hard
to embrace the notion of genuine, authentic paradox as when deep wisdom
calls to deep. For years, I longed for some integrative process in my teaching, a
more holistic connection among learning, analysis, and research. Feminist approaches to research had first drawn me to this more integrative mode of
knowing, particularly the work of Shulamit Reinharz in a book about her training as a social scientist and the need to integrate her own values and practices in
"experiential analysis" *(On Becoming* 336). I felt drawn to the more creative, alternative ways of both conceptualizing and doing "research" Reinharz described in *Feminist Methods in Social Research.* At the end of a chapter about
"Original Feminist Research Methods," she summarized an emphasis by some
feminist researchers on innovative social research methods. For some feminist
researchers,

> the feminine spirit is one of breaking free, including breaking free of methodological
> traditions...One of the many ways the women's movement benefited women is in free-
> ing up our creativity in the realm of research. And one of the ways feminist researchers,
> in turn, have benefited the societies in which we live is by the spirit of innovation. (239)

Influenced by Palmer, Reinharz, and the many Quakers who have attended the Meetings of Friends Association for Higher Education over the past ten years, I became drawn to the idea of engaging in both teaching and research as a holistic, spiritually informed, rigorous quest, in which my deepest values could be engaged and supported. In particular, when I read Palmer's summary about how he had incorporated six paradoxical tensions as a classroom teacher, I felt an "aha" of recognition and tried to incorporate these pedagogical principles into my teaching and learning. Here's how Palmer summarized an application of various paradoxes into the learning structure of his classroom teaching:

1. The space should be bounded and open.
2. The space should be hospitable and "charged."
3. The space should invite the voice of the individual and the voice of the group.
4. The space should honor the "little" stories of the students and the "big" stories of the disciplines and tradition.
5. The space should support solitude and surround it with the resources of community.
6. The space should welcome both silence and speech. (74)

While I did not attempt to apply each of these paradoxical goals in my own teaching, this notion of paradoxes became a guiding principle for my attempts to create a learning space in my seminars that reflected creative, holistic responses. In addition, I wished to cultivate a kind of learning that became open to serendipity. Overall, I wanted to build a community of discourse in which individual voices could be heard, paradoxically, within a context of community. I also yearned for a nurturing, creative space in which an understanding of the issues of both "spirituality" and "silence" could be created communally, as part of emergent meanings.

The speaking and writing from Parker Palmer mattered, because he had urged teachers to embrace paradoxical thinking in order to live an undivided life, so that as teachers we can become learners—with all of the confusion, vulnerability, and complexity that this implies:

Paradoxical thinking requires that we embrace a view of the world in which opposites are joined, so that we can see the world clearly and see it whole. Such a view is characterized by neither flinty-eyed realism nor dewy-eyed romanticism but rather by a creative synthesis of the two.

The result is a world more complex and confusing than the one made simple by either-or thought—but that simplicity is merely the dullness of death. When we think things together, we reclaim the life force of the world, in our students, in ourselves. (66)

I felt some deep congruence about the energy that might come from embracing such difficult paradoxes as a teacher. As a teacher, could I really become a deep listener and not simply a speaker and professor? Concomitantly, in a discipline of listening, particularly as a spiritual calling and ministry, could students become transformed learners? As part of my more individualized teaching, I continued to encourage doctoral learners to take risks, to listen to the deepest urgings within themselves, and to find their own way, open to the more creative parts of themselves. In an alternative Ph.D. program, why would one wish to do a conventional, traditional dissertation unless the deeper personal way led there? Why not embrace the potential for inward direction, for a sort of learning that combined, in some feminist ways, head and heart, body and soul, and allowed students to engage scholarship at the deepest level of their lives? Yes, of course, that's what I thought I had encouraged in others; yet, when it came to myself, things were not so clear.

I think that what I resisted the most was relatively simple: In order to engage—fully and with conviction—in this role as contemplative teacher, the sort of professor who made a point of getting out of the way of how others learned, I would need to be open to personal disclosure and vulnerability. Of course, I would need to disclose that I was one of "them," a Quaker, and that much of the approach to learning that valued silence and a certain kind of listening and deep reflection originated from my own experience, both as person and researcher. For all of my talk about encouraging deeply personal, political ways of learning, could I expose my own religious view in these ways? In this Quaker feminist pedagogy, some of the most intimate aspects of my religious identity would become the key processes of learning, particularly with the emphases upon silent reflection and deep listening.

As it happened, I knew some of the feminist and related literature about disclosure and vulnerability, particularly in connection with scholarship. With great pleasure and some awe, I had heard Ruth Behar speak at a National Women's Studies Conference at Skidmore College, and then I read some of her books, paying special attention—because of my advising in the doctoral program—to *The Vulnerable Observer: Anthropology That Breaks Your Heart*. She wrote about the subjectivity of knowledge, the urgency to reveal what happens within the "observer" in research that engages in "participant observation," and she described the painful longings and difficulties about her own journey as an anthropologist.

Behar wrote that when she started to be open to vulnerability, it opened a Pandora's box. After all, she wondered, who knows what will come spilling out? In one of the many moving passages in *The Vulnerable Observer*, she cited a painful, difficult incident that illustrated the ambiguities between ethnography and life:

> What first propelled me to try to write ethnography in a vulnerable way was the intense regret and self-loathing I felt when my maternal grandfather died of cancer in Miami Beach while I was away doing a summer's fieldwork in Spain. The irony was heightened by the fact that I had gone to Spain, knowing that my grandfather was dying, with a mission to gather material for an academic paper I'd been asked to write for a panel on "the anthropology of death." (21)

This kind of disclosure mattered for a number of reasons. As of matter of learning and teaching, personal disclosure provided an access to rather deep personal aspects of learning, at least potentially. This kind of vulnerability had special meaning for me in my teaching. I wanted to become more open to indirection, to the transformations available through other expressions of the imagination. As Thoreau had observed, connecting to his own spiritual pilgrimage as a seeker, he cultivated a deep sense of daily renewal, becoming a worshiper of the dawn: "I have been as sincere a worshipper of Aurora as the Greeks. I got up early and bathed in the pond; that was a religious exercise, and one of the best things which I did" (83). I wanted to promote or encourage this kind of embodied knowledge, a kind of expression that could be open to inward, personal sources, as Thoreau did. In intuitive yet powerful ways, I wanted to promote the kind of learning and teaching that would be more comfortable with an intuitive mode of knowledge, a tacit knowing, an epistemology that joined heart and head, to become an artist of this spiritually informed heart knowledge. From my view, personal disclosure as a form of discourse would allow the learning and teaching to have access to such knowledge.

Of course, I wouldn't inhabit the same sort of borderland identity as revealed by Ruth Behar; however, in my stories, the personal disclosures and details would be much more on display if I really did engage fully in the role of teacher as contemplative artist, a person who has a pedagogical commitment to waiting and listening. Furthermore, as a teacher, I would need to provide a systematic and practical structure in order to ensure that the emphasis in learning shifted from one of competitive argument to one of centered listening.

I thought to myself: Why not organize the learning in my seminar (now focused upon the meanings and uses of silence in theory and practice) as a worship-sharing experience? In other words, could I bring into a doctoral seminar an emphasis upon deep listening, waiting, and being more centered as ways to learn together? What would this mean as a matter of day-to-day work together in this doctoral seminar? Could I do this? Would people come? Would they participate in the structure that I could provide?

The tensions in this approach to learning remained real and difficult. For one thing, I was thinking about asking adult doctoral students, potentially unconnected to Quakers or any other spiritual tradition, to put aside their individual egos, their competitive affiliation with the dominant culture, to reject a way of learning—dominant in traditional doctoral studies—that posited that the most important component of any seminar would be argument and contention. This was a difficult area to consider. After all, in the Union Institute and University Graduate doctoral program as well as any other, faculty must provide a key focus upon how to construct compelling, reasonable, supported arguments. As a professor in this doctoral work, I remained committed to doctoral study that located itself in the midst of the significant literature in the field, provided a critique of the major theories, and then possibly expressed an alternative view of the role of the person who makes knowledge.

I continued to feel extremely vulnerable in offering a doctoral seminar with a focus upon spirituality, silence, and an epistemology of the heart. After all, what did that have to do with the real world of serious scholarship? Where was the credibility? Who cares anyway? Yet I felt drawn to this other, more integrated approach to creating knowledge, a unified field, a direct challenge to the competitive, argumentative way of knowing that came from my upbringing and education. Nagging at me, I heard voices about rigor, rationality, and cognition: What was I really doing by opening myself, in this academic and scholarly sense, to some alternative, feminist perspective about the creation and distribution of knowledge?

In some more personal ways, I felt hopeless and ridiculous about the whole thing. After all, who was I, small-town nothing, high school jock, and dabbler in things of the mind and spirit, to be leading anything that had some deeply spiritual purpose and direction? I also felt a tension between the ostensible standards of traditional doctoral work and the heart's drawing toward some other way of engagement and knowledge. Who was I, product of a high school romance between working-class kids, to assert some kind of Ph.D. level of education that turned away from argument and contention in order to embrace love? On the face of it, that seemed to be absurd; on the other hand, conferring with trusted colleagues, distressed by education completely focused upon the ego and the upset of disturbed people, I groped toward a different kind of learning.

Questions of a Curriculum in Silence

In a practical way, I wanted—at the least—to try out some ideas that had originated from my research, scholarship, and practice as a Quaker. But I wish to emphasize that my coming to this alternative way of knowing and educating originated from a personal desperation about and disgust with disruptive people. In order to move ahead, I expressed a few key questions, what, in good Quaker fashion, I called "queries." In my handout to seminar participants, I identified some of the key issues in this proposed seminar about "Spirituality and Silence" using Quaker language.

In reflecting about goals and objectives for the seminar first, what would it mean to engage with texts in ways that cultivate multiple perspectives? Second, how could the seminar experience promote sharp, direct, and personal engagement with texts and ideas yet also be supportive of development and growth? What might it mean to be "open" and to be "centered" as a learner in this seminar process? Could this be helpful for an engagement with the unexpected and the unanticipated? How could we integrate silence and contemplation as ways of knowing and being in the seminar? How could we use writing as a way of thinking and being?

Finally, I wondered how to promote and model a form of critical inquiry that promotes deeper, open listening as a way of knowing. Could there be a place in the seminar experience for the work of both heart and mind? What could this mean?

In addition to these overall goals, I elaborated a way to engage in "discussion" and invited seminar participants to use what I understood as a Quaker worship sharing approach. The conversation in the large group seminar context should have these characteristics: We would begin all sessions with a few centered moments of silence, in which we would devote ourselves to some meditative, contemplative dimensions of our experience. The discussion itself should have three additional aspects: First, in this large group context, we should hear from everyone (but people could pass) before anyone, including myself, spoke twice. Second, there would not be any cross talk or verbal responses from anyone. This meant that in the larger group of the seminar we would not have a back-and-forth conversation, defined by a few people. Last, the participants would observe a period of silence, or pause, between speakers.

In the handout that I provided, I asked that participants within the larger group conversations consider a number of questions, including whether or not participants heard anything new. Furthermore, I asked that the seminar participants try to cultivate the sort of response that I might consider as "centered." The heart might be involved, I suggested, not the head only, "open" in a position of listening, being receptive and absorptive, whatever that meant to the participants.

In multiple ways, my approach to the seminar became a search for how to shift the discourse from an emphasis upon speaking in order to focus upon listening as a discipline of learning. From my research about Quaker spiritual practices in worship, I knew that such an emphasis upon listening could have transformative implications. My curricular strategies encouraged participants to enter into the role of deep listening as one of the major objectives of the course. In some simple yet provocative way, I asked people to cultivate a different way of paying attention to themselves as well as to others. In fact, one goal of the seminar was to encourage participants to pay attention to other people in some primary and systematic ways.

I found myself in tune with this different curriculum, this way of learning and teaching. This curriculum focused upon a version of the contemplative life made sense for me, as person, teacher, and learner. In the midst of the confusion, chaos, and distraction of a graduate college seminar, I had begun to provide ways in which participants could let go (a little) and enter a space or zone in which absorptive knowing could be enacted, however partially.

This pedagogy of silence and contemplation had its origins in the direct, experiential construction of knowledge that could be possible in Quaker worship. It was deeply personal to be able to share, even indirectly, this coming into the Presence, the opening to the Divine. In an odd, somewhat ironic way, as a professor at this secular institution, with doctoral students from a very wide spectrum of views, ranging at least from evangelical Christian to fiercely agnostic, this practicing of a version of spiritual pedagogy meant that I occupied the role of minister. But here, the ministry was nothing about conversion or doctrine; rather, this ministry brought forward a structure, an approach to learning that placed value upon stillness, contemplation, and silence, all as ways to shift the learning paradigm from one of argumentative assertion to one that emphasized listening, centered responses, and becoming present to others and their ideas.

This was our paradoxical framework: In my role as professor, I asked participants to become "still," to quiet down, to join in a communal exercise of centered listening as ways to learn and to teach; I ended up in the role of a leader who provided a form of secular ministry. I began to realize that it was the structure that mattered the most; this systematic process of engagement demanded centered listening and shifted the approach to learning. In fact, because I had found ways to employ such a structure, this curriculum shifted the learning experience from speaking to listening. From the outset, such an emphasis made sense to me, as I shifted the learning from mostly about the head to at least somewhat about the heart, a shift that emphasized learning as a form of centered, deeply contemplative knowing.

Matters of Structure

In the description of the proposed seminar, I wrote that while there would be some attention to matters of theory, including philosophy and theology in connection with contemplation and silence, the seminar would provide a structured process to explore some of the practical uses of silence and contemplation in education, with particular attention to the work of Parker Palmer and Mary Rose O'Reilley. I defined the major objectives of the seminar as follows: First, participants would be encouraged to prepare and reflect upon a variety of theories about silence and contemplation as ways of knowing. Second, I indicated that the seminar would explore a range of ways to practice contemplative learning, with individual and group exercises about centered listening and other ways of paying attention. Third, I asked participants to bring a completed seminar paper in order for their own texts to become one primary resource in the experience.

There were two assignments in advance of the seminar: first, participants produced one short paper in which they identified at least one theoretical perspective about silence and contemplation and cited one or more sources for their ideas. Also, seminar participants brought twenty-five copies of their papers, and were expected to read the paper aloud to others during the seminar. Second, everyone created a writer's notebook or journal and was asked to be prepared to read from this notebook at times during the seminar.

I structured the reading of the papers as a group exercise in listening: I established small groups of four people during the five-day seminar, and each person in the group read his or her paper to the others. This small group stayed together for the entire seminar period. Also, I stipulated some rules of interaction: In addition to the one person who read the prepared paper, the other three would perform a couple of functions. Each member of the "audience" would pay attention and try to listen deeply to the person who read the paper. It would be okay to jot down ideas and reactions to the paper. I recommended (along with an anecdote from my study in the United Kingdom) responding from the "midriff" and the heart as well as from the head. This audience of three was to offer reactions, comments, and suggestions that included at least one positive, affirming response to the paper. The small group would be expected to share some of the process and results with the larger seminar group.

I instituted a number of common exercises throughout the seminar. For one thing, I asked participants to engage in small-group listening in pairs. After many of the large-group exchanges, under the given rules of interaction, I asked people in the seminar to get into pairs and consider the following questions: Based upon what participants heard (in the large-group session), I asked them to share some aspect that seemed to be new, different, not expected. As a listener, I urged participants to cultivate openness, a receptive aspect, not about judgment but about hearing from the heart or midriff. I asked participants to respond from the midriff or heart about what they heard, then to reverse the process, always keeping in mind to pay attention and listen to the other person.

I had a few additional structures in the seminar. For example, at the opening of each session in the mornings, titled "Daily Observations and Reflections," I included about ten minutes of initial silence. Then, out of the silence, I asked for some sharing from the notebooks or journals of participants, including reflections and reactions from their lives, feelings, ideas—always in the context of deep listening. Also, as part of the ongoing process of the seminar, I asked people to engage in what I named as focused freewriting, using the work of Peter Elbow in *Writing without Teachers,* drawing upon the notion that one's hand, the process of physical engagement with the page, might be a source of unexpected discovery (15). Hence, at least twice a day in this five-day seminar experience, I asked participants to engage in about ten minutes of focused freewriting according to the Elbow formula. The rule was simple: When I indicated "go," participants were required to write, without pause or stopping. Instead of "thinking" or some mental activity in connection with the writing, all were "required" to keep their hands moving on the pieces of paper. As with any of the large-group interactions, participants could share the results of this writing or not, depending upon their wishes. Usually, I would offer a writing prompt connected to the seminar experience with a focus upon ideas and feelings that struck participants in unexpected ways.

This approach to thinking, as a function of the body and connected to the hand, appealed to me in that context of this seminar. I had been a piano major as an undergraduate, and these uses of the hands and the body appealed to me and made sense as a way of discovery and exploration that valued both creativity and serendipity. In addition to this approach to writing as a kinesthetic way to discover meanings, I offered a workshop that drew upon Gustave Reininger's collection, *Centering Prayer in Daily Life and Ministry.* I noted a chapter by Thomas Keating, "The Practice of Attention/Intention" and one by Basil Pennington, "*Lectio Divina:* The Gate Way to the Spiritual Journey and Centering Prayer," helpful when it came to designing my Quaker version of divine reading and contemplation. As Reininger explained, centering prayer and its adaptation of *lectio* could benefit those in the "active life," not only those in monastic settings (40). For example, in my research about Quaker spiritual practices, I had found that some Quakers used a phrase or word to assist them in becoming more centered, deeper as participants in the worship silence. Quakers might repeat a phrase such as "that of God," or "Praise God," or a similar phrase in order to help themselves to enter more fully into the worship. In my seminar, I provided examples of these phrases, such as "I incline mine eyes unto the hills" or "Be still and know that I am God" from the Psalms, as examples of spiritual strategies that some Quakers used as ways to enter into the depth of silent worship, and we explored a version of reading (and responding) as a contemplative practice, keeping a meditative approach to key phrases or words.

Overall, it felt significant to shift the learning from an emphasis upon speaking to listening. I had two goals in mind about this shift: First, I wanted to promote the idea that listening itself could be a dynamic way of knowing; second, I tried to imagine various ways to organize the learning so that participants could practice the skills of listening. Hence, I established a process of listening as participants considered the various texts and their reactions.

For example, I established a period in the seminar devoted to "book discussions." I asked participants to consider the themes of various books and articles that they had read for the seminar in the following format for engagement: first, meeting in small groups of three or four, each person took about ten minutes and talked about the book or article that made the most impression upon them. Second, I asked the participants to come back together and engage in some focused freewriting about what they heard. So, I asked: What did it mean to listen to and think about others' responses to the various texts? Was there anything surprising at all? What did the participants really learn? Were there any particular challenges? I asked the participants of these groups to share some of the focused freewriting illustrations with the large group.

Final Reflections

Implicitly, I had started to develop an approach that possessed a number of connected components, with the pedagogical uses of silence as the center of this learning process. In addition to the uses of silence as a centering device, I identified related components of this discipline, including a focus on listening, a pedagogy that was experiential and embodied, and a kind of learning that had a potential for a tacit way of knowing. I started and ended each day of the seminar with about ten minutes of silence, an invitation or opportunity to settle down, to relax, to let go of some daily tensions. These periods of silence, including the requirements that participants allow some pause, some spacing of silence between conversational responses, meant that the interactions slowed down; the pace became somewhat more reflective (or simply slower), potentially meditative. Hence, the process of our engagement with one another represented a shift from an emphasis upon interruption (which was not allowed) and speed toward an elongated, stretched, slower pace associated with reflection and listening. From my own view, these various periods of silence—even those associated only with waiting for something else to occur—contributed to a learning discipline that emphasized qualities of stillness, getting settled, or in Quaker terms, becoming more spiritually centered. Silence became a form of discipline that could have a consequence of stilling one's thoughts and might allow one to enter into a more quiet, relaxed state of consciousness.

Furthermore, because there was a required pattern of interaction (as defined by my rules of waiting, pausing, only speaking once, with no cross talk), authority started to become flatter, with less hierarchy. With some irony, and not far beneath the surface, I remained deeply in charge, of course. After all, I had established the rules and we played by the structure, process, and discipline that I had articulated. At the same time, however, this modified version of a Quaker worship-sharing format, with its attention to listening, to a slow pace, to a consideration of silent pauses, to a mode of interaction that did not focus on argument or direct response, had the tendency to reduce domination, offering at least the illusion that participants were somewhat more equal. I think that by setting out the rules of interaction, I could get out of the way a little, become a vehicle or conduit for people to learn, but not a person who became in charge of either what or how they learned. I found this aspect of the discipline of Quaker pedagogy to be satisfying, so that—from moment to moment—the focus of interaction could be upon my listening and not upon my speaking in the role of a professor at all.

The pedagogical discipline associated with the uses of silence had other consequences. For one thing, these strategies associated with waiting, periods of reflective and settling down, allowed for a kind of learning that seemed to be distinctively experiential and embodied. Such a pedagogy encouraged responses and learning that originated from within the body, relied upon the experience of the moment, and offered ways to be in touch with feelings and reactions as well as thoughts and ideas. These different periods of silence promoted a certain attention to inwardness and greater relaxation, as well as a variety of exercises about these matters in both large and small groups.

For example, in one exercise of about an hour or so, I asked people to engage together in a walking meditation. I got the inspiration for this exercise from an experience I had at Woodbrooke College, the Quaker Study Centre in

Birmingham, United Kingdom, where I attended a lecture by the Jesuit Father Jerry Hughes. Hughes had engaged in a number of pilgrimages, and he described them as events in which—because of the emphasis on walking—he could never engage in speculative philosophy. While walking, he felt grounded, focused upon the present moment, concerned about his feet, toes, shoes, the traffic, the ordinary, momentary details connected to walking itself. In this walking meditation, I asked participants (in pairs that I generated randomly) to walk around and chat together as a way to "respond" to the afternoon session. I asked them to allow the walking and movement and the physical sensations to have their way in their responses. I urged the participants to do more walking than talking. When the pairs returned from the walking meditation, I asked them to explore their reactions to the exercise through ten minutes of focused freewriting: Write for this ten-minute period, without stopping, and jot down your reactions to the walking meditation; then share these writings with the rest of us.

I intended, both in the focused freewriting exercise and the walking meditation, to reflect the embodied, experiential learning at the heart of this Quaker pedagogy. Because I had had such an intense, satisfying kind of learning as a piano major at Syracuse University, particularly in connection with the significance of practicing, with all of the connected, integrated aspects of touch and mind, I valued similar integrative learning strategies. The uses of the hand and arm as a way of creating meaning in the focused freewriting made perfect sense to me. Walking itself, as both metaphor and practice, allowed for a similarly integrated knowing. The structure of these exercises and related ones encouraged participants to respond from the "heart," to go deeply within themselves as a source of authority and knowing. We participated in the focused freewriting at least twice a day: an exploration of meanings and ideas that had a literal physical embodiment, as the writing itself flowed out of the fingers, the hand, coming out of the entire upper part of the body, hands and arms providing access to the mind.

Of course, one fundamental yet unanswered question remained: What about the potentially disruptive people? What happened to them in the context of this rather different kind of structured learning? Fundamentally, they lurked, like people who are part of computer list serves but only read the contributions from others. Upset, difficult, angry people attended the seminar, yet their difficulties didn't have much of an opportunity to emerge. I remember one of these seminars in the Quaker manner, focused upon these uses of silence and center-ing, in which it wasn't until Day Four (out of Five) that one such person pre-sented his issues to the rest of us.

He was a guy, more or less my age, who had fought in Vietnam and ap-peared to carry enough anger for all of us in the group. In his "turn," as part of a large-group worship sharing, he presented his reactions to the seminar experi-ence with expressions of intense rage, frustration, and hostility. He said that the seminar itself, the readings, its structures and theories reflected intellectual cor-ruption. He felt contempt and disgust, he said. Furthermore, he challenged all of us to realize this fact of corruption and come to our senses by rejecting the present format and trying out some other way.

Interestingly, and with some irony I thought, the rules of the seminar sim-ply held. In spite of the expressions of rage, he didn't set off other people, at least not overtly and publicly. As demanded by the structure, nothing hap-pened: Nobody responded directly to this tirade. After he finished with his dra-matic, very loud, terribly upset outburst, the seminar continued with its slow, deliberate, considered manner, without excitement or emotional trauma at all. At the first break, many of the seminar participants came up to me and offered some words of advice. Some of the participants had gone to other seminars with this person and cautioned that he was terribly difficult and disruptive. These people urged me to carry on with our process as usual.

Essentially, in the midst of this one, loud call for stopping the corrupt seminar, people said that we should continue as usual. After the break, we con-tinued in the style and form of this Quaker pedagogy, attending to listening, keeping the moderate pace, considering the kind of writing and thinking that flowed from paying significant attention to a more still place within ourselves. And what happened to the shocked and angry veteran? I don't know. I think about him as having gained a significant role at the seminar table, reminding me of the violent, abiding, and difficult consequences of war. In my hotel room after this fourth day, I wondered to myself: Could this spiritual and now peda-gogical container be large enough to hold the hatred and violence of the global trauma of war, here embodied in this shocked veteran? Please God, I prayed, allow this form of spiritually informed learning and being to be large enough to contain the kind of grace and healing that this man needs.

Conclusion

I wish that my teaching could be even more centered, more reflective in these spiritually informed ways, with a greater emphasis upon listening and paying attention as a discipline of both teaching and learning. I have the sense that there's something fragile and vulnerable in this process of teaching, which has the intention to become open to the Spirit, to cultivate a deep form of listening as a requirement for learning. These aspects of teaching make for vulnerability and ambiguity. There's significant emphasis upon trusting the process, of a learning that remains open to surprise and serendipity. I find it both difficult and somewhat problematic to let go of my authority or position as traditional professor, as a significant source of knowledge and insight, in order to turn over my role to a different authority. I'm uncomfortable with this because, as the veteran argued, I wonder if I'm copping out, giving up on the potential for intellectual rigor, for the exciting challenges of doctoral-level investigation, full of questions about everything. After all, I want the intellectual rigor and the experiential flow of learning. I crave both head and heart together, integrated, connected, unified.

I have learned a number of distinctive and at times unanticipated things in these seminars about Silence and Spirituality. For instance, it felt satisfying to be engaged in a scholarly as well as a spiritual connection with other Quaker scholars and teachers. As I attended the annual conferences of Friends Association for Higher Education, I realized the depth, both personal and scholarly, of my connections with the participants. It gave me a distinct pleasure to engage in an extended dialogue with such people. Mostly, it seemed deeply satisfying to recognize kindred participants in this Quaker enactment of a discipline of silence, sharing with them in this contemplative way of learning and teaching.

I learned that there was an inner, temperamental congruence between my personal interests and these ways of learning. I liked this approach to teaching in which—with great care and deliberation—I would set up a suitable pedagogical and spiritual container (here the curriculum) so that seminar participants could explore their own constructions of meanings. The emphasis upon a discipline associated with silence made it possible for doctoral learners to cultivate a learning that originated from within themselves, an unfolding of their own spiritual and academic paths.

As a matter of temperament, but with a somewhat different emphasis, I learned that I liked aspects of this curriculum as practice, expressive and embodied. For me, the emphasis upon a discipline of learning that focused upon a construction of meanings through experience made sense. The structure provided ways—at least potentially—for participants to enact ways of knowing that remained embodied and experiential, drawing upon the contemplative energy within their lives.

Overall, this pedagogy, with its emphasis upon inwardness, contemplation, and centered responses, became congruent with the student-centered pedagogy of the Graduate College's doctoral program. I had some satisfaction that the approach emphasized a kind of learning that originated from my own memory and expression. I learned that such a seminar shifted my teaching in ways that worked. Most of all, even though I had set up a relatively rigorous, systematic curriculum in silence and listening, I occupied a teaching role in which I became a connoisseur of listening. For many reasons, this developing role of teacher as listener made sense for me. I could develop skills, really a discipline, about how to settle down, center down in a spiritual manner, and learn to pay attention to meanings beyond the words themselves. I think that this aesthetic and epistemological stance uncovered ways of knowing that felt compelling.

I learned what it could mean to teach as a guide, a conduit that made it possible for others to construct knowledge out of aspects of meditative practices. This kind of knowledge could include analysis, as well as scholarly theory. The contemplative structure provided what I came to understand as a large, expansive, creative container for learning, one that included the heart as well as the mind in the making of knowledge.

ೞ Part Five
Expecting Transformation:
Servant Leadership

CR Chapter Eight

"Live Up to the Light Thou Hast": The Adult Learner

Susan McNaught

It seemed it would be a faculty meeting like any other. After being part of this group for several months, I thought I knew the people and the system. We were gathered around the table in the familiar but somewhat too stuffy conference room, our papers and coffee cups scattered in front of us. We opened the meeting with prayer as we always did. I treasured this obvious way of being who we said we were—what an incredible thing to start a meeting by asking God to guide our work! We shared our concerns and successes. We got to some issue that consumed more time than any of us really wanted to donate and more energy than most of us believed we had. We had discussed and debated, analyzed and advocated, and had finally reached a resolution. It was a hard but rich session. The individuals in this group had some significantly different ideas, to which they were strongly committed. I was impressed, though, with the perspectives of my colleagues and their willingness to hear each other out. As we were ending the meeting and drafting a document to record our decision, one of my colleagues reminded us how important our task was: These words were meant for us but also for future faculty who would not have had the luxury of being part of this conversation.

Luxury? A long, drawn-out faculty meeting that called on every ounce of attention and patience each of us had? Yes! We had been given the gift of being present to make this decision. Now we were offering to faculty members who would come after us the gift of discernment as to how that decision had been reached. Actually, this was not like any faculty meeting I had ever been part of. It was not so much what we did but how we did it—and why. This part was a bit less obvious. No one said that we were doing this because of our faith, but that was exactly what shaped our approach. We were honoring our truth and being stewards of that truth. It may have been a gray winter day outside, but the Light was in that room.

As a non-Quaker teaching in a Quaker institution, I have come to cherish the Quaker traditions as I understand them. I confess that I am a bit of a beginner. My United Methodist traditions have many things in common with those of the Society of Friends, but there are some differences, too. I am always grateful for the grace and mercy afforded me as I learn.

In Friends' worship, one must focus on Christ as inward teacher, being careful to distinguish between insights that come from Him and those coming from one's own thinking and feelings. Quakers are known for their strong peace testimony, for simple living and stewardship, and for an emphasis on equality. They are well known for their support of education and their work for social justice. I knew of all those things when I came to George Fox University to teach. I see evidence of all these values at Fox as well as other beliefs that provide a framework for a Quaker approach to education. As a non-Quaker, I cannot pretend that I have recognized the most important Quaker distinctives. I have noticed the distinctives that seem significant to me. And as a teacher for adult learners, I may have focused on distinctives more relevant for adult learners than for children or for traditionally aged college students. I am counting, though, on the Quaker belief that each of us has part of the truth and that together, we pool our truth for a more complete insight to the truth. I offer my part of the truth.

Inward Light

Three areas of Quaker belief have special relevance for adult learners: the belief in the Inward Light, the belief that truth is emergent, and the belief that people seek truth in community. Each of those beliefs can be examined in and of itself, but they must also be examined as they relate to each other.

Quaker belief in the Inward Light implies that elements of God's spirit are implanted in each and every soul, and that each has direct access to God. My admittedly non-Quaker understanding of this crucial Quaker concept is that each of us has the living Christ within. Others embrace this concept as well.

Donna Markham reminds us of Nelson Mandela saying, "We were born to manifest the glory of God within us. It's not just in some of us; it's in everyone" (ix). This notion of Inward Light has powerful implications for adult education. When we assume the light of truth can be found in each individual, we honor that which is of God in each one.

How does this look in practice? George Fox University offers a unique program for adult learners through its Department of Professional Studies (DPS), designed specifically for adults returning to school to complete management degrees in several areas of study. The Professional Studies Degree programs provide a model for some basic Quaker distinctives. An exploration of these programs may shed some light on how Quaker beliefs can shape an education.

The program reflects the belief in the Inward Light in several ways. One basic Quaker belief is that God has a will for us as individuals and as corporate gatherings. Truly believing that God has a will for us brings us to whatever we do with a greater sense of power. It is not our own ego. It is not some mystical, magical power. It is simply the knowledge that, with God's help, we can see beyond our own fears, preferences, and limitations. We allow God to use all the resources at His command, moving in us and through us. Jan Wood, recorded Friends minister and director of Good News Associates in Seattle, Washington, asks in *Christians at Work*, "If we did our job with God's heart, how might we do our work differently?" (20) This query shapes a Quaker pedagogy that is open to all, trusting, and expecting each person to grow.

As a staff, we come together knowing each of us has a part to play in this plan; every person in this department is viewed as having gifts and graces to be used to teach, to serve, and to support. We are all Christian, but we are not all Quaker; indeed, only two of our four full-time faculty members are Friends. We all seek, however, to honor the Quaker distinctives that form this institution. Each of us teaches and nourishes each other. We accept our differences because our commitment is bigger than the differences. We find delight in the common understandings, and we gain wisdom from working through our differences.

So how is this different from just being very civilized grown-ups skilled at group dynamics? It is different because each of us feels called by God to be where we are; we do not start with ourselves. Quaker or not, each person on this staff reflects the Quaker belief in vocation. Frederick Buechner says that vocation is the place where your deep gladness and the world's hunger meet (119). We are glad to be here. We start with a sense of mission. Our work finds us and as such is sacred. We realize that we are called to be in this particular place at this particular time with this particular group. I treasure these people. I laugh with them; I pray with them; I learn from them. I may disagree with a colleague from time to time, but I know that he has things to teach me. I may know something he does not, so I am called to share what I know. There is more patience and more gentleness with each other, less competitiveness, and more willingness to consider other opinions.

That being said, we do not always agree. Quaker belief in peace does not preclude some fairly rousing discussions. It does not even mean that institutional politics don't crop up from time to time. What it does mean is that there is an incredible commitment to honest dialogue. We honor the Quaker commitment to simple speech. No hidden agendas, no self-aggrandizing, no jockeying for position. It also means that while we seek common understanding, we know there will sometimes be conflict. We use the Quaker decision-making model of reliance on the sense of the Meeting. We know there may be differences of opinion, and we value them because the different perspectives enrich the discussions. We value conflict over competition. Conflict is open and sometime raucous, but it is always communal. Competition can dissolve relationships; conflict is a dynamic by which we test ideas in the open. There is an incredible commitment to honoring the light in each other. And if I am seeking the light in you, I am less likely to cut off dialogue, to bring hidden agendas, to discount your ideas. I may disagree with you, but when we allow the Spirit to be present, egos do not take center stage.

Operating from a belief in the Inward Light requires certain institutional structures. First, if each of us has part of the truth and we all need to share our truth, we need time and place to be able to do that. Meetings cannot be rushed. This does not mean that we dawdle, because we must also be good stewards of our time. It means that we must provide time to thoughtfully consider what we are about. We must get information out to members of our group in a timely fashion so that they may thoughtfully consider the topic. We must allow time during the Meeting for the spirit to speak. We must expect that the most practical matters have their roots in the sacred. "At the most practical level, the decision-making process in a Quaker school has as its purposes arriving at good decisions and helping people become more skilled at sharing responsibility for decisions. It aims to serve people and help them become better servants" (Lacey 48). Each of us must also be aware that we have to hear what God is calling us to do and when God is calling us not to do something. More may not be better. Taking on additional tasks may not be a sign of service, but of hubris. There is an important balance.

Believing in the Inward Light also means that we have structured this as a learner-centered program. The program is structured to help people overcome their inhibitions, behaviors, and belief about learning (yes, you can teach an old dog new tricks!) so that they are ready to learn. With this approach, we switch from focusing on teaching to focusing on learning. All these threads can be woven together; we just need to mind the warp and the woof, pay attention to the pattern, and enjoy the Light that plays over it.

George Fox's degree completion program through its Department of Professional Studies is content based but is collaborative between teacher and student. This is a partnership: DPS provides the structure and the students bring the experience. We emphasize education as a part of living rather than as preparation for it. We see education as transformational. It is only in adulthood that transformative learning (as opposed to formative learning of childhood) can take place. In adulthood, individuals discover a need to acquire new perspectives in order to gain a more complete understanding of changing events and a higher degree of control over their lives (Imel 2), so it is imperative that we address the spiritual, intellectual, and social aspects of our students. In his inaugural address at Yale, Benno C. Schmidt remarked, "Our education in the end prepares us not only for our professions, but for the two-thirds of our life that is not about our jobs, our work, our status. But about daily-ness. About inwardness. About our capacities for affiliation."

Transformative education requires critical reflection on the part of learners. To help students do that, we use such strategies as journal writing, papers called "life labs" in which students apply the concepts they are learning in class to work situations, simulations, and case studies. Students take the theory and their own situations and develop the application. Students deal with the theory at their own level and depth. When writing about organizational structure, Judy wrote about the large, very bureaucratic state agency that she worked for; Barry wrote about the small concrete business he owned. Both were able to apply the theory to their own particular situations. There are standards for how these papers are to be developed, but the content and insights truly emerge from the student. Truly educated people are the people God intends for them to be. We work to help allow that education to blossom.

For learners to truly engage in this kind of learning requires they be active participants in the process. But the process is a duet. The teacher has a critical role, setting the stage and providing opportunities for critical reflection. Teachers can help learners examine their beliefs and how they have acquired them by creating situations in which they can consider how their values, assumptions, ideologies, and beliefs have come to be constructed (Imel 2). The focus shifts from the teacher being glad that students understand the point that the teacher was making, to helping the learners think about what they thought before and why their ideas have changed. The programs may be content based, but they have a learner-centered focus.

Not all university students are aged eighteen to twenty-two; times are changing. Richardson and King report that more and more adults are coming back to school in the United States and abroad (65). Both two-year and four-year colleges are seeing a huge growth in the number of adult students in class. While some colleges still see mostly traditionally aged students in postsecondary education, the proportion of adult students (those over the age of twenty-two at the time of their entry into higher education) has equaled the proportion of traditional students. Some adults move into traditional programs rubbing elbows with traditionally-aged students in traditional college settings. Some adults move into degree completion programs specifically designed for adult students. The aging of the workforce sometimes brings adults back to school as they find they need more formal education in order to compete. As adults mature, they may find that this new level of maturity leads, or even requires, them to seek more meaning in their lives. This could mean completing a formal education begun many years ago. Nontraditional students often return to school because of experience that puts them on the margins—a divorce, blocked promotion, or need to change careers. They may come because they think their children are finally old enough that they can take on more personal goals. Whatever reason brings them into the classroom, they are often in the midst of transition, and most of them are a bit afraid. We need to respect those fears. We need to allow our students to work through those fears. Their Inward Light is directing them. We need to mind the Light.

Another expression of belief in Inward Light is a sense of wholeness: Quakers are committed to living lives that are undivided. Quakers do not separate head from heart, theory from practice, teaching from learning. Quakers do not seem to separate the secular and the sacred—it is all sacred. Understanding that lives are whole pieces grounded in a relationship to God means that everything that is done is worship—everything! It is less a matter of the integration of faith and work than the recognition that our work is our worship and our worship is never work. There is a unity of spirit but not a uniformity. Unity is spiritual; uniformity is mechanical (Willcuts 77). This has powerful implications for education and learning. As Robert Bellah points out in Benjamin Webb's collection *Fugitive Faith,* "Much of our education is based on a stark and stunning separation of the sacred and the secular, to the great impoverishment of our intellectual as well as our moral life" (Webb 6). The Quaker approach to pedagogy is to bridge that separation and to offer a more coherent model to learning, indeed, to life, that emphasizes unity. It is whole in its approach to the task—no compartmentalizing here. It is an awesome wholeness. Work becomes a sacrament and a ministry. No matter what is done, it is an act of religious devotion.

This sense of wholeness can be found in the way curriculum is structured. Any curriculum has two aspects. The explicit one is what we say we are offering: the courses, the majors, the schools. The implicit curriculum includes the patterns or organization or procedures that frame the explicit curriculum: the attitude, time spent, even design of the room.

The whole approach in the DPS is carefully thought out and ordered in a way to serve the students. Rather than the cafeteria style of most universities—one helping of chemistry, two of business, and art for dessert—these programs are complete packages. Courses are designed in a planned sequence so each class builds on the previous ones and provides a foundation for the ones to follow.

Each course is discrete, yet the dynamics established in the earlier ones allow richer and richer dialogues as the program progresses. We move through group dynamics; effective writing; management and supervision; organizational theory and analysis; survey research methods; organizational communication; fiscal and operational management; Christian faith and thought; and values and ethics in the workplace. Topics may be dealt with in different ways in different courses. For example, in the first course, group dynamics, we explore the nature of personal conflict. We deal with workplace conflict in the third course, management and supervision. We look at conflict again in the organizational theory course, as we examine conflicting structures and policies. In the final course, values and ethics in the workplace, the topic of conflict is approached as an ethical issue.

The content is integrated and designed to challenge all the students. The articulated arrangement leads to strong emphasis on interdisciplinary coursework and collaborative learning techniques. Collaboration rather than competition must be the norm. With the emphasis on collaboration, the process shifts from teacher centered to learner centered. For example, instead of spending most of the time lecturing, the instructors facilitate. Instructors introduce topics and then allow students to explore them and to apply their own experience. There is much small-group work where students bring their own experience and expertise. We do not just permit active participation by learners; we require it. We believe all have access to truth, so every voice seeking a hearing must be heard. This emphasis on group discussion and experiential learning harkens back to George Fox's query, "What canst thou say?" Each person must contribute for the program to work. It is a bit like the Quaker approach to ordained leadership. Parker Palmer, in an interview with Benjamin Webb, says that Quakers haven't abolished the clergy; they have abolished the laity (Webb 57). In the DPS, we have not abolished teachers; every person in the class is a teacher.

This is not to say that we, as faculty, do not have a role or that curricular issues are not important; we must do our part. We bring the structure and the curriculum. When a student is transformed, there is always a teacher who ignites the passion, but the student chooses to learn from the teacher. And since each of us shares the Light, the teacher may be the professor, another student, or the learner himself—all of us can play that role. In *Quaker Faith and Practice,* Barbara Windle recalls a comment made by one of Rufus Jones's students at Jones's memorial service, "He lit my candle" (Perkins 107). We need to be candles; we need to be candle lighters. We need to mind the Light.

Minding the Light means that there is a commitment to each and every student from the very beginning. Our admissions staff, our evaluation staff, and our faculty truly look for the Lord in each student. We strive to serve each one and to honor the holy in each one. Some students may work with the admissions staff for months to get everything done before they can be admitted. The admissions staff works with applicants to answer all questions, to help them through the process, and to give them a sense of what the program is. We believe that we have great programs, but we know that they may not be right for some people. We want to serve those who apply to Fox, not just hook them so our numbers look good. For example, this fall a woman applied and was quite eager. She was also involved in a new ministry program at her church, one involving a significant commitment of time. The admissions counselor worked with her to help her understand the juggling she would need to do in order to do both programs. She needed to make her own decision, but she needed to make an informed decision. She elected to complete the program in her church and enter our program next spring. She will be a strong student because she will be coming to the program when she is more able to focus on it.

If there is concern that an applicant may not be successful in the program—a weak writing sample, not enough work experience, or a low grade point on his transcripts—then the admissions committee is convened. We structure the program to be academically rigorous, but we want our students to succeed; we do not want to set anyone up to fail. It is a joint effort. Students must work hard; the institution must serve the student. It is a whole process. Last winter a student applied who was only twenty-three. We do not have a minimum age, but we do require five years' work beyond high school. This student did not meet that requirement. He did, however, have a burning desire for more education, lots of volunteer experience in management-related activities, and an abundant amount of self-discipline that became evident in the interview. He was admitted and is doing well. Another student applied a few months before. The committee suggested that she take some more community college courses and think about starting the program in a year. It was not what she wanted to hear, but the committee did not think that she had the experience that would allow her to benefit from the program. She was most unhappy and entered another program. She struggled and eventually dropped out. She called our program a few months later, asking that her file be reactivated and requesting a list of what the committee had suggested she do before entering. She will enter the program in January. I think she will be ready.

Honoring the Inward Light allows the program to focus on experiential learning, with our students applying their experiences to the theory that they learn in the classroom and then also applying the theory to their experience—

coming full circle. As they share their insights, the emphasis is on turning away from passively received dogma and secondhand truths to looking inward for personal experiential knowing. When we discuss organizational theory, every student can bring examples from his organization—how it works or does not. When we talk about negotiation in the communications course, the scenarios may range from the business board Meeting to a family Meeting, from resolving a conflict with a coworker to dealing with conflict in a church congregation. The settings may differ, but the need for resolution is common. This reflects Quaker pedagogy, which understands that true education is always about learning to connect knowing with doing, belief with behavior. We do not want our students to get all As in coursework and flunk life.

Truth Emergent

Quakers hold a firm belief that truth is emergent. God is with us and continues to speak to us. Someone recently commented to me that God sometimes works on a needs-to-know basis. Part of not always knowing what is happening is the conviction that God is on our side and wants us to understand—as we are ready.

A belief in truth emergent means that we understand that God continues to work; we must be open to continuing revelation. This conveys at least two things to me. The first is that we do not now have all the answers (what a relief), but that God is present and continues to reveal. We seek unity with the creation as well with ourselves and silence allows that. The second aspect of this continued revelation is how it happens. This is where there is a wonderful paradox. Learning demands both silence and noise, both solitude and community. We want lots of noise—people sharing their understanding and experience with others—and we want silence—being quiet enough to allow God to be present. The thing is, we can, and must, have it both ways.

Here is where the waiting in silence comes in. Friends wait in silence to discern God's will. Friends listen! The silence helps create inner space for Christ to enter. We can learn to take off protective and defensive masks—for the first time for some of us. Parker Palmer quotes Nellie Morton as saying that one of the great tasks of our time is to "hear people to speech" (Palmer 46). Quaker pedagogy fosters listening: teachers listening to their students, students listening to each other, and everyone listening for the Spirit within.

A good teacher listens to voices even before they are spoken, making space, being aware, paying attention, honoring the Light in each one. When we are truly attending to each student, we cannot rush the process; we must wait. We must respect the process of God being present at that very moment. Silence gives us opportunity to sort out the merits of ideas being offered. Silence gives us opportunity to sort out what we believe to be true and what we cannot accept—and why. Silence gives us opportunity to put things in perspective. For example, when students are discussing a topic, as the instructor I must be careful to monitor the movement of the conversation but not too eager to jump in and direct it—I rely on the truths that students bring and on the Light being present.

One practice I have found to be helpful is to begin each class with a few moments of waiting in silence. I am open about being Christian and explain about my understanding of Friends "centering down," a Quaker practice of turning away from the noise of the world and embracing the quiet so that God may speak to us. I do this for me and I do it for the group. I do not ask anyone to do anything other than let the quiet be present. My Christian students may take the time to pray; my students who have raced to make it to class on time may take the time to catch their breath; my students who come from hectic days at work may take the time to turn loose of their day. This time allows us to come together. It allows us to hush the world's noise and to listen for the important stuff. It allows us to be gathered.

Teachers in a program like this must set the tone because most of our adult students have come through traditional programs and are used to traditional classroom arrangements: Hush up and listen to the teacher. We need to help them understand that silence is not empty; indeed, the silence that allows us to wait upon the Lord is very full! We need to help our students listen to God, to themselves, and to each other.

Out of the silence can come the noise of learning. We are first quiet so that we focus. When we find that center, the noise that comes from it comes from the silence that birthed it. The centering down allows a noise that is focused, that is respectful, that is prepared, that is joyful. It has been my experience that classrooms that are noisy can indicate that some pretty exciting learning is taking place, people doing things and talking about ideas. "Truth is an eternal conversation about things that matter, conducted with passion and discipline"

(Palmer 104). So noise is important for adult learners too. Those of us who teach in these programs want learners who are passionate about what they are learning. We want learners who can enjoy the other members of their cohort. We want active involvement.

Truth emerges when there is trust. Truth often emerges in informal settings and when people are comfortable. Students in these programs are encouraged to bring snacks to share. A huge amount of bonding occurs over chips and dip! It has been my experience that groups that eat together, whether light snacks or serious potlucks, share more than just carrot sticks. My cohorts who did not bring food did not bond as tightly. I am not sure what the Quaker position on food might be, but in every Christian group that I have ever been part of, there is the realization that breaking bread together is worship as well as fellowship. In the first course, I encourage folks to bring food to share as well as their ideas.

The first course in the program, group dynamics, sets the tone. By the time we get to the second course, the effective writing class, we know each other, like each other, and are ready to reveal a bit more of ourselves. Both of these first classes make way for the rest of the courses. Each course is discrete, yet the dynamics established in the earlier courses allow richer and richer dialogues as the program progresses.

A prime example of truth emerging when there is trust is the dynamic we see over and over during the eighth of the nine courses, the Christian faith and thought class. By the time we get to that course, trust is well established. Even those who are Christian often face this course with mixed feelings. Some are evangelical and enjoy talking about their faith; others may come with deep faith but may not be comfortable talking about it. Most come from Christian traditions different than those of Quakers. Some have had bad experiences in church and really want nothing to do with it. Some are atheists. Some have no experience at all with organized religion. They may be curious; they may come seeking answers; some may come just prepared to endure a course that they know is required by the program. Most emerge from this course very different than when they began it. They do so, in part, because of the material, but mostly because of the trust that has been established, which allows them to ask some complicated questions and examine some pretty basic beliefs, knowing no one in the class is going to judge. The instructor's task is to be hospitable to the students' beliefs so students are able to take their own faith journeys. We can share hope and vision as they become more ready to hear it. All people are on a spiritual journey whether they know it or not; it is an ongoing process. Sometimes it is overt; sometimes it is not. We trust God's time.

Community

The Department of Professional Studies is grounded upon a commitment to community, to the common unity. We believe that God has a will for us as individuals and as corporate gatherings. Community is not simply people who hang out together but is far more complex. The early Quaker, Issac Pennington, wrote in 1667, "Our life is love, and peace, and tenderness; and bearing one with another, and forgiving one another, and not laying accusations one against another; but praying one for another, and helping one another up with a tender hand." (Perkins, 10.01) Community does not depend on professing identical beliefs but on loving one another, accepting responsibilities, sharing, and working together.

One of the clearest ways community is seen is in the development of curriculum. For several reasons, the DPS faculty work together to develop the curriculum for each course. We want all our students to have the richest possible curriculum, and this takes the efforts of all of us. When we produce a commonly developed curriculum, we trust that it is the results of the Spirit in each of us. I might go off on a tangent by myself, but working with my colleagues keeps my interests and passions in balance with those of others. We trust that when we join together to produce this curriculum, we inspire each other to be more creative, more complete, and more thoughtful than we would be if we were working in isolation. Our own vision is widened by the vision of others. This process reflects the Quaker belief that each of us has part of the truth; we must come together and pool our knowledge in order to gain a fuller truth.

Another way we see community in these programs is in the fact that we use a cohort model. Classes are taught as seminars, allowing for greater student participation and built-in support. Students stay with the same group, usually numbering from twelve to eighteen, all the way through the program. This model allows students to learn cooperatively as well as to share professional and personal backgrounds. Students develop relationships and learn about interdependence. This arrangement reflects a paradoxical pair of Quaker beliefs: "each of us has an inner teacher that is an arbitrator of truth and each of us needs the needs the give-and-take of community in order to hear that inner teacher speak (Palmer 152).

Each cohort is usually taught by a primary instructor who teaches at least seven of the nine, or eleven, courses. This arrangement encourages the bonding of the group, allows the instructor to mentor, and provides continuity for the group. The primary instructor is more of a generalist than most university instructors are. Each of us has areas of specialty, but each also is able to teach a variety of courses, partly because we work together to develop them. Because instructors are chosen for their ability to be generalists and for their ability to facilitate group learning, the emphasis is on the learners. Primary instructors coordinate with specialty instructors to maintain continuity for students. Learning requires breadth of outlook. We do not want our students' world to be limited to just the particulars of anyone's individual work.

Even the way that the room is arranged reflects a Quaker approach. Quaker congregations are often arranged in circles or squares so that each person can be aware of everyone else and yet no one person appears raised above another in status. Our classrooms, too, reflect this desire. We structure our classrooms with tables arranged in a square. Each student can see every other student. The instructor and students can easily engage in discussions, and the arrangement makes clear that students will be actively involved in the process. We are all in it together. The classroom itself tells students that each individual is important and that the group is important; it is the old Quaker theme about needing both the individual and the community.

Saturday Seminars are another way to emphasize community. About every three months, all the cohorts come together on main campus. The topics for the seminars vary. Some are leadership oriented; some have a more liberal arts focus. The all-day seminars have several purposes.

First, Saturday Seminars give all the cohorts an opportunity to come together. Students who have almost completed the program can celebrate and share words of wisdom with those who are just beginning. Beginners can talk with those who have successfully navigated the system. They can see that they are part of something bigger than just their small cohort. And since none of the classes are held on main campus (remember, we go to them), they have a chance to experience the George Fox ethos on the main campus at Newberg, where it may be more evident than on the satellite campuses. They see that they are connected to other students and to a bigger system.

Second, students are exposed to a variety of learning opportunities at Saturday Seminars. They can learn strategies for effective leadership or how to maintain a drug-free workplace or the value of mythology in the workplace. Some of the liberal arts topics are fun, too, and not topics our students would be exposed to in any other setting. My personal favorite was when the chemistry professors taught us all how to make silly putty. The point was on practical application. Actually, the point is that all we do has meaning—and that includes play.

Some students appreciate the variety; some do not. We, as faculty, can take the opportunity to help our students understand that even if they personally do not appreciate one particular topic, it may be exactly what someone else needs that day. Not every individual need will be met, nor should it be. This, too, is an opportunity to grow in community and in the Light.

Application Elsewhere

For those who do not teach in Quaker institutions, integration of faith and learning is still possible and may be even more crucial because the outward support may not be there. Each of us truly is called to find ways to honor God and to honor that which is of God in each other. A Quaker pedagogy is less a visible, outward result than a fundamental way of being. It is a centering of spirit, an approach to students and colleagues, a certainty that the teacher is an instrument. When I teach in public institutions, I do not open my classes with prayer. I do, however, pray before class. I need God's presence and guidance. I seek to see God in every one of my students. I ask for wisdom and patience. Do my students know this? Not overtly. Does it matter? Absolutely.

This model of adult education that George Fox uses is only one model of many. How can these Quaker distinctives work in other settings? First, we need to remember that change is an inside job. It is not what I do with this stuff, but what this stuff does to me. Jacques Barzun says, "To become educated is above all things, the result of wishful thinking; but the wish must be for the true state, not for its trappings" (311).

We all educate within a community, and our practices need to encourage the growth and recognition of that community. With our vision, we can help students and colleagues put on new lenses when they are ready in order to see what would be invisible otherwise. For instance, when Melinda came to class without having done the reading for the evening, she announced that she had just been too busy that week and would do better next week. She accepted responsibility for herself, but that was as far as it went. It was a good opportunity to chat about how she not only shortchanged herself but would not be as able to contribute in the small group discussion because she was unprepared. She had shortchanged her cohort as well. It was an opportunity to remind us all that this program is not just about individual achievement but about contributing to the community.

We also feel the importance of the community in the class dynamic. We need to remember that good teaching and good learning cannot be reduced to technique; the teaching/learning process grows from the identity and integrity of the learner and the teacher. Our students learn only when they risk opening themselves. And they are more likely to be willing to risk when we provide a safe place for them to do that. As teachers, we must risk, too, and demonstrate what Parker Palmer calls the courage to teach. This is the courage to keep one's heart open in those very moments when the heart is asked to hold more than it is able so that the teacher and students and subject can be woven into the fabric of community that learning and living require (11). We risk in order to discover connections.

Organizations are communities so we must mind our Light in our organizations, too. We can also create a workspace that feeds our souls and the souls of our colleagues and students. Community is an outward and visible sign of inward and invisible grace. "To teach is to create spaces in which community is practiced" (Palmer 90). To create this community, we may need to push for some institutional or departmental changes. In order to do that, we must first lay some groundwork. In his conversation with Webb, Bellah reminds us that we need conversation in cold times to prepare for the time when widespread social transformation becomes possible (xi). We lay the groundwork for change by first developing relationships and community. We cannot develop policy—even for the department—if we do not have some common understanding and trust.

Community requires us to think about the consequences of who we are and what we do. For instance, a truly learner-centered approach honors the wholeness of the individual, of the group, and of the material. If we want to know what is essential, we must stop thinking the world into pieces and start thinking it together again (Palmer 63). We can help our students make connections between ideas. We help them apply theory and practice. We let our students know that they can honor thinking and feeling. No matter what subject matter we teach or where we practice our craft, we can help our students understand that their hearts and minds are connected—that they must be connected. We can remember that our institutions and our society have limited ways of measuring, and some things that are very valuable are not easily measured. We must make sure that we are using strategy that matches what the research shows about how adults learn and yet remember that not everything will be researchable. I once had a student who was very insecure and as a result was very defensive—all the time. She said she was shy; the rest of us thought of other adjectives. She had a hard time working in small groups because she expected to be intimidated and even when no one was trying to upset her, she saw intimidation. She was a professional victim. Finally, one night, after what seemed like just one more discussion, she sighed. I looked over and waited. "They really are on my side, aren't they?" she realized. Her lesson that night had nothing to do with the content of the text. The lights that go on for our students are not necessarily measured in kilowatts.

Community goes beyond the relationships with each other in the classroom. The most important thing that Quaker pedagogy does is to emphasize connection—connection to God, connection to each other, connection to the material. And we must start at the beginning. So how do we connect? How do we deal with internal realities—in a practical, Quakerly fashion—when we may not be in a Quakerly place?

Connecting reveals God's pull on us. For this to play out, it is imperative that we remember that we are not alone—we have the Living Spirit and we have each other. We know that God is revealed to individuals through models suited to their temperaments and abilities, to communities through models suited to their cultures. Given that—and that is a lot—there are some practical approaches. Each of us, teacher, administrator, student, whatever, must remember that we are children of God called to do God's work. We are all challenged to speak to or answer that of God within others. As George Fox said in his oft-quoted letter, "walk cheerfully over the world, answering that of God in every one" (Perkins 19.2).

What Fox's reminder means in practical matters is that our attitudes precede us. We bring our faith into the classroom not by preaching but in the way we conduct ourselves. Indeed, we bring that same faith into faculty meetings. We must resist the temptation to compartmentalize. We must teach, and live, each day in ways that honor our deepest values rather than in ways that simply conform to the institutional norm. It is our special privilege to confirm the deepest things in our students.

We do not see what is in their hearts and heads by merely looking around. What we see depends on how we see the world—our worldview, our philosophy about what happens and why it does so, our values. We need to help our students identify what lenses they are using in order to view the world. We cannot impose our lenses; we cannot refuse our lenses. I need to respect the worldview of my students, which may be different from mine, and I need to acknowledge my own worldview. We all bring our own values with us everywhere we go, and we need to be honest about the values that we hold.

We know that our students are poised for change—that is why they come to our classrooms. That change will be largely intellectual, but we also know that the most significant spiritual changes are made in midlife. We affirm people in their successes rather than in their failures. Quaker pedagogy expects students to succeed, and how we think of success determines how we approach our tasks. This is where the joy comes in, because we get to help our students define success! Quaker pedagogy asks students to think about what a successful life really looks like. Jack Wilcutts reminds us that the bottom line belongs to God—we must be careful how we measure success (51).

For all of us who teach, Quaker or not, this means being intentional about seeking to understand our own attitudes and approaches—what we say and demonstrate about measuring success. Steven Garber quotes Mark Schwehn as saying that ways of knowing are not morally neutral but morally directive (60). For example, Quaker peacemaking in the classroom is more than consensus-building and conflict resolution. It is the very essence of how and what we teach. George Fox University professor of religion Howard Macy reminds us that the usual translation of *shalom* is peace, but that perhaps a broader definition might serve better—*shalom* as wholeness, harmony, balance, promises kept, reconciliation (102). When we teach business classes, do we consider how people compete without becoming enemies? Are the business practices that we teach examined in the Light of integrity, justice, and love? When we teach writing, do we require integrity in form and content? Do we tell the truth about our own hearts, our living, and the world around us? Do we respect the reader? Do we cherish beauty? Quaker pedagogy requires that we promote peace and that we teach peacefully (though sometimes that requires confronting students and that may not feel peaceful!). Good education is always more process than product.

Being in community and living out God's word require us to find ways to gather for unity—with our colleagues and with our students. A moment of silent prayer, a moment to center down, a moment to focus can provide a huge difference in the way that the Meeting or the class goes. Welcome the silence and listen for God's voice. Out of the silence can come the community. We can work out ideas in the context of friends. Start a book group to explore spirituality in the workplace. By joining together, we expand our own understanding and contribute to the strength and resources of the group.

Gathering for unity also helps us be good stewards of our emotional resources. Richard Foster offers the advice that we must refuse to live beyond our emotional means (91). We must understand our own emotional limits. I like this concept. It comes back to the idea of truly listening for God's direction—we nurture others because we are nurtured. And we must allow ourselves to be nurtured. Mind your own Light as well as the Light of others.

Quaker pedagogy expects rigorous quality education. When we are truly looking for the Light, we are called to extend and to refine our intellectual skills as well as our capacity for compassion. We help our students make connections between ideas. Rigorous education also means that we help our students understand that they absolutely must use both their hearts and their heads. We help our students find a way to honor thinking and feeling. Too often, our society separates these two, but if our students are going to be successful, they must understand that an educated life is not feeling or thinking but feeling and thinking. We seek the unity. We use all the resources that God has given us.

Quaker pedagogy also implies a learner-centered focus. By focusing on the learner, there is more equality. With adults, that sense of partnership is critical. This means using a collaborative mode of learning. We function in community. We meet our students where they are, not where we would like for them to be, and we help them move to where they can be. It means the material, as well as the approach, needs to be relevant to the jobs and life of the students. No fragmentation. It means that the teaching/learning process is dynamic. We need to be open to new Light from wherever it may come.

As we honor the Inward Light in each person, we need to mind the need for servant leadership. We can teach about servant leadership and encourage our students to become servant leaders. Certainly this is a fine concept for a management program. But it is not just content, an idea that we examine like bacteria under the microscope or as a noble theory in management class. We need to become servant leaders ourselves. We serve our students when we provide academic counseling so that appropriate goals are established at the beginning of their programs. We serve our students when we expect the best of them. We serve when we nurture, when we say no because there is a bigger yes, when we believe in the potential and the Light of each student. We serve when we structure for active and cooperative learning. We serve when we insist that classroom location and course schedules are convenient for students. We serve when we believe in our students when they doubt themselves.

When we expect transformation, we need to remember that it may or may not be articulated. I do not have to tell my students that their lives will be transformed. That message is probably not mine to deliver. I just get to know. I get to watch.

We all need to remember that we have the potential to transform lives. If we truly believe that the Spirit is with us and in us, what incredible power that provides! Jan Wood reminds us that "authenticity means showing outside what's real inside" (128). If we're having a real relationship with God, there are natural ways and times this should show. There is a lovely hymn that says, "They will know we are Christians by our love." Witnessing does not mean just saying the words. We witness with everything that we do. Witnessing is about being transparent about ourselves. It goes back to the Quaker understanding that everything that we do is worship, and that truth is emergent. It is all in God's time.

And we also need to remember that sometimes the Spirit may nudge; the work may not be obvious. I remember a student of mine who was quite immature (thirty-eight going on thirteen) who drove me to distraction with his disruptions and bravado. I worked with him, and on myself, to get through the program. During the Christian Faith and Thought course, he announced that he had recommitted himself to God and was a new person. I am counting on God to be able to see that. While I cannot begin to understand what was going on in his heart, I did not see much change on the outside. But it is not about me. It is about him and his relationship to God. Those two need to work it out, and I have every confidence that they will. We need to remember that faith, the things unseen, are at work here. Maybe he had no huge insights, but even a commitment to search would be a good thing. Maybe his baby steps looked faltering to me, but he was making the steps. We know that we mature spiritually in small steps. The life gap between our awareness of God's call and our day-to-day behavior is a sign that God is working in us. The thing to remember is that the process is ongoing.

And finally, we remember that joy is the hallmark of Quaker pedagogy. We are called to live in joyous trust. We can heed Caroline Fox when she advises us to "Live up to the Light thou hast and more will be granted thee" (Crumley-Effinger 80). As we mind the Light in our students, in our colleagues, and in ourselves, we are renewed. And as we mind the Light, we are doing God's work wherever we may be.

❦ Works Cited

Abbott, Margery. "'A Tender, Broken Meeting': Description of a Workshop." *Friends Bulletin,* April 2001.

Adler, Ronald, and Elmhorst, Jeanne Marquardt. *Communicating at Work.* New York: McGraw-Hill, 1996.

Anderson, Chris, Klaus, Carl and Faery, Rebecca. *In Depth: Essays in Our Time.* New York; Harcourt Brace, 1990.

Applebee, Arthur N. *Tradition and Reform in the Teaching of English: A History.* Urbana, Illinois: NCTE, 1974.

Atwan, Robert, ed. *Ten on Ten: Major Essayists on Recurring Themes.* Boston: Bedford, St. Martin's, 1992.

———. *The Best American Essays, College Edition.* New York: Houghton Mifflin, 2001.

Bacon, Margaret Hope. *Mothers of Feminism: The Story of Quaker Women in America.* San Francisco: Harper & Row, 1986.

Baker, Nicholson. "Books as Furniture." *Best American Essays 1996.* Ed. Geoffrey C. Ward. New York: Houghton Mifflin, 1996.

Barzun, Jacques. *Teacher in America.* New York: Little Brown, 1945.

Behar, Ruth. *The Vulnerable Observer: Anthropology That Breaks Your Heart.* Boston: Beacon, 1996.

Belenky, Mary, Bond, Lynne, and Weinstock, Jacqueline. *A Tradition That Has No Name: Nurturing the Development of People, Families and Communities.* New York: Basic, 1997.

Bellah, Robert. *Habits of the Heart.* New York: Harper & Row, 1986.

Blair, Brent. "Divisible Theatre in Divisive Communities." Community fieldwork paper, Pacifica Graduate Institute, 2000.

Blau, Sheridan. "Language as Moral Action." Theme essay for the Call for Proposals for the Eighty-seventh Annual Convention (1997) of the National Council of Teachers of English. Urbana, Illinois: NCTE, 1996.

Bohm, David. *On Dialogue.* London: Routledge, 1996.

Boulding, Kenneth. *Mending the World.* Pendle Hill Pamphlet 266. Wallingford, PA: Pendle Hill, 1986.

Bradshaw, Isabel. "Re-embodying Science: Science Practice as Body Practice." Community/ecological fieldwork proposal, Pacifica Graduate Institute, 2001.

Brinton, Howard H. *Friends for 300 Years: The History and Beliefs of the Society of Friends since George Fox Started the Quaker Movement.* Wallingford, PA: Pendle Hill, 1952.

———. *Ethical Mysticism in the Society of Friends.* Pendle Hill Pamphlet 156. Wallingford, PA: Pendle Hill, 1967.

Brock, Peter. *The Quaker Peace Testimony: 1660 to 1914.* York, England: Sessions Book Trust, 1990.

Brookfield, Stephen D. *Becoming a Critically Reflective Teacher.* San Francisco: Jossey-Bass, 1995.

Brookfield, Stephen D. *Becoming a Critically Reflective Teacher.* San Francisco: Jossey-Bass, 1995.

Brown, Lynn, and Gilligan, Carol. *Meeting at the Crossroads.* New York: Ballantine, 1992.

Buber, Martin. *Daniel.* Leipzig: Insel-Verlag, 1915.

————. *I and Thou.* New York: Scribner's, 1958.

————. *The Way of Man: According to the Teaching of Hasidism.* New York: Citadel, 1964.

Buechner, Frederick. *Wishful Thinking: A Seeker's ABC.* San Francisco: Harper San Francisco, 1993.

Christian Faith and Practice in the Experience of the Society of Friends. London: London Yearly Meeting of the Religious Society of Friends, 1960.

Christian, William A. "Inwardness and Outward Concerns: A Study of John Woolman's Thought." *Quaker History* 67 (1978): 88–104.

Couser, G. Thomas. *Altered Egos: Authority in American Autobiography.* New York: Oxford University Press, 1989.

Cronk, Sandra. *Gospel Order: A Quaker Understanding of Faithful Church Community.* Pendle Hill Pamphlet 297. Wallingford, Pa.: Pendle Hill, 1991.

Crowell, John, and Searl, Stanford J., Jr., editors. *The Responsibility of Mind in a Civilization of Machines: Essays by Perry Miller.* Amherst, MA: The University of Massachusetts Press, 1979.

Crumley-Effinger, Stephanie. "Raising Up the Good: The Universal Ministry in Higher Education." In D. Neil Starr and Daniel L. Smith Christopher (eds.), *Practiced in the Presence: Essays in Honor of T. Canby Jones.* Richmond, IN: Friends United, 1994, 71–89.

Davin, Anne. "A Depth Psychological Review of CalSTAT." Community Fieldwork Paper, Pacifica Graduate Institute, 2000.

Denney, Michael. "Body, Soul, and Medicine: Confessions of an Elder Physician." Diss. Pacifica Graduate Institute, 2001.

Dickinson, Emily. *The Poems of Emily Dickinson.* Ed. Thomas H. Johnson. Cambridge: Belknap, 1963.

Dillard, Annie. *The Best American Essays.* Ed. Robert Atwan. New York: Houghton Mifflin, 2001.

Edgerton, William. "U.S. Quakers: Hybrid Corn?" *Friends Journal,* 47, 6 (June 2001): 68.

Elbow, Peter. "The Doubting Game and the Believing Game: An Analysis of the Intellectual Enterprise." *Writing without Teachers.* London: Oxford University Press, 1973.

————. "Embracing Contraries in the Teaching Process." *The Writing Teacher's Sourcebook.* Ed. Edward P. J. Corbett, Nancy Meyers, and Gary Tate. New York: Oxford University Press, 2000. 54–65.

Epstein, Joseph. *The Norton Book of Personal Essays.* New York: W. W. Norton & Company, Inc., 1997.

Faith and Practice of New England Yearly Meeting of Friends (Book of Discipline). Worcester, MA: New England Yearly Meeting of Friends, 1985.

Forster, E. M. "Anonymity: An Enquiry." *In Depth: Essayists for Our Time.* Ed. Klaus, Anderson, and Faery. Orlando: Harcourt Brace, 1990. 262–270.

Foster, Richard. *Freedom of Simplicity.* San Francisco: HarperSanFrancisco, 1981.

Fox, George. *The Journal of George Fox.* Ed. John L. Nickalls. Philadelphia: Religion Society of Friends, 1995. First published 1694.

Freire, Paolo. *A Pedagogy of Liberation: Dialogues on Transforming Education.* New York: Continuum, 1987.

————. *Pedagogy of the Oppressed.* New York: Continuum, 1989.

Frye, Northrop. *The Great Code: The Bible and Literature.* San Diego: Harcourt, 1982.

Garber, Steven. *Fabric of Faithfulness.* Downers Grove, IL: Intervarsity, 1994.

Garman, Mary, et al., eds. *Hidden in Plain Sight: Quaker Women's Writings 1656–1700*. Wallingford, PA: Pendle Hill Publications, 1996.

George Fox University Mission Statement. *George Fox University Undergraduate Catalogue*. Newberg, OR: George Fox University, 2001.

Gould, Stephen Jay. "A Biological Homage to Mickey Mouse." *In Depth: Essayists for Our Time*. Ed. Klaus, Anderson, and Faery. Orlando: Harcourt Brace, 1990. 290–298.

Greenleaf, Robert K. *Servant Leadership: A Journey into the Nature of Legitimate Power and Greatness*. New York: Paulist, 1977.

Havel, Vaclav. *The Art of the Impossible*. Trans. Paul Wilson. New York: Fromm, 1998.

Heales, Brenda Clifft, and Cook, Chris. *Images and Silence*. London: Quaker Home Service, 1992.

Heller, Mike. "The Recognition of Silence." Unpublished paper. Versions presented at the Annual Conference of the Friends Association for Higher Education (1996) and the College Conference on Composition and Communication (1998).

Hillman, James. *The Thought of the Heart and the Soul of the World*. Woodstock, CT: Spring, 1992.

Hoagland, Edward, ed. "Hailing the Elusory Mountain Lion. *The Norton Book of Nature Writing*. Ed. Robert Finch and John Elder. New York: Norton, 1990. 744–757.

———. "What I Think, What I Am." *In Depth: Essayists for Our Time*. Ed. Klaus, Anderson, and Faery. Orlando: Harcourt Brace, 1990. 362–364.

———. Introduction. *The Best American Essays 1999*. Series ed. Robert Atwan. New York: Houghton Mifflin, 1999.

Horton, Myles. *The Long Haul: An Autobiography*. New York: Doubleday, 1990.

Huntley, John F. "The Judgment and Public Measure of Value in Academic Contexts." *The Journal of General Education* 37 (1986): 280–312.

Hurston, Zora Neale. *Their Eyes Were Watching God*. New York: Harper, 1990.

Hyde, Lewis. *The Gift: Imagination and the Erotic Life of Property*. New York: Vintage, 1983.

Imel, Susan. "Teaching Adults: Is It Different?" ERIC Clearinghouse on Adult, Career, and Vocational Education, ERIC Document Reproduction Service, 1995.

Jung, Carl. "The Transcendent Function." *The Collected Works of C. G. Jung, Vol. 8*. Princeton: Princeton University Press, 1960.

Kalamaras, George. *Reclaiming the Tacit Dimension: Symbolic Form in the Rhetoric of Silence*. Albany: State University of New York Press, 1994.

Keating, Thomas. *Intimacy with God*. New York: Crossroad, 1997.

Keiser, R. Melvin. *Inward Light and the New Creation: A Theological Meditation on the Center and Circumference of Quakerism*. Pendle Hill Pamphlet #295. Wallingford, PA: Pendle Hill, 1991.

Kelly, Thomas R. *A Testament of Devotion*. San Francisco: Harper, 1941.

Kenworthy, Leonard S. *Quaker Education: A Source Book*. Kennett Square, PA: Quaker Publications, n.d.

Kidder, Tracy, ed. Introduction. *The Best American Essays 1994*. Series ed. Robert Atwan. New York: Houghton Mifflin, 1994.

Kimball, Beatrice, and Holden, Joyce. *Dictionary of Friends Terms*. Richmond, IN: Friends United Meeting, n.d.

Knowles, Malcolm. *The Modern Practice of Adult Education; Andragogy Versus Pedagogy*. New York: Associated, 1970.

Lacey, Paul. *Education and the Inward Teacher.* Pendle Hill Pamphlet 278. Wallingford, PA: Pendle Hill, 1988.

————. *Growing into Goodness: Essays on Quaker Education.* Pendle Hill Pamphlet 297, Wallingford, PA: Pendle Hill Publications in cooperation with Friends Council on Education, 1998.

Lifton, Robert. *The Nazi Doctors: Medical Killing and the Psychology of Genocide.* New York: Basic, 1986.

Lopate, Phillip, ed. *The Art of the Personal Essay: An Anthology from the Classical Era to the Present.* New York: Anchor Doubleday, 1994.

Lorenz, Helene, and Watkins, Mary. "Depth Psychology and Colonialism: Individuation, Seeing Through, and Liberation." 2002. http://www.mythinglinks.org/LorenzWatkins. html.

————. "Silenced Knowings, Forgotten Springs: Paths to Healing in the Wake of Colonialism." *Radical Psychology: A Journal of Psychology, Politics, and Radicalism.* http://www.radpsy. york.ca, 2002. Also see illustrated online version at http://www.mythinglinks. org/LorenzWatkins2A.html.

Loring, Patricia. *Listening Spirituality, Volume II: Corporate Spiritual Practice among Friends.* Washington Grove, MD: Openings, 1999.

Macrorie, Ken. *Writing to Be Read.* Upper Montclair, NJ: Boynton/Cook, 1984.

MacWilliams, Deborah. "Embodied Dialogue with Place: Intentional Engagement with the World." Diss. Pacifica Graduate Institute, 2002.

Macy, Howard. "The College of Shalom." *Practiced in the Presence.* Richmond, IN: Friends United, 1994, 99–106.

Markham, Donna J. *Spiritlinking Leadership.* New York: Paulist, 1999.

Martin-Baro, Ignacio. *Writings for Liberation Psychology.* Cambridge: Harvard University Press, 1994.

McQuade, Donald, and Atwan, Robert. *The Writer's Presence: A Pool of Essays.* Boston: St. Martin's, 1994.

Mitchell, Lali. "The Sleeping Lady: Dreaming the Valley." Community/ecological fieldwork paper, Pacifica Graduate Institute, 2000.

Morton, Nelle. *The Journey Is Home.* Boston: Beacon, 1985.

————. "Warriors with Words: Toward a Post-Columbine Writing Curriculum." *English Journal* (May 2000): 42–46.

Nelson, G. Lynn. *Writing and Being: Taking Back Our Lives through the Power of Language.* Innisfree, 1994.

Newman, Daisy. *A Procession of Friends: Quakers in America.* Richmond, IN: Friends United, 1972.

Ojai Foundation, www.ojaifoundation.org.

Olmsted, Sterling. *Motions of Love: Woolman as Mystic and Activist.* Pendle Hill Pamphlet 312. Wallingford, PA: Pendle Hill, 1993.

O'Reilley, Mary Rose. *The Peaceable Classroom.* Portsmouth, NH: Boynton/Cook, 1993.

————. *Radical Presence: Teaching as Contemplative Practice.* Portsmouth, NH: Boynton/Cook, 1998.

————. *The Barn at the End of the World: The Apprenticeship of a Quaker, Buddhist Shepherd.* Minneapolis, MN: Milkweed Editions, 2000.

Orwell, George, "Shooting an Elephant." *The Writer's Presence: A Pool of Essays.* Boston: Bedford, 1994. 96–101.

Ozick, Cynthia, "She: Portrait of the Essay as a Warm Body." *The Atlantic Monthly,* September 1998.

Palmer, Parker J. *Meeting for Learning: Education in a Quaker Context:* Pendle Hill Bulletin No. 284. Wallingford, PA: Pendle Hill, 1976.

———. *The Promise of Paradox: A Celebration of the Contradictions in the Christian Life.* Notre Dame, IN: Ave Maria, 1980.

———. *The Courage to Teach: Exploring the Inner Landscape of a Teacher's Life.* San Francisco: Jossey-Bass, 1998.

———. *Let Your Life Speak: Listening for the Voice of Vocation.* San Francisco: Jossey-Bass, 2000.

Penington, Isaac. "The Inward Journey of Isaac Penington." *Quaker Classics in Brief: William Penn, Robert Barclay, and Isaac Penington.* Wallingford, PA: Pendle Hill, 1987.

Penn, William. *Fruits of Solitude: Reflections and Maxims Relating to the Conduct of Human Life.* Chicago: R.R. Donnelley & Sons, 1906.

Perkins, Elizabeth, ed. *Quaker Faith and Practice: The Yearly Meeting of the Religious Society of Friends (Quakers) in Britain.* Warwick: Yearly Meeting, 1994.

Perls, Frederick S. *In and out the Garbage Pail.* Lafayette, CA: Real People, 1969.

Plato. *Plato: Republic.* Transl. G. M. A. Grube, revised by C. D. C. Reave. Indianapolis: Hackett, 1992.

Potok, Chaim. *The Chosen.* New York: Ballantine, 1967.

Public Conversations Project, www.publicconversations.org.

Quaker Faith and Practice: The Book of Christian Discipline of the Yearly Meeting of the Religious Society of Friends (Quakers) in Britain. London: The Yearly Meeting of the Religious Society of Friends (Quakers) in Britain, 1995.

Reinharz, Shulamit. *On Becoming a Social Scientist.* New Brunswick, NJ: Transaction Publishers, 1988.

———. *Feminist Methods in Social Research.* New York: Oxford University Press, 1992.

Reininger, Gustave, editor. *Centering Prayer in Daily Life and Ministry.* New York: Continuum, 1998.

Richardson, John T. E., and King, Estelle. "Adult Students in Higher Education: Burden or Boon?" *Journal of Higher Education* 69 (1998): 65–88.

Rumi. *Open Secret: Versions of Rumi.* Trans. John Moyne and Coleman Barks. Putney, VT: Threshold, 1984.

Schmidt, Benno C. "Inaugural Address." Yale University, New Haven, CT. September 20, 1986.

Scholem, Gershom. *Major Trends in Jewish Mysticism.* New York: Schocken. 1946.

———. *On the Kabbalah and Its Symbolism.* New York: Schocken Books, 1965.

Searl, Stanford J., Jr. *Voices from the Silence.* Unpublished manuscript.

Simkinson, Anne. "An Interview with M. Scott Peck." *Common Boundary,* March/April, 1993.

Smith, Robert Lawrence. *A Quaker Book of Wisdom: Life Lessons in Simplicity, Service, and Common Sense.* New York: Eagle Brook, Morrow, 1998.

Sontag, Susan, ed. Introduction. *The Best American Essays 1992.* Series ed. Robert Atwan. New York: Houghton Mifflin, 1992.

Steere, Douglas. *Dimensions of Prayer.* 1962; rpt. Nashville: Upper Room, 1997.

Stevens, Barry. *Don't Push the River.* Lafayette, CA: Real People, 1970.

Thoreau, Henry David. *Walden.* Boston: Beacon, 1997.

Updike, John, "The Mystery of Mickey Mouse." *The Writer's Presence: A Pool of Essays,* second edition. Boston: Bedford, 1997. 426–432.

Walker, Alice. "The Black Writer and the Southern Experience." *In Depth: Essayists for Our Time.* Ed. Klaus, Anderson, and Faery. Orlando: Harcourt Brace, 1990. 690–694.

Watkins, Mary. "Imagination and Peace: On the Inner Dynamics of Promoting Peace Activism." *Journal of Social Issues,* 44, 2, 1988.

———. "Depth Psychology and the Liberation of Being." *Pathways into the Jungian World: Phenomenology and Analytical Psychology.* Ed. R. Brooke. London: Routledge, 2000.

———. "Seeding Liberation: A Dialogue between Depth Psychology and Liberation Psychology." *Depth Psychology: Meditations in the Field..* Ed. Dennis Slattery and Lionel Corbett. Einsiedeln, SW: Daimon Verlag, 2000.

Webb, Benjamin. *Fugitive Faith: Conversations on Spiritual, Environmental, and Community Renewal.* Maryknoll, NY: Orbis, 1998.

Weil, Simone. *Waiting for God.* Trans. Emma Craufurd. New York: Harper, 1951.

White, E. B. "Intimations." *One Man's Meat.* New York: Harper, 1982. 2–22.

———. "The Essayist and the Essay." *In Depth: Essayists for Our Time.* Ed. Anderson, Klaus, and Faery. New York: Harcourt Brace, 1990. 728–729.

Whitman, Walt. *Leaves of Grass.* New York: W.W. Norton, 1968.

Wilcutts, Jack. *Why Friends Are Friends.* Newberg, OR: Barclay, 1984.

With People's Wisdom: A Video Interview with Rajesh Tandon. Dir. Ruth Pelham. Highlander Center, New Market, TN, 1984.

Wolf, Dennie. "Creating a Portfolio Culture." *With Portfolios in Hand.* Ed. Nora Lyons. New York: Teachers College, Columbia University, 1998.

Wood, Jan. *Christians at Work: Not Business as Usual.* Scottsdale, PA: Herald, 1999.

Woolman, John. *The Journal of John Woolman and a Plea for the Poor.* Secaucus, NJ: Citadel, 1961.

———. *The Journal and Major Essays of John Woolman.* Ed. Phillips P. Moulton. Richmond, IN: Friends United Press, 1989.

Wright, Charles. *Appalachia.* New York: Farrar, Straus and Giroux, 1998.

Zimmerman, Jack, and Coyle, Virginia. *The Way of Council.* Las Vegas: Bramble Books, 1996.

⚕ Contributors

Anne Dalke is a member of the English Department and Coordinator of the Feminist and Gender Studies Program at Bryn Mawr College in Pennsylvania. She is the author of *Teaching to Learn/Learning to Teach: Meditations on the Classroom* (Peter Lang 2002) and a member of Radnor Monthly Meeting of the Society of Friends.

Barbara Dixson teaches English and English teachers at the University of Wisconsin Stevens Point. As a teacher of teachers, and as a Friend by convincement, she has read, thought, and written for many years about the ways her Quaker understanding informs her teaching. She is a member of Stevens Point Friends Meeting.

Mike Heller teaches literature and writing courses at Roanoke College in Virginia. He has special interests in the personal journal, Quaker journals, and nonviolence. He has written on John Woolman and contemplative writing and is currently coediting a book of Mohandas K. Gandhi's writings. He is a member of the Roanoke Monthly Meeting of Friends.

Richard Johnson teaches English at Kirkwood Community College in Iowa City. He also serves on the Board of Directors of Scattergood Friends School, a college preparatory Quaker boarding school.

Barbara C. Mallonee is a member of the Department of Communication, Loyola College, Baltimore, Maryland. She is a member of Stony Run Friends Meeting and a member and former chair of the Board of Trustees, Friends School of Baltimore.

Susan McNaught has taught since 1996 at George Fox University, a Quaker university in Newberg, Oregon. She works in the Department of Professional Studies with adult students completing management degrees at the bachelor's level. She is an active member of the Association for Continuing Higher Education and of the United Methodist Church. Her service has mainly been in the areas of education, peace, and justice.

Stanford J. Searl, Jr. teaches at the Union Institute and University Graduate College, a self-directed, learner-centered, and interdisciplinary doctoral program in Los Angeles. He has completed a qualitative research project about the worship practices of Quakers in the silent Meeting traditions, has composed a devotional manuscript based upon this research, and is now in the midst of writing a more academic book about it, tentatively titled "Emergent Voices in Quaker Silent Worship." He is a member of the Santa Monica Monthly Meeting in California.

Steve Smith was born into Iowa Yearly Meeting of Friends (Conservative). Since 1968 he has taught philosophy at Claremont McKenna College in California. A member of Claremont Monthly Meeting, he has been active within his monthly, quarterly, and yearly Meeting, as well as with the Friends Association for Higher Education (FAHE) and the Friends World Committee for Consultation (FWCC). He has written for *Friends Bulletin* and *Friends Journal,* and has edited three books by Charlotte Joko Beck: *Everyday Zen, Nothing Special,* and *Now Zen.*

Mary Watkins is a psychologist who coordinates Community and Ecological Fieldwork and Research in the Depth Psychology Doctoral Program at Pacifica Graduate Institute, Santa Barbara, California. She is the author of *Waking Dreams, Invisible Guests: The Development of Imaginal Dialogues,* and coauthor of *Talking with Young Children about Adoption.* She is a member of Santa Barbara Meeting.

Index

STUDIES IN

EDUCATION & SPIRITUALITY

Peter L. Laurence &
Victor H. Kazanjian, Jr.
General Editors

Studies in Education and Spirituality presents the reader with the most recent thinking about the role of religion and spirituality in higher education.
It includes a wide variety of perspectives, including students, faculty, administrators, religious life and student life professionals, and representa-
tives of related educational and religious institutions. These are people who
have thought deeply about the topic and share their insights and experiences through this series. These works address the questions: What is the
impact of religious diversity on higher education? What is the potential of
religious pluralism as a strategy to address the dramatic growth of religious
diversity in American colleges and universities? To what extent do institutions of higher learning desire to prepare their students for life and work in
a religiously pluralistic world? What is the role of spirituality at colleges and
universities,
particularly in relationship to teaching and learning pedagogy, the
cultivation of values, moral and ethical development, and the fostering of
global learning communities and responsible global citizens?

For additional information about this series or for the submission of manu-
scripts, please contact:

Peter L. Laurence
5 Trading Post Lane
Putnam Valley, NY 10579

To order other books in this series, please contact our Customer Service
Department:

(800) 770-LANG (within the U.S.)
(212) 647-7706 (outside the U.S.)
(212) 647-7707 FAX

Or browse online by series:

www.peterlangusa.com